FORMATIVE EVALUATION for EDUCATIONAL TECHNOLOGIES

COMMUNICATION

FORMATIVE EVALUATION for EDUCATIONAL TECHNOLOGIES

Barbara N. Flagg
Harvard University

LEA LAWRENCE ERLBAUM ASSOCIATES, PUBLISHERS
1990 Hillsdale, New Jersey   Hove and London

Lawrence Erlbaum Associates, Inc., Publishers
365 Broadway
Hillsdale, New Jersey 07642

Library of Congress Cataloging-in-Publication Data

Flagg, Barbara N.
Formative evaluation for educational technologies / Barbara N. Flagg.
    p.   cm.
  Includes bibliographies and index.
  ISBN 0-8058-0127-8
  1. Educational technology—Evaluation. 2. Curriculum evaluation.
  I. Title.
  LB1028.3.F57   1990
  371.3'078—dc20
                                        89-7838
                                        CIP

Printed in the United States of America
10 9 8 7 6 5 4 3 2 1

Contents

Contributors

Linda Callahan • Research Communications, Ltd.
Valerie Crane • Research Communications, Ltd.
Shelley Isaacson • ATEX Corp.
Susan Doll Jolliffe • U.S. Productions, Inc.
Saul Rockman • Apple Computer
Leona Schauble • Learning Research and Development Center
William J. Tally • Bank Street College of Education
Kathleen S. Wilson • Bank Street College of Education

Acknowledgments

I am grateful to Gerald Lesser, Samuel Gibbon, and Lewis Bernstein for having introduced me to the fields of formative evaluation and electronic media. The Spencer Foundation supported the early stages of this book. Special recognition goes to my colleagues and students, past and present, who have "evaluated formatively" the many manuscript drafts. In particular, I must mention Karen Hoelscher, Dan Burnstein, and Terence Tivnan. Above all, I greatly appreciate my mother's proofreading and my family's encouragement and enduring tolerance of my preoccupation with this project.

Barbara N. Flagg

Introduction

> *We think that it's a great pilot program! But we need to know what the*
> *kids think. Will they like it? Will they begin to understand just what*
> *folklore is and what it does?*
> —T. P. Butler (personal communication, February, 1986)

These were questions raised by executive producer Terri Payne Butler about Weston Woods Institute's pilot television program, "A Story, A Story." The eventual television series was to help 6- to 8-year-old children understand the nature and process of folklore. Butler had additional concerns:

> This program is a pilot, so we know that we can improve on its appeal and comprehensibility, but we need feedback from the children to direct and justify decisions about any changes. We think our host does a marvelous job in the pilot of "A Story, A Story," but what do the viewers like or dislike about him? Does the pacing of the program help or hinder comprehension of our goals? Which of the stories appeal and why? We think the transitional material, the host-to-audience talks, are on the right level, but do the 6- to 8-year-olds really understand?

To answer these questions, Butler needed to try out her pilot television program with kids. She needed a *formative evaluation*. Formative evaluation helps the designer of a product, during the early development stages, to increase the likelihood that the final product will achieve its stated goals. *Evaluation* in this definition means the systematic collection of information for the purpose of informing decisions to design and improve the product. The term *formative* indicates that information is collected during the formation of the product so revisions might be made cost-effective. The developing products that benefit from formative evaluation range from detergents to history curricula, from rock songs to computer programs. Although formative evaluation may apply also to classroom teaching (Bloom, Hastings, & Madaus, 1971), in this book the process is presented as it pertains to replicable curriculum products. The products of concern in this book are educational or training programs for all ages that use electronic technologies as their means of communication. The technologies considered here include television, microcomputers, videodisc and compact disc,[1] and teletext.[2]

In a foreword to the published proceedings of an international conference on evaluating educational television and radio, Wilbur Schramm (1977), professor of communications, wrote the following:

> Typically a field of this kind which begins without an intellectual father-model begins by trial and error, with many different kinds of contributors, each doing his own thing, before it becomes apparent that all this activity really fits into one field and the different kinds of people in it have something to contribute to one another. Out of this develops a broader and more powerful view of the activity in which they are all engaged. They have been nibbling at related problems; now their activities are ready to coalesce into a field of study. (p.viii)

Since Schramm's observation, the field of formative evaluation has grown informally through project-specific conference papers, limited dissemination of unpublished in-house reports, and isolated articles and chapters in media research and instructional design journals and books. Researchers are still "nibbling at related problems," but widely available collective knowledge about this field is scarce. Moreover, published discussion focused on formative evaluation of computer-based materials is almost nonexistent. This book is intended to fill the gap. It synthesizes

---

[1]Videodisc is a relatively indestructible *analog* storage and playback medium for motion and still video and for two audio channels. Computer control of a videodisc permits immediate random access to video segments or frames in any order. Computer coupling allows for simultaneous presentation of computer-generated text and graphics and also for performance record keeping. Compact discs (CD) are laser read discs that store a thousand times more *digital* data than a floppy disc. Text and graphics applications are commercially available, while those featuring digital audio and digital video are still in development.

[2]Teletext is the one-way transmission of text and graphic information to televisions equipped with special decoders and keypads. A decoder displays on the television pages or frames sent during the vertical blanking interval of a regular broadcast or cable signal. A viewer uses the keypad to call for a particular frame or page.

and elaborates the philosophies and methods of formative evaluation to provide guidance to newcomers engaging in formative enterprises and to provide a state-of-the-art document for the old guard.

This volume has two major purposes: (a) to examine the philosophy and functions of formative evaluation in the development of educational curriculum for electronic technologies; and (b) to review and analyze the formative research designs, methods, and measures useful in developing and revising materials for television and for more interactive technologies including microcomputers, computer-controlled interactive videodiscs, compact discs, and teletext.

WHAT'S IN A NAME?

The practice of trying out unfinished materials and acquiring information to improve curriculum design and production for electronic technologies is not new. Cambre (1981) traced such activities in the development of film and radio in the United States back to the 1920s and 1930s. However, as curriculum development and curriculum evaluation have evolved and matured into defined professions over the last two decades, certain names have been adopted for the various phases of development and evaluation.

Before elaborating on these names, let me point out that the term *program* in this context refers to any replicable educational materials for electronic technologies such as television and microcomputers. *Development* defines the period from the flicker of an idea through the final implementation of the program. Also I concur with the majority of the field by using the term *evaluation* here instead of the term *research*. A minority of practitioners prefer the term *research* because they feel that they are not determining the value or worth of the developing materials. However, practitioners do often test the feasibility of, say, a certain keyboard interface with children; and they do measure the effectiveness, say, of a certain instructional branching sequence. Both of these terms— *feasibility* and *effectiveness*—are included along with *value* in most definitions of curriculum evaluation. For example, in the *Encyclopaedia of Educational Media Communications and Technology*, curriculum evaluation is defined as "the collection and provision of evidence to aid decision making on the feasibility, effectiveness and value of curricula" (Unwin & McAleese, 1978, p. 338). Moreover, the evaluation literature distinguishes between evaluation and research in terms of their purposes:

> The purpose of research is to provide new knowledge, and its methodology is designed to produce knowledge that is universally valid. The

purpose of evaluation, however, is to delineate, obtain, and provide information for making educational decisions. This information is . . . highly particularistic and specific to a decision situation, rather than generalizable to many or all settings. Thus, evaluation methodology is not necessarily designed to produce universally valid information, but information that is valid and useful *within the decision-making context.* (Stufflebeam et al., 1971, p. 140)

In practice, evaluators often use the tools and methods of research. To the extent allowed by practicality, utility, and cost, evaluation meets the research criteria of objectivity, reliability, and validity. Thus, many prefer the compromising name, evaluation research.

In this book I assume four phases of program development and four parallel phases of program evaluation. Later chapters describe the phases in more detail; at this point I simply want to establish a common vocabulary. The names for these phases in practice sometimes vary depending on the scale and kind of program, the developing organization, and the training of the program team members. The names listed are relatively widespread or generic in the development of electronic learning materials:

Phases of Program Development	Phases of Evaluation
Phase 1: Planning	Needs assessment
Phase 2: Design	Pre-production formative evaluation
Phase 3: Production	Production formative evaluation
Phase 4: Implementaton	Implementation formative evaluation
	Summative evaluation

Phase 1: Planning and Needs Assessment. The first stage in the development of an educational product is a period of *planning*. The outcome of this activity is a proposal for the product, defining it in general terms. A proposal (also called a position paper or predesign document) typically establishes the feasibility of the project, defines the audience, outlines the content, states the goals, identifies the media, and describes the usage context.

At this planning stage, evaluation performed to facilitate decisions is called *needs assessment.* Industry trainers may use *front-end analysis,* which is similar in most respects to the needs assessment in educational evaluation (Harless, 1973). The overall purpose of this evaluation is to obtain data relevant to such questions as: Is there a need for the program? Who needs what content? What delivery system is feasible to address the need in what context? Some evaluation structures include this phase within the realm of formative evaluation (Sanders & Cunningham, 1973; Stufflebeam, 1983); however, the majority consider formative evaluation to begin after the planning phase when there is some initial conceptualization to be further developed, improved and revised.

Phase 2: Design and Pre-Production Formative Evaluation. The planning decisions are particularized and reconsidered in the *design* stage. Judgments are made as to specific content and behavioral objectives and specific instructional strategies (e.g., television format; type of interactivity). This period builds on the conceptualization of the planning phase and ends with documents that can be used to guide production. The end point for the design phase and the beginning point for the production phase is indefinite. However, typical design outcomes for educational television are preliminary scripts or a writers' notebook. A writers' notebook details in practical language the content, audience characteristics, and program objectives, and it gives example treatments of the objectives. Given such a base, writers generate complete scripts. Depending on the type of program and budget, a writers' notebook might be skipped and scripts developed directly from the program proposal. For computer-based instruction usually a script or storyboard (script with pictures) is developed, with a flowchart that defines the interactivity of the program. The flowchart at this point may give only major directions without much detail or may be the final version with all computer code specifications.

The collection of information to guide decisions during the design phase is commonly called *pre-production formative evaluation*. The term *formative evaluation* was introduced in 1967 by Michael Scriven and originally referred to "outcome evaluation of an intermediate stage in the development of the teaching instrument" (p. 51). However, 20 years of use has broadened the application of this term to cover any kind of feedback from target students or professional experts that is intended to improve the product during design, production, and initial implementation. Keith Mielke (1985), vice president of research at Children's Television Workshop, succinctly summarized the pre-production formative activities for an educational television project:

> Consider how an executive producer might use the following strategic information about the target audience—existing knowledge level, interests, beliefs, attitudes, and media habits. These can all be estimated with research. The physical and technical possibilities of the distribution system and the receptivity of critical "gate keepers" such as parents and teachers

can be studied. Moving closer to the start-up of actual production, much can be learned from target-audience reactions to existing programming that features some relevant quality of interest, such as the same subject matter, format, or cast. (p. 9)

Additionally, interactive programs may benefit from pre-production testing of possible hardware–software interfaces, types of interactivity, levels of user control, and feedback procedures.

Phase 3: Production and Production Formative Evaluation.   As scripts, storyboards, and flowcharts are developed, camera crews go out and computer programmers write program codes. The project enters the *production* phase. Production ends with an operational computer program, a mastered videodisc, or a broadcast-quality television program, ready to be received by the target group.

To help assure the effectiveness of the program, *production formative evaluators* gather data to guide revisions using experimental pieces of the program (e.g., scripts, storyboards, flowcharts) or using close approximations to the whole program (e.g., rough cut pilots, prototypes, check discs). These not-final versions of the program are tested with the target group and experts for user friendliness, appeal, comprehensibility, persuasiveness, and learning. Such information is considered by the designers and producers along with other data (e.g., time, money) in order to make decisions about the final complexion of the program.

Phase 4: Implementation and Implementation Formative Evaluation. *Implementation* involves placing the program in its designated context with the appropriate target group. *Implementation formative evaluation* means testing the effectiveness of the program under approximately normal use conditions with the intention of still changing the program. A more informal name for this phase is *field testing*. There are only limited changes that are realistically and economically possible at this point. Some computer code and text frames are still manipulable, and minimal audio–video editing in a television program may occur. However, such field testing is typically done to help develop associated print materials or to learn lessons that will feed forward into design and production of future programs.

As the final program is implemented in its usage environment, there may be concern with assessing the intended and unintended impact of the program. This kind of evaluation is called *summative evaluation*. It is usually performed independently of the project; and it is not intended for the program developers but instead for program consumers, purchasers, funders, and so on. Summative evaluation may yield formative information, but that is not its goal.

WHAT'S IN THIS BOOK?

The major concern of this book is formative evaluation or the trying out of design ideas and materials. During three phases of product development—design, production, and implementation, formative evaluators employ a variety of research strategies and methods to collect information from the target audience, program purchasers, and experts. This information is meant to reduce the uncertainty of decision making and improve the chances of educational effectiveness.

This volume has three major parts. The first and third parts were written by the author, whereas the second part consists of case studies written by contributors.

Part 1: The Concept. This section introduces the reader to the concept of formative evaluation of electronic learning materials. Chapter 2 uses three case studies to demonstrate why formative evaluation is valuable in the development of electronic learning materials. Also considered is the question of why project leaders choose not to perform formative evaluation. Chapter 3 presents a philosophy of program evaluation as it relates to the phases of program development and describes when and what kinds of evaluation can be undertaken to serve a project involving television and computer-based programs.

Part 2: The Practice. This section comprises five case studies from a variety of organizations illustrating the practice of formative evaluation in the development of microcomputer software, computer-based interactive videodisc, and teletext. Contributors describe the organization and development phases of their projects, the project decisions dealt with by evaluation, and the methodologies used. These chapters furnish a database for some of the discussion that occurs in Part 3.

Chapter 4, contributed by Leona Schauble, and chapter 5, contributed by Saul Rockman, relate the process of computer software development and evaluation at the Children's Television Workshop and the Agency for Instructional Technology, respectively. Kathleen Wilson and William Tally of Bank Street College of Education present in chapter 6 the formative activities supporting the development of an optical disc discovery learning environment. In chapter 7, Susan Doll Jolliffe describes formative evaluation of training videodiscs at Sandy Corporation. The final chapter of this section, contributed by Valerie Crane, Linda Callahan, and Shelley Isaacson, concerns formative methodologies in the implementation phase of a teletext project at Boston's public broadcasting station, WGBH-TV.

Part 3: The Methods. Building on Parts 1 and 2, and other research, this section recommends strategies for designing a formative evaluation of electronic learning materials. Chapter 9 considers how to develop a formative evaluation plan by reflecting on such questions as: Which purposes will the evaluation serve and for whom? What are the evaluation questions? What methods of inquiry are appropriate? What measures will be used with whom under what conditions? The final three chapters detail and compare the various methods and measures that formative evaluators employ. Each method is analyzed for its purpose, techniques, advantages, and disadvantages. Chapter 10 deals with issues of measuring user friendliness, which refers to the user-machine interface of computer-based programs. Chapter 11 examines issues of program reception, including attention, appeal, and excitement. Finally, chapter 12 discusses issues of outcome effectiveness, whether those outcomes be motoric, cognitive, or attitudinal.

This book is meant for newcomers to formative evaluation. For students of instructional design, curriculum development, and curriculum evaluation, the book can function as a supplementary textbook. Current instructional design texts and evaluation texts treat the topic of formative evaluation briefly, if at all. This volume allows students and faculty to explore this important curriculum development process in greater depth, particularly with respect to electronic technologies. Practitioners including researchers, instructional designers, curriculum developers, and project managers can use this book as a guide to develop formative evaluation plans for their own projects. Although the book concentrates on educational and instructional curriculum of the sort currently developed for schools, continuing education, and informal learning situations such as museums, the majority of the book applies also to training projects in industry settings.

REFERENCES

Bloom, B. S., Hastings, J. T., & Madaus, G. F. (1971). *Handbook on formative and summative evaluation of student learning.* New York: McGraw-Hill.

Cambre, M. (1981). Historical overview of formative evaluation of instructional media products. *Educational Communication & Technology Journal, 29*(1), 3–25.

Harless, J. H. (1973). An analysis of front-end analysis. *Improving Human Performance: A Research Quarterly, 4,* 229–244.

Mielke, K. (1985, October 8). The role of research in children's programs. *Current,* p. 9.

Sanders, J. R., & Cunningham, D. J. (1973). A structure for formative evaluation in product development. *Review of Educational Research, 43*(2), 217–236.

Schramm, W. (1977). Foreword. In T. Bates & J. Robinson (Eds.), *Evaluating educational television and radio: Proceedings of the International Conference on Evaluation and Research in Educational Television and Radio* (pp.vii–viii). Milton Keynes, England: The Open University.

Scriven, M. (1967). The methodology of evaluation. In R. Tyler, R. Gagné, & M. Scriven (Eds.), *Perspectives of curriculum evaluation* (pp. 39–83). Chicago: Rand McNally.

Stufflebeam, D. L. (1983). The CIPP Model for program evaluation. In G. F. Madaus, M. S. Scriven, & D. L. Stufflebeam (Eds.), *Evaluation models: Viewpoints on educational and human services evaluation* (pp. 117–142). Boston: Kluwer-Nijhoff.

Stufflebeam, D. L., Foley, W. J., Gephart, W. J., Guba, E. G., Hammond, R. L., Merriman, H. O., & Provus, M. M. (1971). *Educational evaluation and decision-making*. Bloomington, IN: Phi Delta Kappan National Study Committee on Education.

Unwin, D., & McAlesse, R. (Eds.). (1978). *Encyclopaedia of educational media communications and technology*. Westport, CT: Greenwood Press.

I

THE CONCEPT

2

Formative Evaluation
in Decision Making

> *Will Lee, a character actor who played Mr. Hooper, the storekeeper on "Sesame Street," since the children's program went on the air 13 years ago, died of a heart attack Tuesday night at Lenox Hill Hospital. He was 74 years old.*
>
> —"Will Lee" (1982)

This tragic event had wide repercussions among the "Sesame Street" staff at the Children's Television Workshop (CTW) in New York City. What were they to do with Mr. Hooper's character in their ongoing series?

Should "Sesame Street" follow the typical practice of prime-time television, that is, ignore the event and substitute another actor for Will Lee? Or should "Sesame Street" avoid the issue by having Mr. Hooper move out of the neighborhood, perhaps joining his brother in Chicago? The economics of this solution appealed since previously aired non-street segments using Mr. Hooper could continue to be shown.

Or should "Sesame Street" meet the issue of Mr. Hooper's death head on, attempting to explain it to the almost 7 million 3- to 5-year-olds in America who watch the program? This latter choice was the most acceptable to CTW. The "Sesame Street" staff were mature in their understanding of the audience and confident of their ability to deal with emotional issues in a way that was not true in the initial years of the series.

But making the choice to treat the issue of Mr. Hooper's death on air took the producers no further in terms of designing the actual program.

The production staff was faced with the decision of how to handle the death of a popular character in a way that would not negatively affect the distant preschool viewers and might possibly be turned into a positive educational experience. Basically, the producers needed to know how to deal with death and loss for their young and impressionable audience.

Formative Evaluation.   To help guide their decisions concerning the Mr. Hooper program, producers turned to their formative evaluation staff. Formative evaluation refers to the process of gathering information to advise design, production, and implementation decisions. In this chapter, we discuss how the "Sesame Street" formative researchers studied preschoolers' understanding of death to develop guidelines for the scriptwriters and how researchers tested effects of the prebroadcast program.

In addition to the "Sesame Street" case, this chapter relates stories of how formative evaluation is valuable in the decision-making process during the design of computer software and videodisc. These concrete examples of how formative evaluation works in actual production settings are meant to provide the reader with an understanding of why evaluation is used during program development. The chapter portrays how the formative evaluator obtains information relevant to a program issue and then renders diagnostic feedback facilitating decision making. The discussion of each case explores the interaction between producers and researchers, outlines the evaluation questions investigated, discusses briefly the research methods that were applied and the findings, and summarizes the solutions that production finally developed. The intent of this chapter is to present short but complete cases of effective formative evaluation to give evidence as to *why* formative research is valuable in program development.[1] Later chapters examine the philosophy and methods of the program evaluation process as it applies to electronic learning materials, detailing when and what to evaluate and how to test whom.

THE CASE OF "SESAME STREET"

Pre-Production Formative Evaluation

The initial question that the executive producer of "Sesame Street" posed to Valeria Lovelace, in-house director of research, was whether it was feasible to deal with the issue of death with preschoolers. The an-

---

[1]Most of the information in this chapter was obtained through personal interviews with the identified researchers, designers, and producers over the period of March 1985 to July 1986.

swer, after researching the academic literature and polling experts, was not only was it feasible but there was agreement about the basic messages to communicate: (a) that Mr. Hooper had died, (b) that he would not be coming back, and (c) that he would be missed. Based on this information, a script was written and discussed in general staff meetings in which the researchers represented the child audience's viewpoint. For example, when the writer suggested using video clips from previous programs in remembrance of Mr. Hooper, the researchers demurred. They reasoned that young viewers would see the live-action Hooper as indication that he was still alive. Still photographs were substituted. Eventually the script passed through readings by advisors and staff members and was taped as a show.

But would the viewers actually watch the program segments dealing with Mr. Hooper's death and would they understand the messages? More important perhaps, would there be unintended effects resulting from the emotional aspects of the program? Were there changes the production staff could make in the program before broadcast that would maximize communication of its message and minimize negative effects?

Production Formative Evaluation

To provide feedback to the producers on these questions, the formative evaluators showed the prebroadcast program to preschoolers (Lovelace, Schwager, & Saltzman, 1984; Sesame Street Research, 1983). Three- to 5-year-olds viewed segments about Mr. Hooper's death in small groups and were individually interviewed to appraise their understanding of the main messages. Comprehension was high for 4- and 5-year-old children. Additional groups of preschoolers watched the complete hour-long "Sesame Street" program, while observers recorded their viewing behavior to determine the appeal of the program. Appeal of the Hooper segments was comparable to adjacent segments of different content. Thus, the short-term evaluation findings for comprehensibility and appeal were positive. But what about possible long-term unplanned reactions, such as sleep disturbances?

To estimate longer term effects, the evaluators asked 20 pairs of parents and preschoolers to watch a short segment on Mr. Hooper's death, at pickup time at their day-care center. About 10 days later, parents were questioned by telephone as to any effects they observed after the viewing. No negative behaviors were reported, and those children who initiated conversations discussed the facts with no emotional overtones.

The benefits of formative evaluation data in terms of impact on audience learning and behavior are not easily documented unless one sets up an experimental comparison between the program before changes and the program after changes. This kind of comparison rarely occurs given the usually limited time and budgets of formative evaluators. However, audience research such as that carried out by Lovelace's staff can give producers an understanding of the strengths and weaknesses of a program presentation. This feedback reduces uncertainty and facilitates decisions to maximize the program's potential to affect an audience in a certain way. The formative evaluation gave the "Sesame Street" production team confidence that the program would meets its objectives, and it aired with much publicity on Thanksgiving day in 1983.

Broadcast. I viewed the Thanksgiving "Sesame Street" program with my 4-year-old son, having told him nothing about the content. He watched the show with his usual intensity with no visible signs of emotional response, whereas I was drying my tears surreptitiously. Death is not something with which most preschoolers have personal experience, even Bambi's mother's death scene leaves preschoolers emotionally dry-eyed. However, it became apparent weeks later that my son had absorbed cognitively the information in that Thanksgiving show. We were reading a "Sesame Street" book in which Mr. Hooper's store was pictured, and my son commented in a matter-of-fact tone: "That's not Mr. Hooper's store any more now. It's David's store. Mr. Hooper is dead." Fan mail received by CTW after the broadcast indicated that my family's experience was not atypical.

Summary

The original production decision of how one can deal positively with the issue of death on television for a preschool audience was addressed through the offices of formative evaluation. In this case, formative evaluation played a role during the design phase of the television program, using the method of literature review to develop script guidelines. The evaluation staff also acted later during the production phase in their audience test of appeal, short-term comprehensibility, and longer term unplanned effects. Observation during viewing and child and parent interviews provided information for the executive producer to make the decision to air the program.

At the Children's Television Workshop, the "Sesame Street" project team has many players, including several researchers who concentrate their energies only on formative evaluation. This group is one of the few in America to have the time and money to carry out extensive formative work such as that previously outlined. Actor Will Lee died in December 1982, and 11 months later a well-tested show about his death was aired. Yet formative evaluation need not be expensive or even require separate personnel in order to be valuable in the development of a product, as will be evident in the next case of a computer-controlled videodisc.

THE CASE OF "THE BUSINESS DISC"

Early in 1984, Ademola Ekulona and Joanne Strohmer of Maryland Instructional Television (MITV) received the commission to design an innovative educational computer-controlled interactive videodisc. With just the two of them as the core project team, Ekulona played all the major production roles, whereas Strohmer performed as the design and research staffs. Members of the Service Corps of Retired Executives in Maryland functioned as content advisors for the disc.

As the producer described it, "The Business Disc: How To Start and Run a Small Business" is a

> simulation which leads the user through the steps of creating a successful small business by requiring him or her to make planning decisions, then experience twelve months of running a business based on those and subsequent decisions. Through this simulation, participants can explore a personal dream of entrepreneurship without the risk of testing it in the real world. (Ekulona, 1985, p. 35)

One of the decisions facing this small development team was how to assure the user friendliness of the videodisc without waiting until the mastered disc and computer software were completed. At that late date, budget and time restrictions would limit significant changes. To obtain feedback early enough in the development process to make an economically feasible impact on the videodisc, formative evaluation activities occurred during the design and production phases.

Pre-Production Formative Evaluation

During the late design phase, the evaluation method of paper proofs was used frequently and informally to test the effectiveness of the disc design. Adults who had experience with their own small businesses and those without any experience played the disc—on paper. The paper proof method involved showing individual participants paper sketches of the video or computer screens while reading the narrative storyline to them. After respondents made each business decision, they experienced the next branch of paper screens dependent on that decision. After a few hours of work with a participant, enough information was collected to guide changes in the design.

The revised paper design was then evaluated to check whether those changes were improvements or not. In the continuous testing and revision process, respondents participated repeatedly until fewer and fewer problems turned up. This tedious and labor-intensive technique provided an opportunity to check on the logic of the program design and permitted exploration of a number of evaluation questions about user friendliness at a time when design changes were easily made.

Production Formative Evaluation

Once the instructional design and audio–video production were completed, out-of-house programmers created the simulation software using a check disc, an inexpensive version of the final mastered videodisc. Formative evaluation in late 1985 used the check disc and prototype software with approximately 20 adult volunteers. An observer recorded detailed notes of many hours of individual user interaction.

In an interactive learning environment, it is important that the software program and the hardware system be easy to use. The questions of user friendliness that concerned the developers both at the pre-production and production formative evaluation phases included:

1. Accessibility: Was the information easily accessible? Did users understand what to do next or how to proceed through a decision-making process?
2. Responsiveness: Was the program responsive to the users' wishes? Did users receive timely feedback appropriate to their needs? Did users find all the tools that they wanted?
3. Flexibility: Could users change the parameters in the program to suit their own needs?
4. Memory: Could users retrieve and examine their past business decisions and performance to the extent desired?

These research questions are discussed in more detail here.

Accessibility. One issue of accessibility explored was whether users became lost in the program. Were they anxious about where they had been or where they were going? This was not a problem for participants at the pre-production paper proof stage, so a main tracking function was not introduced into the final design. The check disc testing also did not show that users wanted this information; the program seemed acceptably organized for both knowledgeable and naive participants. It is significant to note here that findings on users' comfort with program organization were similar for both early paper proof and later check disc stages. Thus, to evaluate program logic, researchers can obtain user opinions about less expensive paper versions of a videodisc and validly generalize from those data to the final videodisc.

Another aspect of accessibility investigated with paper versions was the appropriateness of wording and completeness of directions. For example, when users were instructed to fill out a cash flow statement, it was clear that additional directions were needed and that not all the instructions could fit on the bottom of the screen in a legible manner.

Although the paper proofs technique focused on program organization and wording, the check disc allowed the best test of accessibility because users had to interact with the keyboard actually in front of them. To illustrate, the videodisc's introduction taught the keyboard functions slowly to the user, but check disc field testing indicated the need for supplemental help screens reviewing which function keys to use for specific data entry sequences.

Responsiveness. During both pre-production and production phases of formative evaluation, all users felt comfortable with the responsiveness of the system. They judged the feedback mechanisms and branching logic of the simulation acceptable, and few requested more didactic instruction or feedback. Some participants at the paper proof stage expressed the need for additional tools to help them learn; for example, several users suggested a computer notepad, which was added to the final version.

Flexibility. Some users showed frustration during the paper proof stage that they could not go back and change their minds about business decisions they had made earlier in the program. Because learning from the consequences of your decisions is the philosophy of a simulation, the developers did not design the program to adjust to users' hindsight. Nonetheless, the check disc evaluation revealed that some limited user control for reviewing or changing material was needed. Users wanted to be able to review video material just as they might ask someone to repeat something they had said, so programmers introduced the capability to skip back multiple times in the video presentation. Also production formative evaluation showed that users frequently did not have all the information they needed at one sitting or that they wanted sometimes to choose an alternative business direction after an initial decision had been made. In response to these observations, the ability to change one's data entry or branching path was allowed in the program to the extent that such a change would be possible in real life. As a case in point, if you had discussed an urban business location with a realtor but had not signed a contract, you could change to a suburban location; however, if you had signed a contract, the change of mind would not be permitted. Once the user passed certain data entry points or video points, change or replay was made impossible.

Memory. "The Business Disc" allows users to work on screen with various business forms, such as a loan application, that are useful to a small business. Participants in the formative evaluation suggested that completed forms in hardcopy would be handy to study and review while making future decisions in the program. Hence, the revised disc provides a list of forms and those that users fill out are available to print.

Summary

The designers of "The Business Disc" applied inexpensive formative evaluation techniques to try out the user friendliness of the videodisc. Accessibility and responsiveness of the videodisc were investigated during the early design phase by testing paper versions of the disc. The additional user friendliness categories of flexibility and memory were probed during the later production phase by testing the check disc using prototype computer software. Such user pretesting is cost effective because changes at these points of product development are relatively inexpensive as compared to changes to the final mastered and programmed version. Early formative evaluation can maximize the videodisc's educational effectiveness for the least cost.

In the first two cases of this chapter, we have seen formative evaluation functioning during the design and production phases of an educational television program and a computer-controlled interactive videodisc. Formative evaluation can also play a role in the implementation phase of a product as in the next case of a microcomputer program.

THE CASE OF "PUPPET THEATER"

Steve Ocko, developer of "Puppet Theater" for Microworlds Learning Inc., intended his computer-based writing program for use with young elementary school children. But the schools he had worked with also wanted software to meet the needs of fourth graders. Did that request mean an entirely new program or could "Puppet Theater" be stretched or reconfigured for the older age groups?[2]

---

[2]This discussion is based on projects for a formative evaluation course taught by the author, Spring, 1985. Students—K. Bernstein, D. Cherenson, T. Feingold, I. Holland, and B. Wallace—worked in cooperation with the "Puppet Theater" developer, Steve Ocko.

"Puppet Theater" encourages young users to engage in two primary activities. First, they can design two puppet characters on the computer screen by a mix and match method choosing from an inventory of shapes, colors, and costumes. Then users choose names and voices for each puppet. Second, the children can use the keyboard to type whatever they want each puppet to say. The letters, words, or sentences appear on screen, and the users can direct the computer's voice synthesizer to "read" the material back. The puppet's mouth moves in concert with the words. The dialogue for the puppets can be saved and played back as a performance, thus the title "Puppet Theater." With this talking typewriter tool, children can work individually or in collaboration with others. The written script and an alphabetical list of words used is available in hardcopy.

Implementation Formative Evaluation

Ocko worked closely with the evaluators to define the research questions underlying his implementation decision of whether "Puppet Theater" would have to be revised to be used with fourth graders. Research questions included, for example: Would fourth graders find the puppets appealing? Would they accept the voice quality available on the Votrax synthesizer? Were the writing patterns of the older children different from the younger ones, so that changes should be made in the program to facilitate the older children's uses? Did the format allow for successful collaboration between older users? The evaluators applied a range of methods to examine: (a) appeal—how much the users liked different parts of the program; (b) responsiveness—how well the program responded to users' inputs and wishes; and (c) flexibility—how flexibly the program could adapt to users' needs. These issues are discussed in more detail here.

Appeal. Older users found the program appealing as indicated through user observation, interviews, and frequency of program use. They enjoyed the concept of designing the puppets and making them perform in a show. Although the developer expressed concern that fourth graders would be critical of the synthesized quality of the speech, the evaluators found that this age group accepted the voice quality as typical of "computer talk."

However, a small group of the students hesitated in their use of the program because of worries about spelling. Spelling errors often became obvious during the computer vocalization of the words. Some students used this feedback to correct their errors; some even enjoyed playing with the sounds of spelling errors; but others felt uncomfortable with such verbal correction. To increase the appeal of "Puppet Theater" for this cautious group, Ocko proposed to add a word list tool to help users find correct spellings.

The program as it was designed for the younger audiences appealed for the most part to the older age group. However, as is shown later, the older students occasionally wanted the program to do more than it could. At these points, the appeal of the program suffered.

Responsiveness.   The expectations of the older users in terms of responsiveness of the system were not met entirely. Many complained that the verbal feedback was too slow. Observational data yielded user comments such as "If I type faster, will the words come back faster?". Further, the timing of the verbal feedback was frustrating to the older user. Many wanted to type in longer dialogues before hearing their words spoken. Accordingly, Ocko planned revisions to allow the user more control in terms of the timing of the verbal feedback; however, speeding up the feedback would require a different hardware and software configuration.

Flexibility.   "Puppet Theater" is a writing tool that gives children a great deal of control over many parameters; for example, the look of the puppets, the pitch of their voices, and which puppet speaks what words. The more sophisticated older users, however, wanted more flexibility, more control, and more real-life options than were available in the program for beginning writers. For example, in postuse interviews, many evinced the desire to animate the puppets and to use scenery and props in their stories. Additionally, older users were frustrated by the restricted amount one could type for each puppet and by the inability to change words that were previously saved. In response to such findings, Ocko proposed the inclusion of special effects tools to create set designs and props, and a scrolling text window was planned within which simple text editing could occur.

Summary

Ocko found the research data of his out-of-house formative evaluators to be constructive in reconfiguring "Puppet Theater" for implementation with older elementary school users. In response to feedback from user observation and interviews, the designer planned additional tools to increase the program's appeal, responsiveness, and flexibility for these more sophisticated authors.

WHY EVALUATE?

As evidenced in these three case studies, the main reason for performing formative evaluation is to inform the decision-making process during the design, production, and implementation stages of an educational program with the purpose of improving the program.

Design Phase

Producers, writers, and software designers typically rely on their own personal and professional experience for ideas about their target audience. As the experiences and characteristics of the target group diverge from those of the design and production group, pre-production formative evaluation takes on a more critical role. Design decisions benefit from knowledge about the existing competencies of the target user—their knowledge of the content, attitudes toward the content, interests in the content, and their experience with the medium. Choices of television format and interactive strategies should be tested with the target group for "there are no theories of pedagogy so well established that one can say, without tryout, what will prove educative" (Cronbach, 1963, p. 677). For example, when the "Sesame Street" staff grappled with the decision of how to deal with death for preschoolers, research on children's conceptual understanding of death provided information useful in scripting the program, and the research staff's feedback on how preschoolers comprehend the medium of television helped guide the production.

Production Phase

Trying out early versions of instructional materials for electronic technologies can reduce expensive production mistakes by providing timely and cost-effective feedback for revisions. User observations gave producers of "The Business Disc" feedback to improve user friendliness before the instructional program reached a stage where changes were cost prohibitive. A wide range of audience/user reactions can be assessed at early production stages; among these are attention, comprehension, information retention, personal involvement, and user-machine comfort. Production formative evaluation "is an advisable substitute for trying to second guess the aesthetic preferences and intellectual astuteness of the target audience" (Bertrand, 1978, p. 7).

Ordinarily formative findings are only one piece of information that determines the revisions in a program during the production phase. Economics, politics, deadlines, and intuitions are other inputs to the project manager's decision-making process. Occasionally the evaluation data will be strong enough to dictate abandonment. As a case in point, in the first year of planning for "Sesame Street," a series of episodes called "The Man from Alphabet" tested poorly with preschoolers on appeal and comprehensibility (Connell & Palmer, 1970). This storyline was dropped from the program lineup, and the lessons learned were applied to production of other program formats.

Implementation Phase

Additionally, formative evaluators can collect information during the implementation of a program in its intended setting. Implementation formative evaluation can help developers to: (a) fine tune the material for its educational setting, (b) further define the remainder of a series in development, or (c) reconfigure a program for a different context or a different user group. The latter function appears in our case of "Puppet Theater" in which the developer reworked the writing program and added tools in response to formative data from users older than his originally defined target students.

Even implementation data for computer-based interactive videodiscs can be used to revise computer programmed text displays. For example, Dan Burnstein (Personal Communication, February, 1987) of the Harvard Law School Interactive Video Project reported that users of a simulation videodisc on trial advocacy skills have provided data to guide revisions and additions to the computer text feedback screens.

NonFormative Formative Evaluation. Occasionally formative evaluation is used for purposes other than facilitating the formation of effective program materials. One of these purposes is public relations, where the studies are seen as ways to obtain early exposure and praise; the other purpose is accountability, where funders need some confirmation that the project is going to be successful. Research for public relations or accountability has a different audience for its findings than formative evaluation and also requires answers to different questions from those posed by formative evaluators. Both of these functions are inappropriate for the formative evaluator who is dedicated to the improvement of the educational materials.

Evaluation of Formative Evaluation. The notion that audience/user feedback and teacher/expert criticism can lead to improvements in one's curriculum has commonsense appeal, and certainly anecdotal support for the process abounds. But does the notion of the effectiveness of formative evaluation stand up to empirical testing?

The answer to that question is yes, as far as the limited amount of experimental research allows us to generalize. Studies cited in review by Baker and Alkin (1973) on the effects of formative evaluation indicate that programmed print instruction and televised instruction revised using empirical data yield better student performance than unrevised versions. The few experimental studies published since 1973 support this conclusion also (Baghdadi, 1981; Kandaswamy, Stolovitch, & Thiagarajan, 1976; Nathenson & Henderson, 1980; Scanlon, 1981; Wager, 1983).

A critical study by Rosen in 1968 (cited in Baker & Alkin, 1973) found that intuitively revised programmed print instruction was less effective in improving student performance than versions revised with the aid of evaluation feedback. Fleming (1963, cited in Cambre, 1981) obtained similar results with televised instruction where film revised using learner data was determined to be superior to film revised by subject matter experts. Robinson (1972) went a step further and trained developers to interpret the formative data with a set of revision rules; programs revised by the trained developers produced higher student performance means than programs revised by the untrained.

The empirical evidence, such as it is, testifies to the benefits of formative evaluation. Moreover, no research evidence supports the conclusion that data-based revision of instructional materials produces lower student performance.

WHY NOT EVALUATE?

Good business practice dictates that a product's problems be ironed out before it is marketed. Certainly every snack food and toothpaste on the grocery shelf was tested frequently during development with employee panels and consumers. "Nielsen data on testing of products show dramatically that those products which are tested stand a 3 out of 4 chance of succeeding while those products which are not tested stand a 4 out of 5 chance of failure" (Crane, 1985b, p. 31). And yet a 1971 analysis of educational materials showed that

> of the sixty "best sellers" among textbooks . . . less than 10 percent were field-tested before publication. . . . barely 7 percent of 633 programmed instructional materials in major curriculum areas had empirical support, and only about 1 percent of 233 materials used in broadcast television instruction had been learner-tested. (Komoski, cited in Anderson, Ball, Murphy, & Associates, 1976, p. 241)

In the 18 years since that survey, the practice of formative evaluation with electronic learning materials has grown, somewhat due to the requirements of select government funders. Nonetheless, such agencies typically encourage one-time studies of a pilot or prototype (Crane, 1985a; Nelson, 1980) rather than earlier and more frequent testing as advocated in this book. Further, many educational projects funded outside of these government agencies continue to be designed without benefit of formative evaluation.

Truett has attempted to document the practice of field testing by educational software producers and publishers. Of 56 software businesses responding to a 1983 survey (14% return rate), 70% reported doing some field testing, mainly with teachers (Truett, 1984). Of 125 companies responding to a 1985 survey (32% return rate), 82% reported doing some field testing, mostly with six or fewer teachers in local schools (Truett & Ho, 1986). Gathering teacher feedback is apparently common practice among Truett's respondents, but one wonders about the evaluation philosophy of the large percentage of nonrespondents.

There are many reasons why formative evaluation is not a given in the development of educational materials for electronic technologies. The major excuses are ones of time, money, human nature, unmet expectations, measurement difficulties, and lack of knowledge. Each of these reasons is expanded on here.

Time.   The majority of curriculum developers are under pressure to produce by certain deadlines. The first task to be short-circuited under time pressure is formative evaluation, because it is possible physically to produce some sort of product without such research. However, early project planning and continual supervision of the intertwined dance of production and evaluation help circumvent problems, so that formative findings can be communicated in time to be functional in project development and revision.

Also, when pressed for time, evaluators can choose research designs and formative techniques that have quick turnaround times and still provide useful data. Some computer-based technologies allow fast and accurate access to target group information. For example, with the Program Evaluation Analysis Computer, viewers register their responses to a television presentation by pressing keys on individual hand-held units. Using a microcomputer, the data can be converted quickly to a graph of the group response. This technology provides immediate evidence of television program appeal and credibility (Nickerson, 1979; see also chapter 11, this volume).

In certain circumstances, time can be saved by using small numbers of respondents. Some research has shown that formative information from observing very few students can significantly improve instructional effects (Kandaswamy et al., 1976; Robeck, 1965, cited in Baker & Alkin,

1973; Wager, 1983). Large production groups sometimes set up ongoing formative environments to collect daily information from small samples of target students. For example, when Tom Snyder Productions developed home software for children, students were invited after school to a computer playroom where they could use the company's early prototypes or could choose competing software. Informal but frequent observations by both researchers and designers provided timely and useful formative data (D. Dockterman, personal communication, April 22, 1986).

Thus, the pressure of time on formative evaluation can be minimized by good team management and communication techniques as well as creative use of the full range of formative methods.

Money. As all things do, formative evaluation costs money; however, the amount is usually a relatively small percentage of a production budget. For example, the typical budget for a federally funded adult telecourse includes 2%–3% for formative evaluation. The real issue is to what extent does formative evaluation save money in the long run by avoiding costly revisions in materials that turn out to be unappealing, incomprehensible, not credible, and so forth. Although there are some studies comparing costs of different formative methods (e.g., Golas, 1983; Kandaswamy et al., 1976; Wager, 1983), research explicitly analyzing the cost-effectiveness of formative evaluation per se is nonexistent. We do know, as discussed previously, that curriculum materials can be improved through data-based revisions. We do not know whether that improvement is significant enough to justify the costs of data collection and revision.

Human Nature. One of the major critics of formative evaluation is the curriculum developer/producer, understandably enough, because it is his or her work that is under scrutiny. Some feel that formative evaluation places constraints on creativity. David Connell, the first executive producer of "Sesame Street," described his early feelings about the formative evaluation process by saying that "there was the risk of intellectualizing the material to death and ending up with a program most notable for its monumental boredom" (Connell & Palmer, 1970, p. 3). Obviously, "Sesame Street" did not turn out to be boring. In theory, effective formative evaluation does not restrict creativity but informs it so as to balance the goals of education and entertainment.

As a case in point, a New York advertising agency recently wanted to increase its creativity, to take more risks and produce less conservative television commercials. The creative director felt that "the opportunity to test ideas in early stages without fear of public rejection will encourage, not inhibit, risk taking" (Prescott, 1987, p. 8). Accordingly, the agency established The Risk Lab, a formative evaluation program that tests partially formed creative concepts quickly and informally with consumers.

Some developers reject the concept of formative evaluation almost as if it "were a sign of cowardice—an admission that they did not trust their own intuitions" (Lesser, 1974, p. 133). On the other hand, project directors have felt satisfaction in having their intuitions verified and relief that poor decisions can be addressed before public dissemination of the materials. As one telecourse project director has commented,

> There is a danger of being insulated from the real world while a project team is in the process of developing course materials. The [formative] evaluation brings the project in touch with the audience and helps to determine whether the hypotheses are on target. (Crane, 1985a, p. 4)

All of us are sensitive to having our work reviewed, but formative evaluation is sometimes harder to accept because it requires the review even before the product is actually complete. Developers sometimes argue that findings on early versions cannot be generalized to final versions with their extra bells and whistles. Relevant to this issue, Crane (1985b) compared rough-cut with finished television materials as to viewer appeal and host ratings. She found that television "program elements and program segments tested in rough-cut form—as segments without transitions, program opening, title, or music—test virtually the same as those segments in the finished product" (p. 24).

The developers who appreciate and use formative evaluation see it as direction from a coach or tutor as if during practice rather than as a final score in the game. Such a view necessitates an evaluator who is responsive to the needs of the project, can collaborate with the creative personnel, understands how to compromise between the ideal research study and the feasible, and can communicate findings in a nonthreatening form so that constructive revision decisions may be made.

Expectations. The flip side of those who reject the philosophy of formative evaluation are those who buy into it with unrealistic expectations. They may be disappointed because formative evaluation cannot produce a formula for a successful television program or interactive videodisc. There are too many variables operating in the design of a curriculum and its implementation in the target setting to think that research can guarantee effectiveness. Further, research cannot substitute for creative scripting, convincing acting, engaging interactive sequences, and so on. Formative evaluation is not the creative and determining force in the curriculum development, but it can be a catalyst for ideas and strategies and can "provide data that reduce uncertainties and clarify the gains and losses that different decisions incur" (Weiss, 1972, p. 4).

Measurement Difficulties. Some educational projects fail to include formative evaluation because they have objectives (e.g., creativity) that are difficult to measure or objectives (e.g., attitudes) that need longer term program exposure to achieve change than is usually possible in a time-pressured formative study. Such projects can still benefit from formative work.

* For difficult objectives, researchers search for the best measurement tools available or create their own with appropriate consideration of validity and reliability. Because development of measures is time-consuming and difficult, it is rare to find a formative evaluation in which it is done with scientific rigor.

For objectives that need long-term program exposure, evaluators make certain assumptions about prerequisite behaviors and proceed to measure those as well as possible. Attitudes are unlikely to change after a single half-hour television program, but the program should affect some behaviors that are prerequisite to attitude change. For instance, formative evaluators will look at respondents' personal involvement with the program, belief in the characters, as well as comprehension and retention of the factual information. Thus, some estimate can be made as to the effectiveness of the one program in encouraging attitude change.

Knowledge. Formative evaluation is often not included in curriculum development because people are unaware of the philosophy and methods. Although the practice of formative evaluation with electronic technologies has been traced back to the 1930s (Cambre, 1981), much of the discussion of this field hides away in unpublished or limited circulation reports or in volumes on general educational curriculum development and evaluation. Although I identify with Eva Baker's (1974) question of whether "writing about a process as complex as formative evaluation [is] a way to improve practice in the area of instruction" (p. 533), this book takes on that task to encourage the use of formative evaluation in curriculum development, no matter what the characteristics of the next new electronic medium.

REFERENCES

Anderson, S. B., Ball, S., Murphy, R. T., & Associates (Eds.). (1976). *Encyclopedia of educational evaluation: Concepts and techniques for evaluating education and training programs.* San Francisco: Jossey-Bass.

Baghdadi, A. A. (1981). A comparison between two formative evaluation methods. *Dissertation Abstracts International, 41,* 3387-A.

Baker, E. L. (1974). Formative evaluation of instruction. In W. J. Popham (Ed.), *Evaluation in education* (pp. 531–585). Berkeley, CA: McCutchan.

Baker, E. L., & Alkin, M. C. (1973). Formative evaluation of instructional development. *AV Communication Review, 21*(4), 389–418.

Bertrand, J. (1978). *Communications pretesting* (Media Monograph No. Six). Chicago: University of Chicago, Community and Family Study Center.

Cambre, M. (1981). Historical overview of formative evaluation of instructional media products. *Educational Communication & Technology Journal, 29*(1), 3–25.

Connell, D. D., & Palmer, E. L. (1970, December). *"Sesame Street"—A case study.* Paper presented at the international seminar on Broadcaster/Researcher Cooperation in Mass Communication Research, Leicester, England.

Crane, V. (1985a). *A study of formative research practices for the Annenberg/CPB projects: The first five years.* Unpublished manuscript, Research Communications Ltd., Chestnut Hill, MA.

Crane, V. (1985b, January). *Formative research for television: Believe it or not?.* Paper presented at the meeting of the Association for Educational Communications and Technology, Anaheim, CA.

Cronbach, L. J. (1963). Course improvement through evaluation. *Teachers College Record, 64,* 672–83.

Ekulona, A. (1985). Videodisc simulations need Level III. *EITV, 17*(9), pp. 35, 50, 64, 65.

Golas, K. C. (1983). Formative evaluation effectiveness and cost: Alternative models for evaluating printed instructional materials. *Performance & Instruction Journal, 22*(5), 17–19.

Kandaswamy, S., Stolovitch, H. D., & Thiagarajan, S. (1976). Learner verification and revision: An experimental comparison of two methods. *AV Communication Review, 24*(3), 316–328.

Lesser, G. S. (1974). *Children and television: Lessons from "Sesame Street."* New York: Random House.

Lovelace, V., Schwager, I., & Saltzman, E. (1984, August). *Responses to death on "Sesame Street" from preschoolers and parents.* Paper presented at the meeting of the American Psychological Association, Toronto, Ontario, Canada.

Nathenson, M. B., & Henderson, E. S. (1980). *Using student feedback to improve learning materials.* London: Croom Helm.

Nelson, B. N. (1980). *Assessment of the ESAA-TV program: An examination of its production, distribution and financing* (Contract No. 300-77-0468). Washington, DC: Department of Education.

Nickerson, R. (1979). Formative evaluation of instructional TV programming using the Program Evaluation Analysis Computer. In J. Baggaley (Ed.), *Experimental research in TV instruction* (Vol 2, pp. 121–125). St Johns: Memorial University.

Prescott, E. (1987, June 7). An agency's turn to madcap ads. *The New York Times,* sect. 3, pp. 1, 8, 9.

Robinson, T. J. (1972). Replicable training in revision techniques. *Dissertation Abstracts International, 33,* 1573A.

Scanlon, E. (1981). Evaluating the effectiveness of distance learning: A case study. In F. Percival & H. Ellington (Eds.), *Aspects of educational technology: Vol. XV: Distance learning and evaluation* (pp. 164–171). London: Kogan Page.

Sesame Street Research. (1983). *Study on show #1839.* Unpublished manuscript, Children's Television Workshop, New York.

Truett, C. (1984). Field testing educational software: Are publishers making the effort? *Educational Technology, 24*(5), 7–12.

Truett, C., & Ho, C. (1986). Is educational software field tested? *The Computing Teacher, 14*(2), 24–25.

Wager, L. C. (1983). One-to-one and small group formative evaluation: An examination of two basic formative evaluation procedures. *Performance and Instruction Journal, 22*(5), 5–7.

Weiss, C. H. (1972). *Evaluation research: Methods for assessing program effectiveness.* Englewood Cliffs, NJ: Prentice-Hall.

Will Lee, 74, was Mr. Hooper on television "Sesame Street." (1982, December 9). *The New York Times,* p. B20.

3

Program Development and the Role of Evaluation

The following comments were heard as 9- to 14-year-olds explored an interactive videodisc associated with the first season of the television program, "The Voyage of the Mimi" (Wilson, 1985a, pp. 3, 11, 13, 14):

"I want to see what everything does."

"The way it works is very good. I like it. All these keys, they move you around."

"We're zooming in, on one specific spot, and you know where that spot is? Ten Pound Island."

"Oh wow! Man!! Oh great!!! We're right in the port" (after zooming in from the USA map to a close-up on Gloucester).

"This is great!"

"It does all I want with the video image."

"The Voyage of the Mimi" videodisc energizes kids. Children respond with similar enthusiasm to the "Mimi" science and math television series and computer software produced by Bank Street College of Education in New York. Teachers report high student involvement and extensive learning opportunities (Storey & Julyan, 1985, pp. 44, 46):

I would say that the excitement level was very, very high and as a group it was certainly equal if not greater than anything that I've seen before. The students got more information in less time and probably retained more because there were different approaches each day. Different approaches spark their imagination in different ways and offer more than I could.

What are the secrets behind these success stories? Samuel Gibbon, executive director of the Bank Street College multimedia project, suggests that "Mimi's" effectiveness resulted from a combination of the project team's experience and talent, good luck, and systematic program development and evaluation.

A systematic approach to program development involves the identification of educational needs, specification of program goals, and design of instructional strategies and events that create effective learning conditions for target students. Evaluation plays changing roles through the phases of program development, but its consistent goal is to maximize the program's potential for success. The previous chapter examined the value of formative evaluation in helping out at one decision point in three different projects. This chapter follows the changes in the formative evaluator's role as a single program proceeds from idea to finished product.

Educators have advocated a systematic approach to designing curricula for any content, audience, and medium since the publication of Ralph W. Tyler's (1949), *Basic Principles of Curriculum and Instruction*. Briefly, Tyler proposed that any curriculum project should have clearly defined goals, should provide environments that evoke within students learning experiences likely to support achievement of such goals, and should evaluate the strengths and weaknesses of the curriculum program in actually producing desired outcomes. Tyler (1949) emphasized a cyclical curriculum development process so that

> as materials and procedures are developed, they are tried out, their results appraised, their inadequacies identified, suggested improvements indicated; there is replanning, redevelopment and then reappraisal. . . . In this way we may hope to have an increasingly more effective educational program rather than depending so much upon hit and miss judgment as a basis for curriculum development. (p. 123)

Since Tyler's book, over 40 models of systematic instructional design have evolved with varying levels of specificity (Andrews & Goodson, 1980). Despite the proliferation of models, "the general tasks constituting a model of instructional design . . . are generic in that they may be applied across differing purposes, emphases, origins, uses, and settings" (Andrews & Goodson, 1980, p. 13). On perusal of documentation of program development models for different electronic media, one finds many commonalities. The course of action followed by educational television production companies such as Children's Television Workshop (Palmer, 1983; Young, 1983) and TVOntario (Nickerson & Gillis, 1979) parallels that of microcomputer educational software design companies

(MECC, 1984) and that of interactive videodisc developers such as Wicat Systems (Campbell, Tuttle, & Gibbons, 1982) and Systems Impact (Hofmeister, Engelmann, & Carnine, 1986).

For television, software, and videodisc, this chapter outlines four generic phases of program development and four simultaneous phases of evaluation activities to inform the decision-making process

Phases of Program Development	Phases of Evaluation
Planning	Needs Assessment
Design	Pre-production Formative Evaluation
Production	Production Formative Evaluation
Implementation	Implementation Formative Evaluation

This chapter presents a philosophy of program evaluation as it relates to the major phases of development. The chapter describes the phases of program development and, using examples from "The Voyage of the Mimi" multimedia project, illustrates the nature of the decisions at each phase and the various roles that evaluation plays in facilitating decision making.[1]

PHASE 1: PLANNING AND NEEDS ASSESSMENT

We can trace the beginning of "The Voyage of the Mimi" back to a request from the U.S. Department of Education for a multimedia project in science and mathematics for upper elementary school children. In response to that request, executive director Sam Gibbon and his colleagues at Bank Street College of Education proposed a television series with supplemental materials to include books, microcomputer software, and interactive videodisc (Bank Street College, 1981).

The beginning of Gibbon's project is typical for an educational or training curriculum, entailing a period of planning and analysis that culminates in a formal or informal proposal for funding or for action. Establishing the need for and feasibility of the project is the main intent

---

[1]Unless otherwise referenced, details of the "Mimi" project were obtained through interviews with Samuel Y. Gibbon, Jr., Executive Director, Cynthia A. Char, Research Scientist, and Kathleen Wilson, Videodisc Project Director, during the period of July to November 1986. Note also that print materials support the "Mimi" series but are not considered in the discussion here.

of this initial stage. The research tasks performed to supply a foundation for decisions at this point constitute what is variously called a *needs assessment* or *front-end analysis*. During a needs assessment, the major planning questions call for defining the three areas of content, audience, and medium and setting. These areas are discussed further here.

Content. In the early proposal stage, the Bank Street team searched for answers to these content need questions:

- What is the need for a greater understanding of science and math?
- What science and math content needs to be communicated?
- What content justifies the investment, given limited resources?
- Is that content being addressed sufficiently with current curriculum?

Poring over science and math texts and curriculum evaluations yielded a diverse range of significant content for 8- to 12-year-olds. But the critical issue was which content to place their money on. Through recurring discussions with scientists, teachers, and media experts, the development team distilled a set of overlapping thematic areas for the curriculum, including for example: energy, ecology, and processes of change.

Audience. The reports and experts drawn upon for content information offered testimony also for need and feasibility questions about the "Mimi's" target audience or users:

- Who needs this content?
- What are their characteristics with respect to the program content (i.e., their knowledge, interests, attitudes)?
- Is the target group of sufficient size in the educational setting to justify the content and media chosen?

As the "Mimi" team pursued answers to these questions of need and feasibility, they fashioned an audience profile that supported the evolution of general guidelines for the design of the project. For example, review of learning literature indicated that the target group learns best from models with whom they can identify; accordingly, Gibbon concluded that the "Mimi" television series sought to present "'scientists, mathematicians, and oceanographers as real people who do everyday things like washing dishes, besides conducting experiments'" (Reinhold,

1986, p. 29). Likewise, large variability in student conceptual knowledge and learner interests pointed to by teachers and classroom observations resulted in the proposal of multilevel microcomputer and videodisc materials to accommodate a range of abilities, interests, and learning styles (Char, 1985).

Medium and Setting. In addition to considering planning issues of content and target group, the "Mimi" team asked needs assessment questions with respect to each medium in the classroom setting:

- Which content needs can best be met with television, microcomputers, or videodisc, taking into account their special medium and usage characteristics?
- Which media formats can best appeal to the target group and communicate the content effectively?

To make initial broad stroke decisions about the educational content and formats of the television component of the "Mimi" project, executive producer Gibbon drew upon his prior experience with pre-production formative evaluation generated by the "3-2-1 Contact" science show team of the Children's Television Workshop. This research surveyed 8- to 12-year-olds' knowledge of and attitudes toward science as well as their preferences for various program formats (Mielke & Chen, 1983). The Bank Street team noted in these findings that interest in whales cut across gender and age groups and that dramatic television formats were highly appealing. Thus, half of the "Mimi" series is a continuing adventure/drama and the other half is documentary format.

The "Mimi's" dramatic story format chronicles the adventures of young scientists studying whales from the deck of an ocean-going research vessel. The narrative engages the children's emotions and curiosity and motivates them to identify with the characters who also appear in the "Mimi's" documentary-format expeditions. The expeditions take the viewer to visit people doing research related to topics introduced in the dramatic episodes.

The Bank Street team's pedagogical philosophy and recognition of the role of computers in schools guided the decision that the best use of microcomputers in the "Mimi" project was to permit groups to interact with the technology and to encourage the use of computers to solve problems in ways that scientists do (Char & Hawkins, 1987). Consequently, proposed software formats included simulations, data-gathering and graphing tools, and programmable environments. In addition, the software echoed the television storyline.

To help establish which videodisc formats were feasible for the science content and target user, existing discs were analyzed for appealing and effective educational features. Acknowledging this research and the Bank Street pedagogical approach, the disc formats proposed were to encourage "active exploration and inventiveness," to be "developmentally appropriate for children," and to be suitable for a variety of "potential school usage patterns" (Wilson, 1985b, p. 1).[2]

Summary

The needs assessment role of evaluation during the planning phase of an electronic learning project is to help identify needs, set priorities, and determine feasibility of programs to meet those needs. The gathering of information to facilitate initial decisions about content, audience, and media entails: (a) reviews of existing relevant research studies, test data, and curricula content; (b) consultations with experts including program managers such as teachers; and (c) measurement of target audience characteristics. The planning decisions are then reviewed and elaborated in more detail in the next phase of design.

PHASE 2: DESIGN AND PRE-PRODUCTION FORMATIVE EVALUATION

The design phase particularizes the proposal of the planning phase and ends with *design documents* used to guide production. During this period, decisions are made specifying content, defining desired learner outcomes, and delineating presentational strategies. The amount of detail and specification that appears in design documents depends on the type and size of the project and the organization of team personnel.

For example, Children's Television Workshop develops a design document called a writers' notebook that "translates the curriculum goals into practical language, expands upon their definition and suggests teaching strategies. . . . The notebook is intended both to set the producers and writers on a sound course, where child development and learning are concerned, and to spur creativity" (Young, 1983, p. 14). Such resource notebooks may be superfluous where writers are in-house and actively involved in the project definition, as in the case of the "Mimi" television team—draft scripts for two pilot shows served as the design phase outcome.

---

[2]The videodisc component of the first season of "The Voyage of the Mimi" was funded by SONY Corporation of America.

The design documents for computer-based materials typically consist of a flowchart detailing the logical flow of what will be shown when and a script and storyboard describing the presentation. For example, the flowchart of a computer-based interactive videodisc is

> the skeleton upon which all other components will hang. . . . Here you'll decide what menus will be shown, what answers accepted, what segments reviewed, and what data collected from the viewer. You'll also choose whether a segment is to be videodisc motion, videodisc still, videodisc text or graphic, or computer text or graphic; and whether there will be sound and which of the two possible soundtracks you'll use. (Utz, 1984, p. 41)

The videodisc design document also includes a script and storyboard that "is the flesh we attach to the flow chart's skeleton" (Utz, 1984, p. 41). The script and storyboard specify video scenes, narration and sound, text and graphics, and branching instructions.

The initial design documents roughly outline the program with more and more specification as the project moves into the production phase. There are currently few standard formats for computer-based design documents; each organization and project develops what is appropriate for its working needs.

Pre-Production Formative Evaluation. The role of evaluation during the design stage is to feed the team information that will contribute to and increase confidence in decisions about content, learner outcomes, and presentational strategies. Typically this means that researchers call upon the eventual users, both students and teachers (or program managers).

For students, evaluation might ascertain:

- their knowledge of and interests in the proposed content;
- their interests in, understanding, and usage of the intended medium;
- their attitudes toward the content and medium;
- their responses to existing or draft materials that embody some potential program feature such as content, characters, interactivity, or format.

For teachers or the eventual program managers, evaluation is concerned with such issues as:

- their understanding of target learner characteristics;
- their receptivity of the proposed content and medium;

- their perceived utility of the program within current curriculum practices;

- classroom management of the medium.

During the phase of pre-production formative evaluation for "The Voyage of the Mimi" project, a teacher advisory board evaluated proposed content ideas, identified learner characteristics important for materials design, proposed media features that they felt discriminated effective science programs, and outlined management issues for using media in the classroom (Char & Hawkins, 1987).

In addition, evaluators elicited 8- to 12-year-olds' reactions to potential story themes and story characters with a variety of methods. Students assessed the appeal and comprehensibility of a set of existing television materials on whales, computers, and sign language (given that a deaf woman was among the television cast). Classes of the target age group read printed stories with themes of deserted islands, whales, and navigation and discussed their curiosities, interests, and problem solving approaches. Exposure to print descriptions of characters and videotapes of cast auditions produced student ratings on appeal, credibility, and personal identification. The project team discussed the findings of these studies in their deliberations on content and pilot scripting.

For the "Mimi" interactive videodisc, pre-production evaluation activities built on the research findings of the TV and software components. Further consultation with teachers and content experts helped guide decisions about the videodisc database and interactivity. Additionally, various program features were evaluated at early stages with student users; for example, comprehension of icons was tested first using drawings on paper and then later using graphics on screen.

Summary

As a function of pre-production formative evaluation activities, researchers for an electronic learning project include the target audience and teachers (or program managers) in the process of making design decisions about content, objectives, and production formats. Further, experts in the subject matter, the medium, and the target audience may critically appraise the program at this time. Pre-production studies generate strategic information (Mielke, 1985) to help guide the creativity of designers and reduce the uncertainty of some critical decisions. As a project moves into production, attention turns to gathering tactical information (Mielke, 1985) about specifics of the product as it develops.

PHASE 3: PRODUCTION AND PRODUCTION FORMATIVE EVALUATION

The production phase begins when the design document reaches a usable form, although it may still be incomplete. There are innumerable decisions made during the transition from design to all-out production. The art of *production formative evaluation* comes in choosing which decisions are vital enough to warrant data collection—which decisions will make a significant difference in the effectiveness of the program. The role of formative evaluation at this point is to try out developing versions of the program with student users and program managers to map out the weaknesses and the strengths of the program. Then weaknesses can be eliminated and strengths replicated before the program is finalized.

"When formative evaluation is conducted properly and the results are communicated to conscientious production staff, the usual risks encountered in producing a successful series are minimized" (Nickerson & Gillis, 1979, p. 6). This does not mean, however, that formative evaluation guarantees success or that formative evaluation is the cause of success. Formative findings allow the learner a voice in the proceedings during the development of the product. How that voice is responded to depends upon time, money, and program design, and also depends upon the creativity, interpersonal relationships, and mission of the team members.

Production Formative Evaluation. To help assure the effectiveness of educational materials, production formative evaluation uses early versions of the program to gather feedback from target users and program managers (e.g., teachers). Evaluators test television scripts and storyboards as well as paper versions of computer screens, flowcharts, and prototype interfaces. Even interactive videotape can mimic some aspects of a videodisc for early evaluation (Hofmeister et al., 1986). Such cost-effective tryouts of development versions reveal gross problems in the program design, for example, ineffective instructional strategies, lack of character appeal, inappropriate language levels, confusing icons, and difficult control options. Also such testing highlights those aspects that are strengths in the program.

As the program versions change to better approximate the final materials, production formative evaluation looks at more subtle and complex user-processing responses. Outcome effects are measured also. Approximate program versions—rough-cut television pilots, operational software prototypes, low-cost check discs—are tested with the target group for appeal, comprehension, persuasiveness, and user friendliness. Further, evaluators keep an eye out for unintended effects of the program.

For example, characters incidental to the main storyline may show inappropriate behaviors (not caught by the director) which viewers pick up and imitate.

Evaluators communicate the formative findings and action recommendations to the designers, producers, and programmers who weigh them along with data on time, money, personnel, and so on, when making revision decisions for the final program. Note, however, that formative evaluation is of little use at this point if the pilot versions cannot be modified. Under those circumstances, the findings inform the development of other programs of the same or similar projects.

Production formative evaluation takes a different role if a project is in series production, where the pilot format has been tested already and many programs are being produced based on that template. For example, at the Children's Television Workshop where most projects are large scale series, the role of the evaluator during series production is as spokesman for the audience:

> Once volume production is underway, short-term data-based feedback loops from the target audience are no longer feasible, logistically or financially. What then is the research contribution to design and production? Professional judgement. The researcher can represent the viewpoint of the target audience as an in-house advocate even in the most hectic of production schedules. At CTW the executive producer typically formalizes some system of checks and sign-offs by both Research and Content departments at various points in a production process. (Mielke, 1985, p. 9)

However, most of the significant directional changes in a project occur earlier at the pilot-testing stage, when the production staff has not committed themselves entirely to a certain point of view.

As "The Voyage of the Mimi" team worked on two dramatic/adventure pilot television shows, researchers tried out scripts with the target audience. The effort was phenomenal, because the turnaround time allowed was minimal. A draft script was received at 6 p.m. one day and multiple-choice questions and group-discussion questions were composed and copied. The next day saw researchers reading scripts aloud to whole classrooms and then administering questionnaires and conducting classroom discussions. Evaluation questions covered comprehensibility of vocabulary and certain points of information as well as credibility and appeal of the characters. By the end of that day or sometimes on the third day, findings were available to the writer and producer.

Eventually the two pilot "Mimi" television programs were complete enough for economical tryouts with a large group of viewers. Ten test sites furnished about 600 fourth- to seventh-grade respondents. The goals for this study were to measure appeal of the storyline and characters and to measure comprehension of the dramatic story and science-related story content. The production formative evaluation used multiple measures including observations, paper-and-pencil appeal rating sheets, computer-based viewer response units to estimate moment-to-moment interest during viewing, and questionnaires and small group interviews to assess comprehension. Because the head writer was part of this research effort, the findings could be put to use immediately on the next set of scripts, although an extensive report was also written up to support revisions of the pilot shows (Char, Roberts, Vibbert, & Hendrick, 1982).

In addition, formative evaluation activities enlightened the production of the "Mimi" computer software programs. Target age users responded to the appeal and comprehensibility of program screens presented in paper and computer versions. Evaluators explored attributes of user friendliness with early storyboards and mockups of the software. These were tried out with children "to see how they made sense of the program, and whether they could figure out what was possible to do with the software, how to get around the program" (Char, 1985, p. 8). Designers modified the text and structure of the program given the formative feedback. Children played also with operational prototypes. The observations of these sessions led to the development of multilevel software:

> For example, testing of an early prototype of the Bank Street Laboratory revealed that many children were confused by temperature/time graphs. In particular, the notion of time as represented by a horizontal line or axis was novel and confusing to many children. Thus, the initial conception of the software was augmented to include a series of 4 graphing subprograms . . . building up to [an understanding of] a line graph of temperature over time. (Char, 1985, p. 6)

The production of the "Mimi" Level 3 interactive videodisc[3] benefited from formative evaluation of a Level 1 version. The Level 1 disc con-

---

[3]The *level* of a videodisc as originally defined by the Nebraska Videodisc Design/Production Group (Nugent, 1980) is prescribed by the hardware configuration, not the amount or quality of user interactivity. Level 1 involves a consumer model videodisc player that allows random access to specific pictures and picture sequences, permits dual-channel audio, and provides VCR-type user controls such as freeze frame, forward, and reverse action of single frames or video sequences in slow motion and normal speed. Level 2 requires a videodisc player with a built-in microprocessor which adds some memory and programmability to the Level 1 capabilities. Level 3 interfaces a Level 1 or Level 2 videodisc player to an external computer, making a system with memory for record keeping and with data processing for complex instructional sequences and computer-generated text and graphics.

tained segments from two "Mimi" television episodes and 22 text frames and photos of, for example, maps, charts, and whales. Evaluators investigated issues of user friendliness, appeal, and comprehensibility through observations of eight children, who experimented with the disc and Level 1 control options. For example, the observers found that "the sequence of close-up views of the Gloucester coastline did not feel to some [users] like movement along the same map up or down the coastline, despite a descriptive text frame describing this movement" (Wilson, 1985a, p. 5). This finding produced the recommendation that the Level 3 disc "include visual organizers in the form of overlays on overview maps, to show the sequence of close-up views marked on the smaller scale maps" (p. 5). Such a computer-generated overlay was developed for the Level 3 "Up and Down the Coast" subprogram. Later testing of this part of the Level 3 disc with users showed the effectiveness of the modification: Five of the seven respondents "understood the function of this overlay and seemed to perceive the maps that followed as a sequence up and/or down the Gloucester Coast much better than the Level 1 subjects, who had no such organizer" (p. 11).

Summary

The process of production formative evaluation for electronic learning materials involves revising a program based on feedback from try outs of early program versions with the target group. Such information can maximize the program's potential for success. Materials can be tested in their early phases of scripts and flowcharts and in more complete versions of pilots and prototypes. Information on user friendliness, comprehensibility, appeal, persuasiveness, and more can give the team confidence in their production decisions and revisions. In addition, subject matter specialists can assess the content accuracy during the production phase.

PHASE 4: IMPLEMENTATION AND IMPLEMENTATION FORMATIVE EVALUATION

When a program reaches its final phase, it is implemented in its designated setting with the target audience. In projects where program changes are still possible, the role of formative evaluation is to test the effectiveness of the program under near normal use conditions. *Implementation formative evaluation* (or the field test, as it is informally known) collects data to:

- fine-tune the material for its educational setting;
- pinpoint program management problems;
- aid development of supplemental program materials (e.g., teachers' guides);
- feed forward into future design and production decision making.

"The Voyage of the Mimi" evaluators asked teachers in 13 fourth- to sixth-grade classrooms to implement two dramatic/adventure television episodes, one of three software programs, a teacher's guide, and student activity books, over a period of several months (Char, Hawkins, Wootten, Sheingold, & Roberts, 1983). Teachers submitted background facts on their curriculum and teaching habits; and then, as they used "Mimi" materials, the teachers recorded their usage patterns and their reactions. Classroom observations, student interviews, and teacher interviews supplemented the day-to-day teacher journals.

The field test findings demonstrated that teacher training with the materials and elaboration of the teacher's guide to support classroom management were critical: "Teachers' knowledge of science directly affected their recognition of the scientific concept and potential inherent in the software" (Char & Hawkins, 1987, p. 217), and the type of software "did not automatically rest in a conceptual niche of computer experiences commonly found in schools" (p. 218).

Summary

Implementation formative evaluation for an electronic learning project is concerned with how the program operates with target learners in the environment for which it was designed. Curriculum products rarely stand on their own. They usually require some support network to introduce them to the user, to mold them for individual differences, and to assist the user in transferring the new knowledge, attitudes, and experiences to the real world. Field testing helps designers see how their final products will really be used by program managers with target learners. This feedback aids the development of program management support materials and affects design of future programs.

Implementation formative evaluation should not be confused with *summative evaluation*. The latter measures the impact of the final program on users, usually by comparing learners who have been exposed to the program with learners who have not received the program. Such impact data are used to assess program accountability.

SUMMARY

> Briefly, the systems approach to instructional design involves the carrying
> out of a number of steps beginning with an analysis of needs and goals, and
> ending with an evaluated system of instruction which demonstrably suc-
> ceeds in meeting accepted goals. (Gagné & Briggs, 1979, p. 5)

Evaluation of the system of instruction occurs throughout the development of the program. At each phase the role of evaluation changes as the
production decisions required change. To contribute to the decision-
making process of the designers and producers, the evaluator gathers
pre-production information as well as feedback on program versions
from the target learners, from program managers such as teachers, and
from experts in the content, the medium, and the learner. The goal of
formative evaluation is to maximize the potential effectiveness of the
final product.

The concept of formative evaluation is consistent across educational
technologies; evaluators work cooperatively as part of the project team to
represent the target group during the molding and remolding of the
program. However, the concept put into practice is interpreted differently for specific projects. Different project teams place their priorities—
including time, money and personnel—on different phases of development and evaluation. Different inquiry approaches and research methods are employed for different media, contents, goals, and target groups.
How the concept of formative evaluation is variously interpreted is the
theme of the second part of this book.

The second part of this volume comprises the following five chapters
that are case studies of formative evaluation as practiced in specific organizations on specific electronic learning projects. Chapters 4 and 5 consider the development of microcomputer software; chapters 6 and 7 look
at formative evaluation of interactive optical discs; and chapter 8 discusses the implementation formative evaluation of a teletext magazine.

In each chapter, the contributing authors describe their organization's
structure, ranging from a three-man production team with an outside
formative researcher (chapter 8) to a large consortium of educational
agencies with staff evaluators (chapter 5). The learning programs include home-based personal computer software and videodiscs for children (chapters 4 and 6), school-based software and teletext for elementary and secondary levels (chapters 5 and 8), and corporate training
videodiscs (chapter 7).

The chapters review the developmental phases of programs, the project decisions dealt with by formative evaluation during each phase, and
the methods used to gather feedback from program users, program

managers, and expert critics. Some chapters emphasize pre-production formative evaluation (e.g., chapter 5); some place a priority on trying out prototypes (e.g., chapter 6); and others concentrate on the final implementation phase (e.g., chapter 8). However, all of the chapters demonstrate the importance of starting research early in the development process, maintaining a close relationship with the program decision makers, and providing timely, relevant and specific information for design and revision.

REFERENCES

Andrews, D. H., & Goodson, L. A. (1980). A comparative analysis of models of instructional design. *Journal of Instructional Development, 3*(4), 2–16.

Bank Street College of Education. (1981). *Development of a television series on science and mathematics education which incorporates interactive television and microcomputers* (Proposal to the U.S. Department of Education). New York: Author.

Campbell, J. O., Tuttle, D. M., & Gibbons, A. S. (1982). *Interactive videodisc: Design and production (Workshop Guide)*. Orem, UT: Wicat Systems. (ERIC Document Reproduction Service No. ED 244 580)

Char, C. (1985, April). *"The Voyage of the Mimi": Formative research in the design of television and software on science for children*. Paper presented at the meeting of the American Educational Research Association, Chicago.

Char, C., & Hawkins, J. (1987). Charting the course: Involving teachers in the formative research and design of "The Voyage of the Mimi." In R. Pea & K. Sheingold (Eds.), *Mirrors of minds: Patterns of experience in educational computing* (pp. 211–222). Norwood, NJ: Ablex.

Char, C., Hawkins, J., Wootten, J., Sheingold, K., & Roberts, T. (1983). *"The Voyage of the Mimi": Classroom case studies of software, video, and print materials* (Research Report). New York: Bank Street College of Education, Center for Children and Technology.

Char, C., Roberts, T., Vibbert, M., & Hendrick, D. (1982). *"The Voyage of the Mimi" project in science and mathematics education: Pilot show evaluation* (Research Report). New York: Bank Street College of Education, Center for Children and Technology.

Gagné, R. M., & Briggs, L. J. (1979). *Principles of instructional design* (2nd ed.). New York: Holt, Rinehart & Winston.

Hofmeister, A. M., Engelmann, S., & Carnine, D. (1986). *The development and validation of an instructional videodisc program* (Research Report). Washington, DC: Systems Impact.

MECC. (1984, November). *Instructional design of courseware*. Pre-conference workshop at the MECC '84 Educational Computing Conference, Minneapolis, MN.

Mielke, K. (1985, October 8). The role of research in children's programs. *Current*, p. 9.

Mielke, K., & Chen, M. (1983). Formative research for "3-2-1 Contact": Methods and insights. In M. J. A. Howe (Ed.), *Learning from television: Psychological and educational research* (pp. 31–56). New York: Academic Press.

Nickerson, R., & Gillis, L. (1979). *Information for decision making during television production: The OECA model* (Office of Project Research Report No. 19). Toronto, Ontario: Ontario Educational Communications Authority.

Nugent, R. (1980). *An overview of videodisc technology* (Project Paper No. 4). Lincoln, NE: University of Nebraska, Videodisc Design/Production Group.

Palmer, E. L. (1983). Formative research in the production of television for children. In M. Meyer (Ed.), *Children and the formal features of television* (pp. 253–278). Munchen: K. G. Saur.

Reinhold, F. (1986). Video educator Sam Gibbon: The man who looks through kids' eyes. *Electronic Learning, 6*(3), 28–29.

Storey, K. S., & Julyan, C. L. (1985). *The integrated design and use of computers and television in education* (Tech. Rep. No. 85-20). Cambridge: Educational Technology Center, New Technologies Group.

Tyler, R. W. (1949). *Basic principle of curriculum and instruction.* Chicago: University of Chicago.

Utz, P. (1984). The early stages of producing an interactive videodisc. *AV Video, 6*(11), 40–43.

Wilson, K. S. (1985a). *Mimi I prototype videodisc formative research.* Unpublished manuscript, Bank Street College of Education, Center for Children and Technology, New York.

Wilson, K. S. (1985b, August). *The "Voyage of the Mimi" disc: Development of an exploratory learning environment for children.* Paper presented at the conference on Interactive Videodisc in Education and Training of the Society for Applied Learning Technology, Washington, DC.

Young, S. A. (1983, Fall). The CTW Model. *CTW International Research Notes,* pp. 12–15.

II

THE PRACTICE

4

Formative Evaluation in the Design of Educational Software at the Children's Television Workshop

Leona Schauble*
Learning Research and Development Center

The Children's Television Workshop (CTW) is known for pioneering a television production process that incorporates evaluation throughout, from needs assessment through final summative evaluation. In fact, the production process, and consequently the research that is one element of that process, takes different forms for each of the Workshop's projects. These forms depend on the different content domains, program formats, target audiences, project budgets and schedules, and the working styles and personalities of the project teams.

Production and evaluation are not woven into one static model; rather, their relationship is in continual evolution, both within the duration of any project, and from project to project. CTW has had 20 years of experience in tailoring research models to production efforts that have varied from domestic to international versions of television programs, from short televised informational announcements to magazines; from activity kits to books; from puzzles and toys to multimedia programs for schools. In computer software, too, CTW staff members have needed to learn about the features of the medium and then to evolve new production models including formative evaluation that are responsive to both the characteristics of the medium and to children's educational needs.

This chapter's discussion of formative evaluation in computer software is necessarily a snapshot of processes that are still changing as staff members continue to explore new methods and fine-tune old ones, mod-

---

*At the time of drafting this chapter, the author was Director of Research of the Software Group at Children's Television Workshop.

ifying both research and production to explore ways of achieving the best results in the most efficient fashion.

CTW'S INVOLVEMENT IN COMPUTER SOFTWARE

Although the Children's Television Workshop is best known for its experiments in educational television programming for children ("Sesame Street," "The Electric Company," "3-2-1 Contact," "Square One TV"), CTW has also applied formative research to the development of projects using other media. CTW's initial involvement in computer software development, for example, began with plans for Sesame Place, a "Sesame Street" theme playpark for families. Plans for the playpark were under way in 1979 before the current widespread interest in computers as vehicles for children's education. At that time there was very little computer software for children, and what did exist was not appropriate for a large public gallery filled with crowds, different age groups, inexperienced users, and rapid turnover of visitors. To address these problems, CTW formed a small in-house development group charged with planning the Sesame Place Computer Gallery's computer system and its software.

Over a period of about 3 years, the team planned and set up a networked system of 50 personal computers, encased in colorful protective steel housings with keyboard overlays, to give children as young as 3 years old some basic and friendly interactions with the computer. The team developed approximately 55 computer programs for children in three age ranges: 3–6, 7–10, and 10–13.

Over time, the Computer Gallery software team became a division within CTW called the Software Group. The group's mandate is to produce engaging and empowering software for children in age groups from preschool through preteen, and for use in various settings including homes and schools. The Workshop's primary intent is to make good computer materials widely available to children. The main role of research within this practical context is to inform the design of a product before its development is completed.

There are several important things to note about this formative kind of research as it has been performed within the Software Group. Its primary purpose has been to help engineer a better product, not to extend a generalizable body of knowledge. In fact, because production decisions are best informed by the study of specific materials in particular contexts, production "recipes" are not likely to be forthcoming from formative research studies. The research has had to be performed within the constraints of project resources and inexorable production deadlines, and the research questions have been formed by the need for decision-making information, rather than by theoretical interests. Finally, we have not considered the research process completed when the data have been collected, analyzed, and reported. Rather, researchers have learned to use their experience, opinions, and insights in knowing when to go beyond the data in making recommendations about the design of a software program. In that regard, researchers are also members of the production team.

FORMATIVE EVALUATION OF TELEVISION VERSUS COMPUTER SOFTWARE

Although the Software Group could draw upon CTW's experience with research in television, the computer medium stimulated new research questions and gave a new slant to the familiar questions. These adjustments were required partly because of differences in the intrinsic features of computer software and television and partly because of the kinds of television projects and software projects attempted so far by CTW.

For example, research planning for CTW's television series has been given focus by the fact that the television programs within a series are usually similar to one another in fundamental ways: theme, characters, content, and format. Thus, research questions and methodologies appropriate to one program in the series can often be applied to others as well. In contrast, the software programs produced so far by CTW have been single-concept programs that share little common ground in content or in format. Because each software production team typically works simultaneously on four or more single-concept programs, the team researcher must assemble and apply a mosaic of research methods to address the unique set of research questions raised by each program. In effect, each program has required a tailor-made research plan.

Another important difference between research in television and in computer software rests on the fact that television material is prepared for one-time, or at most, for few-time use. With computer software, on the other hand, one cannot know how long any user will spend with a program or with any portion of the program. Computer software for homes and schools is used over and over, throughout some indefinite period of time. This means that both the software and the research performed on the software must account for the user's interaction with the material over time. To look for changes in the use of the software over time, software researchers frequently must use short-term longitudinal methods, which are logistically more complicated and more expensive than cross-sectional methods that address differences across age groups on a single presentation of the material. The software and the research must also incorporate some theory of what that change may be like, and how we expect the user to negotiate it.

Television is basically presentational in its form, whereas computer software is basically interactive. The consequences of failing to comprehend adequately a computer program are much more serious for the user than the consequences of failing to comprehend every moment of a television program. Should a viewing child fail to understand a particular "Sesame Street" segment, there is a fair chance that he or she may understand the segment that immediately follows, or the next. Not every "Sesame Street" segment needs to work for every child. But every software program has to work—in some fashion or another—for every child for whom it is intended.

Of course, this is not to downplay television researchers' responsibility to assure that the media conventions employed in a program (ripple effects, pans, fades, zooms, etc.) are understandable to the intended viewer. However, the consequences of any particular misjudgment on the part of the television producer may not be very serious: The viewer's attention may flag for a moment and may need to be recaptured by the next segment. Software producers cannot afford the consequences of a failed experiment; they must be meticulous about assuring the comprehensibility of a program's media conventions. Menus, icons, modes, windows, and the like must be understood to be used. The mode of interaction with the computer—keyboard, light pen, graphics tablet, touch screen, joystick, mouse—must be both meaningful to the child and also within his or her powers of motor coordination. The program must be designed in such a way that it encourages the child to develop functional mental models of the task and the program itself.

Fortunately for software researchers and producers, it is more feasible in software to revise programs that do not turn out quite as we had hoped. Intelligently planned software is generally less expensive to revise during production than is television. On the other hand, it is true that software development simply holds more surprises of all kinds than television does, for producers and researchers alike. The television and software production technologies are in different states of evolution. In television, the producers and writers responsible for making creative decisions about programming are very knowledgable about the technology of television production. They know what can be done with television, and they know how it is done. They know its symbols and conventions, and, just as important, its logistics and economics.

In contrast, software producers are still searching for cost-efficient ways of melding creativity and technical competence. An aesthetics of software is still in its infancy, and the development of such an aesthetics has been severely constrained by the limitations of the personal computers widely owned today. To complicate matters, few writers, producers, designers, artists, and musicians know how to program computers. And unfortunately, on today's microcomputers, implementations simply cannot be neatly divorced from design decisions (although some researchers have argued that design and implementation should be separated; e.g., Bork, 1983). The Software Group's experience has been that it is impossible to draw a clear line between design and programming, and few individuals are talented in the mix of educational vision, programming wizardry, and artistry that good educational software requires and deserves.

CTW's response to this problem has been small production teams that include representatives of several disciplines who work together to forge a common point of view and a series of software programs. A team typically includes several programmers, whose role is not just to write code but to serve as bona fide members of the design team. It includes a software editor who writes print and documentation, an artist who performs the graphic design, and a musician who composes music and sound effects. The software editor, the artist, and the musician work together to forge the aesthetic coherence of the programs. One or more researchers serve during design as experts about children's capabilities and preferences. In addition, they plan and perform formative evaluation on the programs while they are being created. A project manager leads the group toward a consistent educational and aesthetic point of view, mediates among representatives of the various disciplines in the design process, and manages the project.

PROGRAM DEVELOPMENT

There is not a "typical" computer software program, so there is no one process typical of development. There is also no one typical research plan; rather, for each program, the researcher must patch together a practical plan designed to address the particular questions which arise in the design of that program. However, it is possible to think of the research on each program as being shaped by three general questions: (a) What makes us think this program will be engaging to children? (b) What makes us think children are likely to learn anything meaningful from this program? (c) What makes us think children will be able to understand and work with this program? Ways of addressing these questions will be different for home products and for school products, for preschool materials and for programs for older children. However, it is possible to describe some of the paths that software development might take, as a means for discussing some ways in which the Software Group has addressed these questions with formative research.

PLANNING AND NEEDS ASSESSMENT

Before any program is designed or produced, staff members participate in an intensive process of product definition. The content and positioning of software products is defined within the Software Group by a combination of needs assessment, marketing considerations, and by an assessment of the strengths and interests of the staff members within the group. The major role for formative evaluators within this phase is needs assessment and content research.

Researchers review literature in the relevant content domains, which often involves gathering and integrating points of view from various fields including education, psychology, cognitive science, computer science, artificial intelligence, communications, and the particular content areas. Commonly, researchers consult with outside experts in the content areas. The Software Group, like CTW's television production teams, occasionally hosts seminars that bring together CTW staff with university researchers to explore the boundaries of a content area or to discuss the future direction of the Software Group in relation to the educational needs of children.

Once the content has been identified, the researcher will continue gathering information, with the goal of preparing a position paper that recommends an educational point of view commensurate with the Software Group's philosophy, style, and resources. Also performed at this point is a systematic review of competitors' software that addresses the same content or that embodies some treatment being considered by the Software Group.

Researchers may assemble panels of parents and teachers to discuss children's needs within the content area or to comment on existing products in the marketplace. For example, during one needs assessment period, researchers identified several parent–child pairs who owned the target microcomputer. We invited the parents and children into the Workshop to spend an afternoon using several classes of educational software products for children. We then asked the parents and children into separate rooms to talk about the activities that were most fun, most educational, easiest to work with—and why. The discussion also centered on the kinds of alternatives to existing programs parents would like to see.

During the planning phase, and throughout the production cycle, formative evaluation is guided by the producers' needs for information. An important part of a researcher's role at CTW is to identify the questions that will help enlighten real decisions that must be made.

For example, prior to designing a new project for 8- to 12-year-olds, researchers interviewed the producers about what they felt they needed to know. Producers had several questions about appeal: What do children in the age range like in computer games and activities? What do they dislike? Are there age and sex differences in preference? What kind of programs that currently do not exist would children like to have?

To respond to these questions, the researchers performed a study at a summer computer camp where children would have well-formed opinions about computer materials. Because we were interested in watching while the software was used frequently and over time, we selected a residential camp. During the 4 weeks of the project, 110 children participated. Methods included gathering background information by means of written questionnaires, small-group observations, interviews with small groups of children, and more intensive interviews with pairs of children.

The core of the research were the observations conducted during afternoon workshops. Every afternoon, children would work with software in pairs for about 45 minutes. Every week the researchers would rotate the software materials. Collectively, the programs represented four different classes of software material, each of special interest to the producers because it related in some way to their upcoming plans.

While the children worked, at least two observers were present to take notes on the children's reactions to the materials and any difficulties they were having. In general, the observers helped the children when they encountered insurmountable difficulties, but for the most part they tried to remain as unobtrusive as possible. At the end of each workshop session, researchers asked the children to evaluate each software program according to a prepared interview. Researchers also administered a questionnaire to gather information on the children's computer experience, electronic game experience, expectations and perceptions of the computer camp, and other background information. Finally, researchers performed in-depth interviews with 30 pairs of children to further explore some issues related to sex differences and computer use.

The research report (Revelle & Honey, 1983) included not only an analysis of the observational and interview data but also production recommendations that went beyond the data to formulate creative suggestions about the ways in which that information might be put into application.

PRE-PRODUCTION FORMATIVE EVALUATION

Idea Generation. Once the product point of view has been formulated and the needs assessment and content research are complete, the production team is responsible for generating or finding viable concepts for individual software programs. This process is one of the most challenging for an ongoing production group. It is routine to explore 30 or more program ideas for every one idea that proves to be feasible. All the practitioners on the production team are included in this brainstorming process. During the process, formative researchers serve as a content resource for the team, identifying literature, resources, and possible expert consultants to illuminate the process. In addition, they serve as child advocates, reminders to the group about whether or not the ideas being considered are on target in relation to the needs, preferences, and capabilities of children in the target group. Although field research is not usually a standard part of the brainstorming process, a researcher may try out an existing program or idea with children, if there is a serious question about the promise of an approach that is under consideration by the group.

The brainstorming process culminates in the selection of a limited number of specific concepts for computer programs. These concepts are worked out in some detail, usually several pages describing the fundamentals of the activity, the suggested design of the child interaction, and possibly some sketches of screen designs.

Prototyping. Most often, the concept paper raises more questions than it answers. There are always too many unknowns: Will children want to use this activity? Will they understand particular features of the design? Is there a principled way of choosing among alternative solutions to a particular design problem?

Occasionally, these questions can be explored in a preliminary way before any code at all is written. Sometimes a simple paper-and-pencil mockup can be used to try out an approach. In one case, team members wondered whether preschoolers would be capable of assembling puzzle-like pieces on a computer screen. The team felt more confident about proceeding with the design when the researcher reported that children could perform a similar operation with pieces drawn on large sheets of paper.

Sometimes a researcher can find in an existing program, some form of a convention, format, or treatment in question. For example, one design group was considering whether preschoolers would be able to understand the idea of scrolling off a main picture to a selection page where options could be "picked up" with a cursor and brought back to the scene. A researcher found the same idea implemented in another program, and by testing the existing program with young children, she assured herself and the design team that the idea was viable.

Within almost every program, however, design questions are sure to arise that fail to lend themselves to paper-and-pencil testing, and that have not yet been addressed in any competitors' product that we can find. For this reason, the CTW Software Group has adopted the practice of fashioning prototypes that are for the express purpose of performing research with children and for providing the team with a feeling of what it will be like to use the completed program. *Research prototypes* are quick and dirty, stripped-down versions of the activity. They embody some essential features of the activity, most typically, the user's ability to interact with the activity through the computer.

These research prototypes are made to be eventually discarded; they are not regarded as hopeful first tries at a completed program. Because of this, they embody some features that the final program will not have, and the team has to plan these carefully. If the prototype is too unlike the final program, research performed on it will fail to provide useful information about children's ability to use the final program. On the other hand, elaborating a prototype beyond necessary is a waste of valuable time. Research prototypes are usually written quickly in a high-level computer language, and thus they also sacrifice some elements of the final program; for example, the ability to portray graphic objects moving swiftly and smoothly on the screen. Because prototypes hardly ever include sophisticated art work or sound, they are better used for exploring the child's ability to comprehend and interact with the activity than for exploring the appeal of the final software program. A common practice is for a programmer to prepare a prototype so that the researcher will be able to adjust the parameters of the program during testing. This gives the researcher the capability of performing systematic tests of alternative versions of the program.

One such prototype was prepared for a home computer game called "Taxi." "Taxi" is one of a series of games designed to encourage cooperative play among pairs of children. Together, two children operate a taxi company. They pick up and deliver passengers to destinations on the screen by "driving" small taxis around maplike representations of major cities. Each child controls his taxi by means of a joystick.

As they worked on the design of this game, the production team had several questions: How fast should the taxis move? Would children learn over time to control the taxis with the joystick controllers? Would children be frustrated in their attempts to get the taxis to stop? How wide or narrow should the streets in the maps be? Would it be more difficult to "drive" on diagonal or curved roads? Exactly how should the initial instructions be worded?

Experience had taught the design group that children like games that they can begin playing easily but that quickly offer increasing challenge. They were sure that there was some correct combination of easiness and difficulty that the game should have, but how easy is easy enough? At what rate should the difficulty of the game increase?

The research prototype was designed to allow the researcher to set different speeds for the taxis, so that he could try out several alternatives with children. The narrowness or width of the streets in the simple prototype "town" was also variable by the researcher. In addition, the prototype included a "beep" sound each time the taxi was bumped into the curb of the street or into a building.

As with most prototypes, the researcher tested several children at each of several ages within the range of interest. He worked successively for 3 days with each child. Each day, the researcher recorded the number of passengers that the child managed to pick up and deliver within a 7-minute time period. In addition, he was able to track the children's increasing ability to "drive" the taxi over time by noting the number of "beeps" per 7-minute period across the 3 days. By systematically varying the prototype, the researcher could identify certain combinations of taxi speed and street width that were associated with a rising number of delivered passengers and a falling number of taxi bumps. Similar kinds of research helped provide information about how children learn to stop the taxis and how the streets should be shaped. Researchers carefully noted which verbal instructions and prompts seemed helpful to the children as they learned to use the prototypes, and this information was useful in designing the game's instructional sequence.

Research prototypes are valuable not only because they permit field researchers to address specific design questions, but for two other reasons as well. First, the prototype serves as a focus of communication for members of the design team. It is frequently the case that members of the group have different internal visions about the program, and the disagreements frequently fail to come to light until the programmer creates a prototype, which serves as a common reference point. Alavi's (1984) research confirms that prototyping in information systems design makes communication on the design team easier and more conflict free. In addition, having a prototype to play with is an important stimulus to the design process. It is easier to imagine enhancements, improvements, and additions to a program when you actually have had some experience in using even a primitive version of it. It is not at all unusual for the practice of prototyping to completely transform the original conception of a program.

Storyboarding. With the results from the prototype research in hand, the design team is ready to build a precise and detailed blueprint for the computer program. These blueprints, known as storyboards, are quite complex; their goal is to specify unambiguously everything in the program.

A storyboard usually has two parts. The first is a flowchart that maps the structure and logic of the entire program. These design flowcharts are frequently complex enough to cover an entire wall when drawn on big sheets of butcher paper.

The second part of the storyboard is a notebook that includes scale drawings of every graphic screen; exact text size, placement, and color on the screen; description of music and/or sound effects; specification of timed events; a delineation of the user's possible interactions with the program at every point; and a plan whereby those interactions can be carried out by means of keyboard or peripherals. Storyboarding is the arena for the real decisions about the features of the program's design, and it is a difficult process of specifying, arguing over, and revising numerous small details. During storyboarding, the programmer serves as the expert in what is technically feasible; the researcher serves as the expert in children's capabilities with computers; the artist serves as the graphics design expert; and the software editor is responsible for the actual creation and continual revision of the storyboard itself.

PRODUCTION FORMATIVE EVALUATION

Coding and Artwork. Once the storyboard is completed and approved, the programmer begins to write the code, while the artist supplies the artwork for the program. Much of this artwork will need to be tested by the researcher. Given the graphic limitations of personal computers, it is necessary that the team be certain children can identify the screen graphics. Preschoolers, in particular, may have difficulty in deciphering a cow from a block of brown pixels.

In a related vein, researchers must test text fonts to assure that a criterion percentage of children can read them. This is necessary because size and shape of screen pixels vary, and artists must create many different text fonts for different programs and different computers. The researcher asks children in various strata throughout the age group to perform a simple recognition or identification task. Revisions are made when images or fonts do not come up to criterion.

Testing the Assembled Program.   Until this point, the researcher has been performing research on pieces of the program, tempering her recommendations with her best guess about how the user will react when those pieces come together into a completed program. This is a risky business at best, because no one knows much about how features of a program—each within the child's range of mastery—might interact to create a system that is too complex to handle. It is important as the program design proceeds to keep a mental tally of the growing demands that the system as a whole is likely to place on the child, and to remain aware that a child who can sort pictures by size may *not* be able to sort pictures by size, find the key that indicates his choice, and press it.

Toward the end of the coding, when the programmer finally has a workable, nearly completed version, the design team gets its first chance to see whether appropriate content, recognizeable images, understandable and readable text, a carefully planned interface, and comprehensible goals do or do not add up to a user-manageable program.

To find out, the researcher will work with several children within the age range. This testing gathers and analyzes careful moment-to-moment observational records of the exact state of the program in relation to moment-to-moment records of what the child is doing. It would be very useful if one could incorporate record keeping into the software of each program, to chart every child's path through the activity (as described, e.g., in Reil & Levin, 1984). This option has not been employed with CTW's programs, because programmers are always working under very tight deadlines and because the code pushes the limits of the host computer. Instead, researchers perform the record keeping, sometimes with the assistance of videotaped real-time records of the screens created by the user. The child's understanding of the program, as well as changes in that understanding over time, can be discovered often only by looking very carefully at subtle changes in patterns of use over time. Analyses of observational data may be supplemented with other methods as well.

One commonly used methodology is to ask children to think aloud while they are using the program (Ericsson & Simon, 1984), and to record and analyze their protocols. The protocols obtained from this thinkaloud method are especially helpful in revealing misunderstandings that do not show up in simple observational records. For example, one preschool-level sorting program asks the user to indicate which "one of these things is not like the others." One screen in this program presents a fourfold display including the numeral 2, the word two, two rectangles, and the numeral 3. Observations, however, indicated that 3-

year-olds frequently selected the two rectangles as the item that "doesn't belong." Asking children to think aloud yielded responses like, "This one doesn't belong because it's an 11." Until several youngsters responded this way, it did not even occur to the designers that they had made an obvious error in arranging two narrow rectangles side by side. In fact, one way of thinking about formative research is that it is the art of making mistakes obvious, by hindsight.

Another method, related to the thinkaloud method, is to use confederates. After a subject has used a program, we ask him to teach a peer confederate, or another researcher, how to use the program. In general, both this method and the thinkaloud method are much more useful with children over 7 than with preschoolers, who tend to stop verbalizing often, when the demands of the program create a kind of cognitive overload.

An additional approach in formative evaluation of CTW software has been to enlist the aid of a small group of knowledgeable children who serve as consultants to the design team through the program design process. The children's role is to act as informants to the designers about the culture and preferences of children. One software project included a "computer club" of children who came to the Workshop regularly three times a week to offer a "kid's perspective" on the program in progress. Because the children worked on the same programs over a year, they became very familiar with the design possibilities and formed sophisticated opinions about which possibilities should be implemented. The children spent a great deal of time thinking and talking about what worked in the designs and what needed to be adjusted, and they became quite articulate in choosing among or proposing their own design alternatives. The children ended up having an enormous influence on the programs; and the process helped shape the children into more thoughtful users of software.

As each round of testing is completed, and as the program moves closer to completion, it becomes more and more difficult to implement changes in the design. The decision to make a particular change lies with the producer, who weighs the researchers' results and recommendations along with other important factors, including project resources and deadlines. However, if one or more prototypes and various pieces of the program have been carefully tested up to this point, rarely is it the case that the research at this stage will bring unpleasant surprises about some unforeseen difficulty with the program. Indeed, it is frequently the case that earlier testing may have already provided advance warning about possible areas of difficulty or decisions that will need to be made. If so, the programmer may have been able to structure her code in such a way as to make certain features of the program more easily modifiable. Moreover, an experienced programmer can also help by thinking early in the programming process about which design decisions will be difficult to change down the line, and which changes will be easy. This planning makes it possible for researchers to set research priorities so as to address first and most carefully those design questions that will be most difficult and expensive to reopen later on.

IMPLEMENTATION FORMATIVE EVALUATION

Once research changes have been negotiated and implemented, the program is considered completed with the possible exception of some fine-tuning. When the software and its accompanying printed materials are finished, but before release to the publisher, researchers will give the materials a try-out over time in settings like those where they will be implemented ultimately.

For example, if the program is meant to be used in homes, we will send several pre-production copies of the software package to families who own the target computer and who have children in the program's age range. A pre-interview collects information about family background, computer use, ideas about education, and software ownership. The program is left in the home for several days or weeks, long enough for the novelty of the new program to wear off. Parents are asked to neither encourage the use of the program nor to restrict use. Over the test period, parents and children keep a running usage diary that records who used the materials, duration of use, frequency of use, and comments.

Phone interviews conducted after the first several days of the trial alert software staff to any serious difficulties with the program or documentation and also serve to remind the families to complete the diaries. Researchers visit the homes once again at the conclusion of the test period to conduct extensive interviews about reactions to the materials.

When the program or package is designed for school use, researchers arrange for the materials to be introduced into classrooms at the appropriate grade levels. They return to the classrooms several times each week to observe the kinds of use the program is undergoing. An important part of the observations includes teachers' interactions with children around the program, and specification of the ways the teachers have integrated the program into their classrooms. Researchers will also keep running records of individual children's use of the program over time. Final interviews with children and teachers complete the testing process.

For example, "Taxi's" final testing was conducted in day camps. Researchers installed computers in camp classrooms and left the "Taxi" game along with two other computer games chosen to serve as a baseline for appeal measures. One of the other games was an arcade game known to be currently popular with children in the target age. The other game was a rather dull and boring, overtly didactic geography game.

Children in the day camps were permitted to use the computer as a free-choice activity during their free time. Researchers asked children to fill out a play slip, indicating age, sex, and game title, every time they played a game. Slips were kept in a nearby box.

Over time, researchers could track the number of playslips for "Taxi" versus those for the popular game and those for the unpopular game. They wanted to know how "Taxi" would compare, once its novelty wore off, to two other activities of known popularity.

The goal of "Taxi" was to encourage children to play cooperatively, to get them to discuss strategies for cooperative play, and to induce them to try to teach those strategies to other children. During regularly scheduled observations in the classrooms and the day camp, researchers tallied instances that matched careful definitions of these goals, and subsequent analysis looked for instances of these behaviors and their increase over time.

By the time the final testing is completed and the results are analyzed, it is frequently too late to make substantive changes in the program, because the project's budget and schedule are nearing an end. The major purpose of the final testing, beyond some fine-tuning, is the further education of the design team, who must learn where their best bets did and did not pay off, and who must always be honing their instincts for forthcoming design challenges.

LIMITATIONS OF FORMATIVE EVALUATION IN SOFTWARE DEVELOPMENT

In spite of its value, we have not yet figured out how to apply formative research to some important problems in software design. One such problem is the case in which a designer has questions about how to implement one small section of what will, over time, become a large complex information system. In the first place, it is difficult to foresee the empirical consequences of making the necessary tradeoffs of consistency, functionality, and learnability in such a system (DiSessa, 1984). It is even more difficult to figure out how one portion of the system may affect the user's ability to understand or use the whole. Although formative research can help in describing how the user is likely to interact with the earliest implemented pieces of the system, it cannot provide any insight about whether the features that facilitate the use of that piece, may complicate the user's understanding of the entire system.

Formative evaluation is far from being able to provide all the answers about software design. Research can help to set the general direction of a software project, and it can help producers to choose among alternatives, but it cannot by itself generate them. Production is still very much an art, not a science. Producers searching for production formulae will be disappointed by formative research (Mielke, 1983). The primary valuable outcome of a conscientiously applied formative research program is a product which is markedly better for the effort. A secondary but also valuable outcome is a production staff who are developing feedback for their growing experience about how children interact with computer programs. In the new field of children's software, where expertise is at a premium, this is a great production advantage.

REFERENCES

Alavi, M. (1984). An assessment of the prototyping approach to information systems development. *Communications of the ACM, 27*(6), 56–563.

Bork, A. (1983). *Computers and information technology as a learning aid.* Irvine, CA: University of California.

DiSessa, A. (1984). *A principled design for an integrated programming environment.* Unpublished manuscript, MIT Laboratory for Computer Science, Cambridge, MA.

Ericsson, K. A., & Simon, H. A. (1984). *Protocol analysis: Verbal reports as data.* Cambridge, MA: MIT Press.

Mielke, K. W. (1983). Formative research on appeal and comprehension in "3-2-1 Contact." In J. Bryant & D. Anderson (Eds.), *Children's understanding of television* (pp. 241–263). New York: Academic Press.

Reil, M., & Levin, J. (1984, April). *Educational software: Interactive design and evaluation.* Paper presented at the meeting of the American Educational Research Association, New Orleans, LA.

Revelle, G., & Honey, M. (1983). *Computer camp study.* Unpublished manuscript, Children's Television Workshop, New York.

5

The Program Development Process of the Agency for Instructional Technology

Saul Rockman*
Apple Computer

There is a continuum of evaluation activities that can be undertaken during the creation of an educational product. The nature of evaluation changes as the product evolves, as an idea becomes a reality. This chapter describes the relationship between the various forms or stages of an instructional product and the various evaluation activities that help make an acceptable and useful product. The relationship is often confounded by the audiences for that product at each stage, that is, the audiences who participate in the evaluation and/or for whom the data have some meaning and utility.

THE AIT CONSORTIUM PROCESS

Before going further, it is helpful to know about the cooperative development process used by the Agency for Instructional Technology (AIT) to develop elementary and secondary school materials. It is the model from which examples in this chapter are drawn. AIT has worked with a consortium of state and provincial education agencies to create television curriculum projects that no single agency could afford to undertake. Through the creation of a consortium, the cost of the project for any one agency is reduced to a manageable size and all agencies have access to the materials they need.

---

*At the time of drafting this chapter, the author, was Director of Research at the Agency for Instructional Technology.

The consortium process, as AIT has been using it, is more than a sharing of costs. Participating agencies contribute by reviewing materials, by discussing the project and its implementation at two or three meetings during the production period, and by participating in evaluation activities. Through this involvement, a feeling of ownership is developed, a sense of commitment is generated, and a willingness to use the materials—and see that others use them—is established. Consortium agencies invest both financial and intellectual resources in a project, often blurring distinctions between research and development, promotion and utilization.

Representatives of the participating agencies become both evaluators and consumers of evaluation data during the development period. Their reactions can and often do influence the project. For the project director and the project evaluation staff, the issue is how to control and productively use the opportunities that exist.

The consortium process, as with all democratic systems, has its limits, its problems, and its failures. I believe, however, that there are elements in the development, production, and evaluation of educational materials that have utility for other projects.

The consortium project discussed in this chapter is a complex and comprehensive one that was established to create eight units of computer and video problem-solving materials for middle school classrooms, to develop in-service plans that introduce and further both the curriculum and the technologies, and to plan and conduct policy studies that help education agencies understand the use of computers in schools. How did this come about?

PLANNING AND NEEDS ASSESSMENT

One of the more neglected areas of evaluation during the planning phase of a program is *needs assessment*. By this term I mean something closer to qualitative market research or needs determination than to the highly quantitative assessment of student achievement based on standardized tests. What do you need to know to establish a project and get it funded, produced, and used? In these gold rush days of the microcomputer, very little effort is spent on deciding what to do, whether it should be done, or who is going to use it. Just produce it and show its relationship to a curriculum area; schools will buy whatever you've got to sell.

A gold rush does not last too long. Schools quickly discovered that an electronic workbook was not necessarily better than a paper one. The highly touted computer revolution to improve instruction quickly became a movement to teach about computers (Becker, 1983; Rockman, White, & Rampy, 1983). A careful needs assessment process could have reduced the haphazard and wasteful efforts of the past few years.

In early 1981, several chief state school officers approached AIT with a concern and a hope. They were concerned that the rapid influx of computers at the school building and district levels was unplanned and often unrelated to instructional needs and tasks. They saw similarities with the introduction of school television more than 20 years ago. They hoped that AIT could help them bring some order to the instructional use of computers as they felt it had with the earlier technology. They were much too optimistic. Nevertheless, we began to look at efforts AIT could undertake, in conjunction with the states and provinces, to assist education agencies with their new responsibilities in technology.

To more fully understand the problems faced by state and provincial education agencies, and to formulate plans that would meet their necessarily diverse needs, we met with the constituency. In the fall of 1981, AIT invited all chief school officers in the United States and Canada to send representatives to one of four regional meetings. With support from Exxon Education Foundation, more than 100 representatives attended from 9 Canadian provinces, 49 states, the District of Columbia, and the Virgin Islands.

These representatives, who were people in curriculum and technology with responsibility for computers in schools, enthusiastically discussed what they were doing and saw a specific role for AIT. Just as in real estate, where location is everything, they saw that the effective use of computers in the schools would be like television, where the program or what appears on the screen is everything.

But what kind of instructional programs did they want? The representatives set some criteria for AIT activities. They wanted an initial project that would focus on matters of widespread and continuing importance to education. They wanted to avoid duplicating the efforts of others, both commercial and noncommercial. And they wanted to take advantage of AIT's experience in technology and curriculum development.

By focusing on problem solving, an area in which AIT had done extensive television work, less effort and money would be required for curriculum development. Previous cooperative projects had dealt with social problem solving ("Self Incorporated"), economic problem solving ("Trade-Offs"), and problem solving as an essential learning skill ("ThinkAbout"). These television series model problem solving in a real-life setting and stimulate thinking and discussion about strategies.

Couldn't these existing materials be the starting point for computer activities? Computer-based problem-solving materials would allow students to practice and extend the skills they see on television by applying them in a controlled, yet responsive environment. Students would view a video excerpt that establishes a problem and then, in small groups, work at the computer to develop and test alternative solutions. Thus, many of the participants believed, a project could bring the best attributes of both media to bear on an issue of educational importance.

Several representatives from these meetings participated along with content and technology experts in writing the proposal and others had a chance to review early drafts. In this way, we not only got evaluative information from the audience for the proposal, but we also obtained their participation and involvement in the development process.

The needs assessment process was important in creating a project proposal that met its ultimate evaluation test in the marketplace. The careful market research we conducted bore fruit in the relative ease with which we were able to fund the project. There were 42 state, provincial, and local agencies who thought enough of the idea to put funds up front to participate. Of the 15 cooperative projects undertaken by AIT, this one received commitments and funds most quickly.

PHASES OF PRODUCT DEVELOPMENT
AND FORMATIVE EVALUATION

Once the planning phase had succeeded, the project proceeded through the design, production, and implementation phases with relevant evaluation activities. The nature of formative evaluation conducted varies with the developmental stage of the product. In the project under discussion, I have identified four stages of product. These fit into the phases of program development and evaluation introduced in the first part of this book as can be seen in Table 5.1.

During each succeeding development phase, the products grow increasingly accessible to students in the classroom, the eventual users of the materials. In the design phase, when the conceptual and illustrative products are mainly print materials, the young students cannot easily become involved in the formative evaluation of the product. Conversely, as the instructional programs move to the computer, adults have more difficulty in reacting to unfinished and imperfect products, whereas students readily participate in helping to improve and perfect the lesson. This does not mean that adults and students should not be involved in each stage, rather that the evaluation tasks at each stage are necessarily different for each group. As the products at each phase of development become available to the evaluator, an appropriate set of questions emerges, consistent with the nature of the product and the needs of the project.

TABLE 5.1
Four Stages of Product

Phases of Program Development	Stages of Product	Phases of Program Evaluation
Phase Two: Design	*Conceptual.* The product is descriptive print covering each lesson's goals and objectives, a summary of video segments, computer activities and print, and a narrative of classroom process for using it. *Illustrative.* The product is a script that takes various forms including complex flowcharts; sample screens with graphics; full scripts with screens, activity. Sequences and coding instruction.	Pre-production formative evaluation
Phase three: Production	*Prototype.* The product is the initial running version of the computer program, often with drafts of associated print, and the video.	Production formative evaluation
Phase four: Implementation	*Operational.* The product is full lesson, including revised computer, video, and print materials available for trials in classroom.	Implementation formative evaluation
		Summative evaluation

This chapter focuses on the emerging techniques and attendant issues as classroom computer materials are developed and evaluated. Many of the evaluation activities are transfers or extensions of evaluation procedures used with consortium projects that developed television materials. There are differences, however, that are based on the nature of the medium and the consortium's knowledge of it.

PRE-PRODUCTION FORMATIVE EVALUATION

Conceptual Stage. The first approximation of the project's instructional materials is the design report, describing the pedagogical approach, content, and classroom process for each lesson. In AIT projects, the design report is a result of the efforts of a team including experts in the subject area and in the technology, classroom teachers, and educational administrators. It lays out the blueprint for the lesson but suggests, rather than specifies, the exact nature of the computer materials. The design report is both a starting point and a reference point for the work of those who create the script or detailed specifications of the computer program as it is to appear on the screen.

The internal project staff and consultants examine the design report for logical consistency and curriculum integrity but turn to the consortium and teachers for a broader evaluation. The internal review is a useful endeavor, bringing rigorous and fully committed minds to bear on the project's conceptual framework (Sanders & Cunningham, 1973). Outside experts in project management, as well as technology and curriculum, can often see problems in the design when those who have created it are too invested and familiar with the material to see them.

The involved group of consortium members help evaluate the design report by carefully reading it, comparing the ideas of the design team to their agency's needs, and responding to questionnaires. Because they are responsible for making the project available to their schools and are responsible often for technology or curriculum in their agencies, they can approach the task with their particular needs and curriculum plans in mind. Fortunately, the range of respondents almost always provides the full range of moderate and extreme responses.

The first meeting of the consortium brings together representatives from each of the participating agencies (and some who have not yet joined but who are close to committing their funds). The agenda has usually been an introduction to the components of a project and an open discussion of the initial design report. Although many of the consortium representatives have responded to questionnaires distributed with the design report well before the meeting, this face-to-face meeting is designed to encourage members to participate. Not all become actively involved, but the opportunity is present.

The process we use to get evaluations and solicit useful information from the consortium is to have small-group meetings led by a member of the consortium. Project consultants and staff members serve as resource people, commenting only on technical issues or responding to direct questions. The small-group leaders are responsible for synthesizing the comments of their group, providing detailed notes of specific issues to the design team, and reporting the overall reactions to the large group for general discussion. This technique creates a common understanding of the curriculum and identifies weaknesses and political problems in the design. Furthermore, issues raised by the earlier questionnaires can be followed up by giving the small-group leaders notes and questions to guide their sessions.

Although many issues are discussed concerning the design report, rarely are decisions about the curriculum and instructional design made during the heat of battle. Cooler heads need to synthesize the data from the meeting, from the expert consultants and from another group of evaluation participants.

Teachers are the ones responsible for deciding how and when to use the materials and even whether they should use them at all. So, in addition to administrators representing the consortium, focus groups of teachers permit further detailed evaluations of each lesson. These adults work more closely with the eventual student user than the consortium representatives, and they have a different vested interest to protect. By bringing together teachers who have been using computers and those who have not yet begun, teachers who use television and those who do not, and teachers who teach problem solving and those who do not, we can get a good sense of the issues facing the classroom as teachers anticipate how they might incorporate this project into their daily plans (Agency for Instructional Television, 1983).

Teachers looked not only at the curriculum fit but also at the technology fit. They were most concerned with how they were going to manage their classroom's use of the materials: scheduling the small groups, access to the school's one computer, and assessing the results of using the lesson (e.g., tangible or testable lesson products). They were quick to point out that by adding more media to the existing classroom mix, you add many more complexities to the teaching–managing process. Teachers also noted the increased difficulty of using the computer for complex problem-solving tasks in contrast to the extension of drill-and-practice and workbook approaches they had seen.

These kinds of evaluation data play a modest role in revisions of the overall design document. The responses, however, give some guidance to the curriculum and to the nature of the computer program. They help fine-tune the goals and objectives. The major contribution has been to management issues and the need to incorporate management plans in each lesson.

During the pre-production phase, the respondents have individual perceptions of what the computer materials might look like. They base their perceptions on the written description, their previous experience with computer materials for home and school, and on their hope for an exciting product. It is hard to tap into that dream, to find out if the project can come close to meeting the diverse expectations of the sponsors and the gatekeepers. The data at this stage are useful but limited. Projecting the details of each lesson is practically impossible, but other valuable information about the barriers to implementation and use can be gained.

There are political benefits to involving the consortium and teachers in the evaluation process at this early stage, and in later ones as well (Rockman, 1977). Although the approach is not highly quantitative and formalized, it does create understanding and involvement in the project, often generates a commitment to share ideas about the project and stimulates agencies to get their classrooms to use it as well. This is not an insignificant benefit—creating an unpaid promotion staff while gathering evaluation data for revision of the design document. And having many sponsors all working together provides a diversity of insights that a single funder cannot.

Illustrative Stage.   In the course of product development for a television project, what follows the conceptual work in the design document would be a script. The analogous print material for computer programs looks very different. Depending on the specific group of design and production people creating the work, the product at this stage can be a flowchart of the events, a series of illustrative screens with coding instructions, or even a complex narrative of the programs (Bork, 1980). For the purposes of evaluation, it comes down to finding a way of presenting, in a public and accessible form, the details of what is to appear before the student on the computer screen and the logic behind it.

The script tells the programmer what the finished product should look like, how it should appear, its pacing, and the operations and logic that permit a student to work through it. In that it is written to communicate to a programmer, the script is often not easily accessible to the uninitiated.

The goal of formative evaluation at this stage is to perfect and predict. The curriculum designers and project staff are concerned about curriculum integrity and fit, the potential for use in classrooms, and the various presentational issues (what in television have come to be called formal features). How do we improve the script so that the eventual program will stand a good chance of accomplishing its goals in the normal context of its planned use?

It is a working assumption that changes are easier and less expensive to make when working with a product that is still paper than with a completed piece of electronically mediated instruction. How can a group of computer novices provide valid and useful reactions to a paper script in order to improve it? Although the consortium encompasses a large number of potential respondents, fewer of them are likely to take the time to review a complex script than would react to the design report. But the consortium process calls for the encouragement of all members to participate, everyone should have a reasonable opportunity to respond to scripts. So at the first consortium meeting, several sessions were devoted to helping the participants understand the concept of a computer script and to teaching them to read scripts from previous projects.

As it turned out, the initial scripts for this project were in the form of extended handwritten flowcharts, not easily understood by anyone not involved in the process of writing them (see Bork, 1980). They did not meet the criterion of accessibility.

A second version of the script, in the form of a detailed narrative of the expected progress through the program and illustrative screens of several extended segments, was used. Although this provided a sense of the lesson, it was expensive and time-consuming to prepare the visuals; and detailed, fine-grained analysis of the program was not possible. We could not look at pacing, all instructions, screen placement, and so forth.

With sophisticated computer materials such as we had in mind, neither of these two formats worked out well. Given one lesson with 127 branches, the extended flowchart quickly became too cumbersome to follow. For lessons that used computer tools, such as spread sheets or word processing programs, the narrative soon became meaningless and most illustrative screens were merely frameworks for input, not illustrations.

One of the many changes in the first year of the project was in production agencies and, along with that, came another method for presenting the scripts for outside scrutiny. Scripts for this design and production group consisted of frame-by-frame presentations with coding instructions such as the order and pacing of screen material, cues for branches, and so on. Scripts showed the entire organization of a computer lesson and were extensive, running 200–300 pages in length. Sheer mass prevented these from being easily duplicated, distributed, and read by many people.

We created a different structure to obtain feedback from the consortium and from teachers. A group of committed volunteers was established from the agencies. Although every agency had the opportunity to participate, we reduced the list of willing reviewers to a manageable number by clearly stating the amount of time needed to do a comprehensive review of a script. From that group, a half dozen or so were called to obtain reviewers for available scripts. A person who could not meet a specific deadline for a script was put back into the pool to be called again when the next draft script was finished. Teachers, too, were selected from the approximately 20 who had participated in one of the script design meetings or who had been part of the earlier evaluation activities. That number was increased as other teachers began to participate in other aspects of the evaluation.

Each of the script reviewers was given a structured response form along with the script. It paralleled the forms we had used for television lessons and asked for some information that was collected for all scripts and some that was specific to that lesson. Some common questions referred to the visibility of the objectives in the student material, curriculum fit, age-grade suitability, and insensitivity to social, racial, geographic and gender-related issues. Most script evaluation forms also sought information on classroom management issues. Examples of the specific issues are: ethical issues within programs, vocabulary, suggestions for extending the lesson into other classroom activities, and appropriateness of particular portions of the program.

In addition to the reviews by educators and teachers from across the country, we tried several other techniques to explore the scripts, to identify problems and strengths, and to make changes before the program coding was started. One technique can be called escorted trials. A small group of teachers or students would be guided through successive short segments of the script by a researcher. All information about each frame, including directions to the programs, would be mentioned. For example:

> on this screen, the graphic would appear on the upper two-thirds of the right-hand side. Immediately, the first three lines would appear on the upper right. After a 2-second delay, the question and request for response would come up below it. Another 2 seconds and the request to think about an answer would appear across the bottom. The keyboard would be locked for 8 seconds, so that no response could be typed. Then the cursor would blink and answers would be accepted.

With so much detail, it was necessary to stop, discuss, and review often. The effort required of the researcher and the participants was enormous and quite time-consuming. But at the same time we were gathering data for one lesson, we were teaching people how to carefully read a script, and this prepared script reviewers for additional lessons.

Another technique to try out a script was a simulation of the program using the researcher to play the role of the computer. Although this approach could not work easily for all lessons, it was successfully used for some. Four students sat at a table opposite a researcher. The researcher would present the instructions orally and then provide appropriate script frames to the students. The researcher then became an intent observer and recorder of the discussions that took place among the students as information or choices were requested by the "computer." As the program branched, the researcher would flip through the script book to find the next frame and present it to the students. Repeated trials using this technique would seem to be a reliable and valid simulation of the program in use. Students quickly fell into the spirit of the exercise, and each trial led to increasingly refined observations and recommendations from the researchers.

As in much of psychological research, the hardest part of any study is creating a well-conceived definition of the stimulus. In conducting formative evaluations of television programs, researchers and producers have already arrived at an understanding of the relationship between a script and the finished product. We know where the compromises will be made; we have a common terminology for the portrayal of the events; we have established an intuitive knowledge of how the visual and aural elements will mesh. For many of us with limited experience in creating instructional materials for the computer, we lack the experience with the medium, with a common production process, and with identifying the information that is useful in improving the final product. As the product gets closer to the finished version, we can, in all likelihood, transfer some of our evaluation models and data-collection systems from one electronic medium to another.

PRODUCTION FORMATIVE EVALUATION

Prototype Stage. In AIT's computer/video projects, the production process for the computer materials is not an in-house operation. We have contracted with another agency that works with project staff and consultants to develop a script, to revise the script based on our review and evaluation, and to produce a running prototype computer disk. The first, reasonably error-free version is sent to AIT for review by staff and, if it does not crash immediately, is evaluated. Although some evaluation is conducted by project staff, the continued participation of the consortium is also important.

With a running disk in hand, the term *evaluation* quickly takes on different meanings for developers and users. For developers at AIT, the evaluation we seek is one that will find the mispellings, identify the problems, note what it takes to crash the program, figure out the common user errors and misunderstood instructions. We are committed to the formative evaluation process and we try to improve the programs. We expect, and contractually state, that several revisions are likely to occur until we can reach an acceptable level of product quality.

For user members of the consortium, few of whom have been closely involved with production and most of whom are responsible for acquiring and distributing curriculum materials, evaluation usually means something different. They are familiar with evaluations that assess a product's impact value for the classroom, not ones that are designed to improve a product during production. Everyone wants to evaluate a disk: "Send me the program and your checklist rating form. I'll get the media people to read it over." They are familiar with the forms used by MicroSift or NCTM or EPIE. The first running software prototypes are certain to flunk those tests. Half the documentation is missing; some graphics are not finished; the work might be on two disks when the final product will be on one. We as developers are looking for errors to correct, and they as users are looking for perfection.

Great care and tact are necessary before consortium agencies are involved for this stage. Only protected disk versions are made available with instructions clarified and repeated warnings placed on the disk. The feedback from consortium members is quite valuable and a political necessity, but it must be gathered thoughtfully so that it does not become counter-productive.

When the first disk is available, the perception of a project changes. Up to this point, it was all talk and paper. Now it is its own thing. For people who have worked with the lesson through its evaluation and development, the product is the culmination of significant effort over long duration. For the majority of those who participate in the consortium, the first disk is a long-awaited and rarely considered product of their dollars. The expectations they held at the time of the proposal have matured as a result of the information they received over the intervening months and the sessions they attended at the consortium meeting. The effects of time and training on the consortium are significant. After viewing an initial disk, some are disappointed that their image of the promise has not been fulfilled. Others are pleased that their hopes have been exceeded. And always, everyone sees the need for certain changes. Fortunately, consortium review is but one part of production formative evaluation at the prototype stage.

Evaluation of the prototype program has two major functions. The easiest to describe, although the most time consuming, is debugging the computer program to make it technically perfect. Computer materials are viewed close up, the pace regulated by the student. Teachers will often ignore a minor flub in a film, but educators are intolerant of spelling, punctuation, and grammatical errors in computer programs. Line-by-line, word-by-word, these items must be checked for accuracy. The obvious grammatical error will be missed the first 15 times through and caught on the 16th time.

In addition to errors on the screen, the underlying logic of the program must be checked. Branch-by-branch, frame-by-frame, does the right thing happen next? What do I do with errors? If the choices are A, B, C, or D, what happens when I press R? Do I have to spell all the words in a response fully and/or correctly? Will it take the first four letters as a full response? The machine itself can be a problem. If I press the wrong keys in the right order, will the program blow up? How many different ways can I make it blow up? Trial after trial, hour after mind-numbing hour, someone must go through the program to make sure it meets the expectations for technical perfection.

A second function of evaluation is dealing with the instructional component. Does it do what it was designed to do and in the way it was designed to do it? Both teachers and students are helpful respondents at this stage; editorial reviews by consultants and staff can also identify curriculum errors.

One of the first issues is "does it work for the students?" A researcher can gain a good sense of the program's flow by observing students working through the program alone or in small groups, and by encouraging them to say aloud what they are thinking. In this case, the researcher becomes the measurement instrument, raising issues of reliability and validity. It seems worth the effort to have several trained observers, each working with five or more groups to gain the rigor needed for firm conclusions and thoughtful recommendations for program changes. Following short segments of the lesson, the researcher can interview the students and have them predict forthcoming frames. Also, timing students working through each segment, noting delays and peer discussions, can provide management information for teachers' guides.

This observation system is productive. It helps clarify the instructions, captures the students' language for answers to free-response questions on the computer (which can expand the parsing functions in the program), and provides a good indication of interest and appeal. It is also time-consuming.

Although there may be some ways of capturing responses on a second disk or of videotaping the students as they work, eventually someone has to go through the data. By using observation systems, and having the observers discuss their work between trials, the efforts can be made more precise and rigorous, and the focus can change to incorporate new information as it becomes known. This iterative system has the capability of generating highly useful information about the program that facilitates revisions.

The technical activities in evaluating a prototype disk must be repeated as each old version is replaced by a newer (and we hope, improved) version.

Having a program that meets the technical criteria and seems to work with students does provide some confidence in the quality of the instructional product both to the producer and to the consortium. The evaluation is incomplete, however, without some indication of how the lesson will work in the classroom, for as the project's participants often noted, "How can 30 students all get to the one computer without disrupting the class?"

IMPLEMENTATION FORMATIVE EVALUATION

Classroom Trials

For the previous stages of product development and evaluation, I have written from my experiences as a project director, evaluator, and consultant in instructional computer projects. This stage of the *operational computer product* is one for which I have no direct experience as I write this. I do, nevertheless, bring to this aspect of product evaluation 15 years of experience in evaluating television projects in the classroom and a growing understanding of how computers are used in schools.

In classroom trials of television or film projects, an early version of the product can be used. There are few management problems (the entire class views at once), technical issues can be explained away and are easily understood by teachers and students, and machine breakdowns are unlikely. We can do and have done classroom trials with roughly edited versions of the video programs, often without music tracks; we can videotape storyboards and use voice-over narration to serve as the product.

Field trials are designed to examine the products under conditions that approximate normal use. With computer materials, you have to begin with an operational product, a reasonably perfect technical product. From there you can explore whether students learn what they are supposed to learn and whether teachers can handle the various project components with ease.

In a project that includes video, computer, and print materials and that can be used by individuals, small groups of students, or even entire classes at the same time, one certain problem teachers will face is logistics. Add to that the classes with one or two computers in their rooms in contrast to computer labs, where both need to use the materials effectively. Teachers will have a management problem. Classroom trials should begin to identify how these problems might be handled. What are some ways teachers assign students to groups? What do students do at their seats while others are using the machine? How much material can be covered in a single 45- or 50-minute class period? What subject matter connections to the video and computer programs are made by teachers and students? The questions go on. Moreover, there are learning outcomes to be measured with a variety of instruments.

The outcome for classroom trials can be revisions in the computer and/or video program. More likely the revisions will be in the student or teacher print materials or in the instructions for classroom activities. At this stage, it may be prohibitively expensive to change the electronically delivered instruction but still rather easy to change the print. Earlier evaluation activities would have caught major curriculum problems in the video and computer programs.

Information about classroom management is necessarily part of the teacher guide and what is derived from classroom trials is immediately useful. The insights gained on management issues have a bearing on in-service and promotion activities as well. In teacher training, one mandatory question will be "How do I use the project under (specify) conditions?" Promotion, however, is a secondary benefit to the consortium agencies participating in the classroom trials. They have early access to the materials, they have an opportunity for their utilization staff to observe the project in place before in-service begins, they have teachers who have tried the materials and can speak to its utility (Rockman, 1977).

Although classroom trials seem cumbersome to conduct, as well as expensive, they have a wide range of benefits. Having some, but not necessarily all lessons in a multiunit project, undergo classroom trials, may be sufficient. Time, staff, and money rather than need may determine the extensiveness of these activities.

The usefulness of evaluation has been demonstrated in instructional technology repeatedly over the past decades (Cambre, 1981). In television and film, as the design and production process became increasingly more sophisticated, the evaluation techniques did also. We can probably expect similar growth in the evaluation of computer materials. In television and film, we turned to technology to help improve our measurement of students' responses—eye movement cameras, event recorders to study attention, automated response recorders to collect data, and galvanic skin responses (GSRs). Although not all technologically sophisticated data-collection devices proved useful in understanding the effects on mediated instruction, progress was made. I would expect that we will also develop a technology to help evaluate computer materials and that it, too, will begin to help our understanding of instruction in that medium.

The resources available for the development of instructional materials have diminished over recent years and, along with that change, has come a reduction in the amount and quality of formative evaluation. In a marketplace looking for a fast return on a minimum investment, reducing evaluation is a certain cost savings. Although this "penny-wise and pound-foolish" philosophy may have short-term benefits for producers, it is detrimental to the quality and utility of instructional products. Perhaps the training efforts of business and industry can show education the value and cost effectiveness of thoughtful evaluation. Until then, we need to look to some of our work in television and explore how to transfer economically the lessons we have learned to the development of instruction using the computer.

REFERENCES

Agency for Instructional Television. (1983). *Teacher verification of the provisional design* (Research Report #88). Bloomington, IN: Author.

Becker, H. (1983). *School uses of microcomputers: Reports from a national survey* (Interim Report #2). Baltimore, MD: The Johns Hopkins University, Center for Social Organization of Schools.

Bork, A. (1980). Preparing student-computer dialogues: Advice to teachers. In

R. P. Taylor (Ed.), *The computer in the school: Tutor, tool, tutee* (pp. 15–52). New York: Teachers College Press.

Cambre, M. (1981). Historical overview of formative evaluation of instructional media products. *Educational Communication & Technology Journal, 29*(1), 3–25.

Rockman, S. (1977). The function of evaluation in cooperative projects: The AIT experience. In T. Bates & J. Robinson (Eds.), *Evaluating educational television and radio* (pp. 56–60). Milton Keynes, England: The Open University Press.

Rockman, S., White, D., & Rampy, L. (1983). Computers in the schools: The need for policy and action. *Educational Technology, 23*(11), 13–18.

Sanders, J. R., & Cunningham, D. J. (1973). A structure for formative evaluation in product development. *Review of Educational Research, 43*(2), 217–236.

6

The "Palenque" Project: Formative Evaluation in the Design and Development of an Optical Disc Prototype

Kathleen S. Wilson
William J. Tally
Bank Street College of Education

The "Palenque" project has been a collaborative effort between Bank Street College of Education in New York City and the David Sarnoff Research Center, Inc. (formerly GE/RCA, Labs) in Princeton, New Jersey. The primary goal of the project has been to create an interactive optical disc prototype for children to use with their families at home. The prototype is based on Bank Street's "Second Voyage of the Mimi" television series and demonstrates some of the unique features of GE's digital video interactive (DVI) technology.[1]

As part of the design and development process, we undertook a series of formative evaluation efforts, observing children using the prototype as it has evolved to help inform our ongoing design decisions about issues of appeal, comprehensibility, and user friendliness. This chapter describes the development of "Palenque" and the evaluation activities carried out during its prototyping phases.

---

[1]Digital video interactive (DVI) technology was announced by GE in March 1987. The technology was developed by GE/RCA's David Sarnoff Research Center, Inc. in Princeton, New Jersey. This technology uses CD-ROM (compact disc-read only memory) to store compressed digital information. CD-ROM is an mass storage optical disc in which data are pits in a reflective surface and are read by a laser beam. DVI allows playback of full-motion, full-screen digital video, in addition to three-dimensional motion graphics, high quality digital audio and digital still video and text.

OVERVIEW OF THE "PALENQUE" PROJECT

The collaborating team envisioned both the design and the development (production and programming) of the "Palenque" prototype as exploratory research efforts. In terms of pedagogy and interface design, we have been guided by several of the biases that are at the heart of much of the research and educational product development work at Bank Street College. For instance, we subscribe to the idea that learning should be an active enterprise guided by children's interests and curiosity, which takes into account their actual experience of the world. We are also committed to formative evaluation in the design of new learning materials. In terms of production, programming, and technical research, we have used the "Palenque" project as a vehicle for developing and testing a highly interactive optical disc prototype that demonstrates a variety of design concepts, filming techniques, and programming innovations. The collaborating team has experimented with state of the art optical disc (videodisc and CD-ROM, see footnote 1), digital audio and motion video (DVI), high resolution color graphics, and computing technology. We incorporated into the design of "Palenque" as many of the advanced features of this technology as possible, given the time, money, and human resources available to us.

Thus, we have tried to create a rich, multimedia, database environment for children and their families that piques curiosity and fosters self-guided exploration, information seeking, and decision making. The optical disc prototype allows children to explore a Maya ruin in the Yucatan, called Palenque. We designed an experience that allows children to browse freely, make choices about what to see, when, and where, and discover things along the way as they explore.

"PALENQUE" PROTOTYPE DESIGN DESCRIPTION

Content. The "Palenque" optical disc prototype (Wilson, 1987) is based on themes, locations, and characters from the "Second Voyage of the Mimi" television series produced at Bank Street College. In the TV show, a cast of scientists and children explore the Yucatan's Maya ruins and learn about ancient Maya culture, archeology, and related sciences. Our "Palenque" prototype incorporates this theme to the extent that the user's experience is based on the ancient Maya site, Palenque, and on the perusal of a "Palenque" information database.

Target Audience and Context for Use. "Palenque" has been designed for use by children in the 8- to 14-year age range at home with their families, rather than for use in classrooms. The age range coincides with the target audience for Bank Street's "Second Voyage of the Mimi." With a nonschool learning environment in mind, we experimented with intuitively accessible interface conventions in an attempt to create an interactive experience that is easy to learn to use, appealing, and comprehensible to a wide variety of users. We have tried to create an inherently motivating environment that is informative and at the same time fun for family members of all ages.

Interactive Formats. The information in "Palenque" is structured implicitly to allow for user-directed exploratory *experiences,* rather than being explicitly structured as tutorial sequences or directed activities and games. One of our design goals has been to create an interesting visual, auditory, and textual database environment in which information in many formats can be browsed through spatially and thematically by children. In addition, we have experimented with visual menus, the use of pictographic icons, and window-based interface conventions that might make navigation about the disc motivating and comprehensible for young users. There are six basic components to the "Palenque" prototype:

1. Video overviews. Video segments introduce the prototype and the three major interactive modes of "Palenque": explore, museum, and game.

2. Explore mode. A virtual travel experience encourages exploration and open-ended discovery by allowing users to "walk" or "run" around the archeological site at Palenque. Users indicate with a joystick which direction they would like to travel and which places they would like to visit. The camera's viewpoint is that of a person walking on the site—the user sees what the visitor would see. Video zooms into places of interest, 360 degree pans and tilts, and a dynamic you-are-here map all complement the walking feature of explore mode. Thus, in this component of "Palenque," the information is stored and accessed spatially, so that users must visually walk to locations on the site to learn more about them.

3. Museum mode. The optical disc contains a multimedia database of information relevant to the Palenque site, including text, still photographs, drawings, motion video, graphics, sound effects, and audio narration. Users browse through virtual theme "rooms" to learn more about such things as Maya glyphs and the tropical rainforest. In the

museum, information is hierarchically structured and accessed thematically, so that users can browse through categories of information presented in greater or lesser detail, as desired.

4. Game mode. Available in the museum's theme rooms are games and activities such as putting back together fragmented glyphs and constructing your own jungle symphony.

5. Characters. Three characters serve as companions, guides, and content experts in the prototype: a young teenager and a female archeologist from Bank Street's "Second Voyage of the Mimi" TV series, and an archeologist from National Geographic who specializes in Maya studies.

6. Simulated tools. Users can explore the Palenque site and museum with simulated tools, including a camera, a photo album, a compass, a tape recorder, and a magic flashlight. The magic flashlight permits users to see buildings as they looked before reconstruction began or in the days of the ancient Maya.

DESIGN AND DEVELOPMENT OF "PALENQUE"

A traditional instructional design sequence usually involves a process that begins with needs assessment and the generation of goals, then proceeds through design, production, and programming, with formative and finally summative evaluation. Due largely to the experimental nature of our project, we, on the other hand, have pursued several ongoing efforts at the same time—each informing the other—a process similar in some ways to the rapid prototyping and iterative design process described by Brown (1986).

These parallel and iterative efforts encompass research (content research, production experiments, formative evaluation with children, and technical experiments with evolving DVI/CD-ROM technology (see footnote 1); design (treatments, scripts, and storyboards); production (filming in Mexico, studio production in the United States as well as postproduction and disc mastering); and programming.

Formative Evaluation. We performed a series of formative evaluation studies as the "Palenque" prototype evolved through preliminary check discs, three videodisc prototypes, a CD-ROM based prototype, and many versions of accompanying software. We observed child users during every development stage, looking at issues of ease of interaction, appeal, and comprehensibility. We studied such things as children's understanding of virtual travel and 360 degree user-controlled panoramic views, their use of spatial organizers, the ease and accessibility of our multimedia database and characters, and the effectiveness of a joystick as an input device. The results of these successive observational studies led to changes in the evolving design that were implemented in each new disc and software prototype.

The remainder of this chapter details the evaluation activities for two "Palenque" prototype phases: a preliminary prototype phase from September 1985, through January 1986, and a final prototype phase from February 1986, through September 1987.

PRELIMINARY "PALENQUE" PROTOTYPE PHASE

Parallel design, evaluation, production, and programming efforts were underway as we developed our preliminary prototypes. Our evaluation activities to facilitate decision-making comprised:

- front-end analysis (i.e., content research, review of existing design conventions, review of related audience research);
- pre-production formative evaluation (i.e., audience understanding of and interest in the content);
- production formative evaluation (i.e., testing of the preliminary prototypes with children).

Our production and programming efforts during the preliminary prototype phase included:

- a scouting trip to Palenque;
- development of a virtual travel videodisc prototype;
- creation of a visual database prototype.

Based on the results of our evaluation, production and programming efforts, our design efforts resulted in:

- a final treatment; and
- a preliminary design document for the final "Palenque" prototype.

We limit our discussion here to the evaluation activities we pursued, omitting discussion of our experimentation in design, production, and programming.

Front-End Analysis

Content Research. The "Palenque" project staff had access to background information on the ancient Maya and the Yucatan that was collected by the Bank Street "Mimi" project (Howland & Seidel, 1985). In addition, library research, museum visits, a trip to Palenque, and consultation with content specialists contributed to decisions made concerning appropriate content and themes to cover, given our target audience and home usage context.

Review of Existing Design Conventions. Products similar to our proposed "Palenque" prototype in either theme, technology, or format were collected for analysis with an eye toward finding useful models for our design efforts. For instance, we looked at how themes of archeology and ancient Maya were handled in different media (e.g., board games, books for children such as the *Choose Your Own Adventure* mysteries, videotapes, films, and computer software). We reviewed software and videodiscs with visual databases, exploration and adventure formats, surrogate travel formats, and visual menu structures to discover what visual cues and organizers were used to structure highly visual material. Reviewing these products helped give us some idea of the relative strength and weaknesses of the several media our "Palenque" prototype would combine, in relation to the Maya and archeology themes.

Review of Related Audience Research. Previous research at Bank Street, conducted with our target audience, provided some guidelines for the evolving design of the preliminary prototypes. Formative evaluators for the "Second Voyage of the Mimi" had assessed the knowledge, attitudes, and interests of 8- to 14-year-old children concerning such topics as Maya glyphs, exploring ruins, dating artifacts, and Palenque (Howland & Seidel, 1985). This research suggested to us, for example, that children's initial difficulty in understanding Maya hieroglyphic writing could be reduced when glyphs incorporated readily recognizable shapes or the names and faces of human figures.

Additionally, a study of children using database software in classrooms yielded some interesting findings relevant to our "Palenque" design (Freeman, Hawkins, & Char, 1984). We learned, for example, that children had difficulty using traditional database software (DBMS), originally designed for business environments. The text-based databases required users to understand a large number of prompts and to manipulate different keyboard control keys. In essence, the study concluded that existing text-based databases were inappropriate for children in classrooms. The research suggested that databases might be more successful if they incorporated more discursive or intuitive modes of access as well as visual supports such as films, maps, and photos.

Finally, formative evaluation conducted with children using a videodisc based on Bank Street's first "Voyage of the Mimi" TV series led to several recommendations for future optical disc design (Wilson, 1985). For instance, target audience children enjoyed and understood the use of a videodisc as a multimedia database to be explored or browsed. The use of nautical maps and timelines, as highly visual spatial menus, proved successful in motivating children's exploration of the disc contents. Users also easily mastered navigation around the disc environment using pictographic icons superimposed on video images. Computer-generated zooms and special effects for transitions and conceptual highlighting added to the comprehensibility of various visual sequences. Other strengths of the videodisc revealed by the formative evaluation were the high realism of the motion video sequences (e.g., characters and animals), sounds (e.g., songs and voices), ability to control motion video and audio segments, and the ease of use of the keypad input device. These recommendations were incorporated, to the extent possible, in the "Palenque" design.

Pre-Production Formative Evaluation

Two studies constituted the pre-production formative evaluation for the preliminary "Palenque" prototypes. In the first study, we explored children's concepts of time, maps, and spatial relationships, using paper maps, photographs, and print materials. In the second study, we assessed children's understanding of and interest in Maya glyphs, bas-reliefs, and an on-camera archeologist. As stimuli, we employed photographs, replicas of glyphs, a videotape of an archeologist, and the narrated story of Palenque's great ruler, Pacal.

These studies were formative in nature; they were intended to inform evolving design and development efforts rather than to discover or test hypotheses. For this reason, we used small sample sizes and students at the same school—Bank Street School for Children, which is a private school in New York City. The first study involved 15 children, aged 8–13; the second study, 19 children, aged 8–12. For 50 minutes, pairs of children were interviewed and asked to do various tasks, while the researcher observed, took notes, and audiotaped the sessions for later reference.

From the first study we discovered several things that were considered in our "Palenque" design discussions. First, most of the children had no sense of the time period of the ancient Maya, nor did they have a sense of the evolution of a site over time: its abandonment, ruin, overgrowth by the rainforest, eventual discovery and archeological restoration. In terms of spatial relationships, most children were adept at grasping the relationships between different views of the site, for example, recognizing the same structures from different angles and distances. Aerial views aided this orientation process.

From the second study, we learned that children were interested in the story of Pacal, the 12-year-old ruler of Palenque during its heyday, who was buried in a sealed tomb inside the Temple of the Inscriptions. The children also enjoyed the story of the discovery of the tomb in 1951 by Alberto Ruz. Further, they preferred carved panels showing people more than panels showing just glyphs. Although the children needed help recognizing the important elements of many glyph images, they liked comparing elements in different representations of glyphs, particularly glyphs with recognizable objects such as animals.

The findings from these two studies helped guide decisions about the design of prototype materials.

Production Formative Evaluation

We designed two research prototypes to simulate different proposed features of the final "Palenque" prototype. For the visual database prototype, we used Filevision software for Apple's MacIntosh computer, which allowed us to simulate several features of our proposed database, including a library with different rooms and a dynamic map of the Palenque site. This prototype eventually evolved into "Palenque's" museum and game modes described previously. For the virtual travel videodisc prototype, we employed a Sony SMC-70 computer, Sony LDP 1000/A videodisc player, and a Sony color monitor. This prototype was a precursor for the explore mode.

Studies of children using these research prototypes guided our further design decisions. The sample sizes were small (10–22 children, aged 9–14) from Bank Street School for Children and an East Harlem public school. Children used the visual database for one 50-minute session and the virtual travel videodisc for one or two 45-minute sessions. The children were interviewed and observed using the prototypes in pairs. We observed pairs rather than individuals because we felt that we would learn more about their thoughts while using the systems if they were in a situation to verbalize to a peer. Also, we felt that pairs or small groups would be a likely usage pattern in a home setting.

In each session children interpreted and acted on a series of novel screen formats by manipulating an input device. To assess appeal, comprehension, and manipulation of each format, researchers followed an outline of questions such as "What is this a picture of? What do you think you can do here? What do you think just happened? Why?" Researchers recorded spontaneous comments, noted program selections, and audiotaped sessions for later confirmation of observation data. Children were also asked to indicate at the end of the sessions which parts were their favorites, which they did not care for, and what they would change to make the program better and more fun.

Visual Database Prototype. The main evaluation questions for the visual database study were: To what extent can children make use of the range of options available? How appealing is it to move around a visual database structured as a library with different "rooms" and a dynamic map of the Palenque site? How appealing is the content of the database? In general, we found that the children were engaged by both the content and visual nature of the Filevision program as well as by the capabilities of the technology. Some of the children's comments were as follows:

> "It's not a game; it's more like a quest. You go into different rooms and find information about things."
>
> "Oooh fresh! We're IN this room! Did you make this picture?"
>
> "It was fun seeing the computer picture change into something different. You get a whole new room and say, 'Hey neat, what can we discover here?'"

The idea of discovering, exploring, and revealing embedded or "hidden" text and images was especially appealing. The most attractive features of the dynamic map were the temples and the rainforest. The realism of the reference room template appealed because it was more than "just words." Children did not recognize the main template as a library, as libraries are seen as places for books; therefore, we changed the allusion from library to museum.

Virtual Travel Videodisc Prototype. For the videodisc prototype study, we were interested in the following: Do children feel as though they are "in" the surrogate travel space and "moving through" it, rather than simply viewing a succession of still images? To what extent do spatial organizers, such as a mime leading the way on a jungle path or marking an intersection, help children orient themselves? Do children understand a 360 degree camera pan as a rotated horizontal view with no forward or reverse movement through space? Do they know when they have rotated a complete 360 degrees versus 180 degrees? Do users obtain any meaningful information from the pan?

Overall, we found that the novelty of self-directed movement around the Palenque site was very appealing and engaging, as were the capabilities of the technology. The children commented in the following manner:

> "Neat . . . it feels like you're a person walking around. Try to run. Whoah, we're RUNNING down this path (makes a sound like a motor). We're going to fall (off the bridge)—splash! Be careful, don't walk on the grass."

> "It's a way to see other parts of the world without going there . . . I wish I could go there . . . I feel like I've almost been there."

Most children demonstrated a sense of location and movement around the site. Their comments indicated that the realism of the video images was an advantage, making exploration in and of itself very appealing. The children eagerly pursued simple search activities and selected most frequently of all icons, the arrows controlling movement. The most attractive locations on the site were the rainforest area and the Temple of the Inscriptions, where users liked visually climbing up the steps.

The mime, included for spatial orientation, was salient both as a reinforcement to the travel arrows and as a landmark. Beyond this, children simply enjoyed seeing people on the site. These people often helped to establish a sense of scale and were thought to be good guides.

Some design conventions were observed to be less successful than others. For example, the simple forward and reverse arrows were often read as "up" and "down," not "forward" and "reverse." In addition, our child explorers wanted the 180 degree option more often than it was available on the disc. However, the children did not select pans often and did not completely understand them. The most appealing and understood pans were the motion video pans. In contrast, the resolution of the digitized and unwrapped fish-eye pans was quite low and the continuity of the still frame pans was weak. In all cases, children wanted to control the pans themselves.

The design conventions in the visual database and virtual travel videodisc that were difficult or confusing for the users were revised and tested in subsequent versions of the "Palenque" prototype.

FINAL "PALENQUE" PROTOTYPE PHASE

As the digital video interactive technology (DVI) reached its final stages of development at the David Sarnoff Research Center, the "Palenque" project team aimed at producing a CD-ROM based prototype for use as a DVI demonstration. During this phase, our research efforts included content research, production and programming research, and formative evaluation. These research efforts combined to inform the design of the prototype as it evolved through a series of revised videodisc and software prototypes, which were used on a system designed to simulate features of the developing DVI technology.[2]

The first two prototypes in this phase were check discs. These videodiscs were incomplete and temporary in many ways but had enough of the final images and sounds on them to permit the programmers, designers, and formative evaluators to proceed with their work, without having to wait for the final disc. These check discs and accompanying software included virtual travel paths and branches, joystick control, dynamic icons, 360 degree pans and tilts, the camera and photo album features, the menubar and icon panel and a preliminary museum menu. Two additional videodiscs were mastered after the check discs; they contained the previous information and additional information, such as the video overviews and museum theme rooms. A preliminary CD-ROM based prototype was mastered early in 1987 for use as a DVI demonstration for GE/RCA.

Production Formative Evaluation

Target audience children used each successive disc/software version at Bank Street's Center for Children and Technology. We created a living-room-like setting to provide a testing environment that felt more like a home than a classroom, as our intended context for "Palenque" was the home. We decided not to conduct any testing in actual homes because of the fragile and bulky nature of our DVI simulation system. The observations made during our testing sessions led to ongoing design revisions that were storyboarded and then programmed in an ongoing feedback loop between researcher/designers and programmers. Our research concerns focused primarily on general issues of appeal and comprehen-

---

[2]The DVI simulation system used in the final "Palenque" prototype phase included a number of components chosen to simulate various features of the evolving DVI technology. The components included an IBM PC-AT with extended memory; an AT&T Targa graphics board; a custom digital audio board; an IBM monitor; a stereo color RCA monitor; a Sony LDP 2000 videodisc player; and a Gravis three-button joystick.

sibility and on user friendliness, that is, children's ability to use various interface conventions.

User Friendliness.   In terms of the interface, we observed the ways that children used the menubar, icons, screen conventions, joystick for travel and joystick for cursor control. Our evaluation questions included: How quickly did children learn the interface conventions? How easy was it for them to navigate through the system? How well did they seem to understand it?

Appeal.   We observed the degree to which using "Palenque" held children's attention and interest and which features were most utilized. We tried to answer questions such as: How appealing were each of the components—explore mode, museum mode, game mode, and characters? Which content areas were of the most interest—the ruins of Palenque, the tropical rainforest, or the Maya glyphs? Which media formats or combinations of formats were appealing—audio, text, motion video, still photographs?

Comprehensibility.   We recorded the ways that children seemed to use the rich and often complex screens, the variety of interactive options, and the thematic and spatial organizational structure. General evaluation questions were framed: Are children getting anything meaningful from the "Palenque" experience? Can children make sense of and use the range of information and interactive features? Does the organization of information in thematic and spatial structures make sense to the users?

Study 1

For the first formative evaluation study in the final phase, we observed 25 target-age children using "Palenque" in pairs for 45 to 60 minutes. Researchers again noted program selections, recorded users' comments, and asked questions to assess users' comprehension of the system.

At this time, within the primary components of the prototype, the following features were available:

- Video overviews—the first half of a motion video overview with the teenage character, C.T.
- Explore mode—virtual travel at the Palenque site in two speeds with revised arrow icons to facilitate turns and feedback; a you-are-here map.

- Museum mode—the glyph room with audio narration by the female archeologist, Terry.
- Simulated tools—a dynamic compass to use with several pan/tilts of Palenque; a camera and photo album (with two text input formats for testing); a preliminary magic flashlight to see past views of Palenque.

Our evaluation issues encompassed user friendliness, appeal, and comprehensibility: How do children use and understand the major features, such as explore, museum, camera, album, map, and pans? How effective is the joystick as an interface device? How effective are the interface conventions, such as the menubar, icon panel, cursor control, and so on? What kinds of helps do users need? How appealing are the motion video and audio, especially the characters?

In general, users found the real characters, motion video, and high quality audio of "Palenque" most appealing. Their comments reflect their attraction to these features:

"Hey, we're walking . . . can we bump into anything? Are we going to crash?"

"I liked being able to control where you're going, to listen and walk around, to find out about glyphs . . ."

"Most games aren't about learning, this is fun learning—you help yourself learn."

"I've never seen a real person on a disk before."

The joystick conventions were mastered in a short time by all the children; at most it took 15 minutes, usually with no help from the researcher. The challenge of mastering the joystick conventions was the source of much of the game-like feel of "Palenque." Requests for help usually were for information about icons and menubar options and how to get the cursor or make selections with the cursor, although users often figured these things out by themselves when asked by the researchers to try. The C.T. and Terry characters were "real people" whom the children liked having as guides and companions.

The results of this formative evaluation led to many recommendations for modifications to the design. Some of the changes increased user control within the system components; for example, revising the turns in explore mode so that users can step through leading turns rather than be led through automatically; allowing for exiting from the video overview; permitting on/off control of museum mode audio narration; and providing the option of scrolling through text.

Other changes were meant to improve comprehensibility of the interface conventions such as reassigning the joystick buttons so that "map" is
available as an icon on the screen, revising the "go back" icon from a
gesturing fist to the words "go back," and highlighting images in the
museum glyph and rainforest rooms that can be selected for further
information. We also revised to increase appeal; for instance, we added a
white glove to the cursor hand so that it would not look like a "flying
chicken."

Study 2

The second formative evaluation study during the final prototyping
phase involved a new sample of children using "Palenque" repeatedly
and using the system with a structured assignment. Over a 4- to 6- week
period, four pairs of 12-year-old children were observed for four 1-hour
sessions. During the final two sessions, the children completed a hypothetical archeologist's logbook using the "Palenque" system. Researchers
recorded their observations of users' comments, questions, and behaviors; audiotaped the sessions; and videotaped directly from the system
(without a camera).

The available features in the "Palenque" prototype at the time of this
study included all of the features mentioned in Study 1, with the Study 1
revisions, plus: three motion video overviews; in explore mode—ambient
audio, a "jump" map feature, motion video travel tips, motion video
question/answer segments; in museum mode—information zooms, a revised museum menu; and in game mode—a rainforest room "symphony"
game.

While we focused on appeal, comprehensibility, and user friendliness,
these issues were looked at within the additional framework of repeated
sessions and a structured assignment. Thus, we were interested to see
whether the features children found interesting and useful changed with
prolonged use and an explicit goal to guide their information seeking.

The following discussion may give an idea of how well children were
able to understand and use the range of interactive options available to
them:

> Ch1: "Let's see what's over there." (They jump with jump map
> feature.)
>
> Ch2: "What's that temple in front of us?"
>
> Ch1: "Ask C.T." (They select C.T. travel tips icon.) "It's the Temple of
> the Sun."
>
> Ch2: "Which one is it on the map?"

Ch1: "I don't know. Let's try the eyes; we can look around" (They select the eyes icon which presents a video pan.)

Ch2: "Oh, look, we're smack dab in the middle of lots of temples. See (pointing to the map) here's the Temple of the Sun."

Ch1: "Let's (jump) over there. I don't think we've been there."

We found that children who had spent 4 hours with the "Palenque" system were still eager to come back and continue playing with it. The introduction of a simple scavenger hunt game (the archeologist's logbook) promoted great interest and involvement with nearly every aspect of the system. The new features—video overviews, jump map, ambient audio, motion video travel tips, rainforest symphony—were useful, engaging, and informative.

This study also led to several recommendations for revisions to the "Palenque" design. Most of these changes involved improvements to the interface conventions: revising the means of accessing the overviews; eliminating the "pop-and-drop" feature of some icons; placing the "turn around" arrow in the icon panel; redrawing ear and movie camera icons; and eliminating text input via a "dynamo labeller" by using only the "soft" keyboard. Attempts to increase appeal resulted in the addition of more album pages and more ambient audio and the enlargement and increased detail of the jump map.

SUMMARY

The "Palenque" project involved concurrent and iterative processes of design, evaluation, production, and programming over a 2-year period. Because our goal was to produce research prototypes, rather than products, we perceived our mission to be one of experimentation in many areas, including the development of design conventions that reflect our pedagogical biases, content and theme development, interface design, production techniques, and technical implementation. For this reason, our collective research efforts in the areas listed above were the essence of the project, rather than byproducts or activities conducted after product completion.

By creating and evaluating a series of prototype discs and software, we were able to use the reactions of child users to catch design problems early, before they became major problems that we could not afford to spend the time or money to revise. Thus, the ongoing activities of the formative evaluators served to inform the efforts of the designers, producers, and programmers. By observing children representative of the target audience actually using the successive "Palenque" prototypes, the formative researchers were able to bring reactions from "real-world" child informants to the design and development process. In this way, the creative hunches and intuitions of the designers, producers, graphic artist, and programmers were confirmed, modified, or unconfirmed, as the case may be, relatively early in the development process, as an ever more appealing and comprehensible product for the target audience emerged.

REFERENCES

Brown, J. S. (1986). From cognitive to social ergonomics and beyond. In D. A. Norman & S. W. Draper (Eds.), *User centered system design* (pp. 475–486). Hillsdale, NJ: Lawrence Erlbaum Associates.

Freeman, C., Hawkins, J., & Char, C. (1984). *Information management tools for classrooms: Exploring database management systems* (Tech. Rep. No. 28). New York: Bank Street College of Education, Center for Children and Technology.

Howland, J., & Seidel, J. (1985). *Internal formative research memos for the "Second Voyage of the Mimi" Project* (Research Report). New York: Bank Street College of Education, Center for Children and Technology.

Wilson, K. (1985, August). *"The Voyage of the Mimi" interactive video prototype: Development of an exploratory learning environment for children.* Paper presented at the Conference on Interactive Videodisc in Education and Training, Society for Applied Learning Technology, Washington, DC.

Wilson, K. (1987, April). *The "Palenque" optical disc prototype: Design of multi-media experiences for education and entertainment in a non-traditional learning context.* Paper presented at the meeting of the American Educational Research Association, Washington, DC.

7

Formative Evaluation of Interactive Training Materials

Susan Doll Jolliffe*
U.S. Productions, Inc.

Each year a greater number of organizations and companies are exploring the use of interactive videodisc to meet their training and information delivery needs. Yet, it is only recently that work has begun to devise some methods for evaluating the product during development. This chapter discusses some of the issues and techniques concerning formative evaluation of interactive videodisc. In particular, we look at some of the methods that have been used at Sandy Corporation. Since 1984, Sandy Corporation, a Michigan-based training and communication company, has developed interactive videodisc programs for Fortune 100 companies. Sandy Corporation's interactive videodisc development teams have formulated some methods of evaluation that allow the examination of the program's appeal and comprehensibility at various stages in the development process.

The field of formative evaluation is still just beginning in the area of interactive videodisc. The search for creative and effective means of conducting formative evaluation on such a highly interactive and visual medium, at the early stages, represents a challenge for formative evaluators and interactive videodisc designers. The ideas here are some first steps toward addressing this challenge.

---

*At the time of drafting this chapter, the author was a videodisc designer at Sandy Corporation.

THE INTERACTIVE VIDEODISC DEVELOPMENT PROCESS

Prior to a discussion of evaluation techniques that can be used during the development process, a look at the process itself is necessary. The process described here is a 13-phase process developed by Sandy Corporation, based on the company's experience on a number of projects. Interactive videodisc is an integration of three media—computer, audio, and video—into a single, cohesive package. This means the development process requires a careful combination of planning, analysis, creativity, and execution of design.

During the development process each activity must be carried out in an appropriate and timely fashion. Thus, in order for the process to take place smoothly and effectively, a systematic development approach is needed. This approach requires that the steps in the process, project evaluations, and project staff be carefully orchestrated to achieve a quality product. The 13-phase process, and the steps within the phases, represent a systematic development approach to interactive videodisc. Figure 7.1 provides a flowchart for the development process.

Planning Phase

Phase 1: Conduct Project Launch. This phase follows the final approval of the proposal and initial program treatment. The entire project team participates in the launch meeting. This meeting includes a review of major program goals, discussion of the development process, clarification of roles and responsibilities, and concurrence on the project schedule. The meeting emphasizes the importance of cooperation and promotes *espirit-de-corps* among the team members.

Phase 2: Conduct Analysis. The scope of the analysis phase will vary with the requirements of the program. During this phase, the program goals, strategies, and content are defined and organized. Interviews and document research are conducted to determine:

- audience needs,
- audience profiles,
- tasks and task sequencing,
- need-to-know items, and
- environmental learning issues.

100

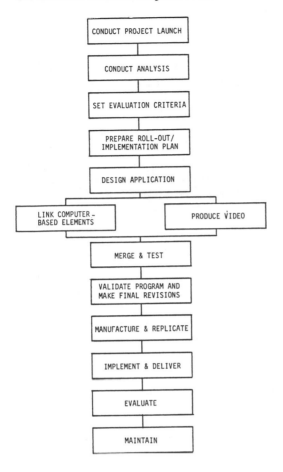

FIG. 7.1. Flowchart for interactive videodisc development process.

Phase 3: Set Project Evaluation Criteria. In this phase, the overall project goals are identified and benchmarks for measuring the effectiveness of the project are established. These benchmarks, for example, may include course cost per student hour, training effectiveness, or student acceptance. Phase 4 consists of developing a plan that documents the audience, strategies, and tools for effective program delivery and usage. This plan is developed upfront to promote program usage from the beginning of the project and to ensure a greater return on program investment.

Phase 4: Prepare Implementation Plan. A plan is developed that documents the audience, strategies, and tools for effective program delivery and usage. This plan promotes program usage from the beginning of the project and ensures a greater return on program investment.

Design Phase

Phase 5: Design Application.   This phase includes the careful definition of measureable objectives, with content to support them. Further, it includes the conceptualization and detailed description of treatment for each content segment by discrete media elements, including video and audio scripting, computer-based activities, and program structure. A program test plan is then established. Finally the design phase includes an integration of the components into a final storyboard of the program before any video is shot or screens are finalized and linked. Formative evaluation of storyboards yields data for revision decisions.

Production Phase

Phase 6: Link Computer-Based Elements.   In this phase the screen images are finalized following storyboard formative evaluation and validation. The computer logic that links the media components together is also generated. Provisions are made for tracking any reporting data that are required, such as a learner's progress through a course or usage information on a program.

Phase 7: Produce Video.   All audio and video sequences are developed using the specifications set forth in the design document. This phase includes all aspects of production, from pre-production planning to mastering of a check disc. It also includes planning videodisc geography to minimize videodisc search time.

Phase 8: Merge and Test.   In this phase, the computer and videodisc components are integrated and all sequencing and branching are verified. The test is conducted according to a test plan developed during the design phase and also includes proofreading screens and checking all program logic.

Implementation Phase

Phase 9: Validation and Final Revisions.   During the validation phase, a quality assurance analyst conducts a final independent assessment of the program against the program standards. This phase also includes validation by representative end-users in a field test of the program. Revisions are made based on the results of the validation sessions.

Phase 10: Manufacture and Replicate.   In this phase, copies of all materials including the videodisc(s), program diskettes, user-implementation materials, and program documentation guides are prepared.

Phase 11: Implement and Deliver.   In Phase 11, the program is delivered to the end-user audience, using the implementation plan developed in Phase 4.

Phase 12: Conduct Project Evaluation.   The summative evaluation phase measures the attainment of overall project goals using the benchmarks set in Phase 3. Evaluation may include analysis of reports generated by the program's recordkeeping components, as well as data collection through such techniques as surveys, interviews, or focus group sessions.

Phase 13: Provide Ongoing Program Maintenance.   This final phase provides for necessary on-going maintenance, including appropriate debugging, revisions, or updates to be released to the end-users.

FORMATIVE EVALUATION WITHIN THE DEVELOPMENT PROCESS

This section describes some of the techniques that can be used for formative evaluation within the various phases of the development process. Three phases of evaluation are considered here: (a) needs assessment during the planning phase; (b) pre-production formative evaluation during the design phase; and (c) production formative evaluation during the production phase. Examples of formative evaluation carried out on various projects are used to illustrate process, as well as potential results, for each phase of evaluation discussed.

Needs Assessment

During the planning phase, the program takes the shape eventually of an outline format, consisting of content points organized into major headings, with several content subheadings under each major heading. Evaluation at this stage can address content and learner needs by measuring the following:

• Comprehension: In terms of completeness of the content picture, what information is extraneous; what information is missing? Also what sequences of information make sense to the learner; are there some typical paths through the content that learners would need to take or would choose to take?

• Interactivity: In terms of the levels of interactivity this audience might feel comfortable with, do these learners require many paths? Does the audience indicate they want or need a high degree of control or should the program itself exercise control of the process?

In terms of both comprehension and interactivity, some of these broad issues might be examined in the early stages of the program's development. In terms of methodology, a structured focus group of sample end-users might participate in the evaluation of the content outline.

Focus Group.   During the focus group, participants would be divided into teams and each team given a stack of 3 × 5 notecards with main content headings in all capitals and subcontent points for each heading in lower case. Participants would then be asked to sequence the cards in an order that makes sense to them—adding cards or taking away cards as appropriate. Follow-up presentations and structured discussions would review the major comprehension and interactivity issues more specifically after each group completed sequencing their notecards.

This method proved to be very effective for a project in which the client wanted the program segmented into a series of modules that could be used as a part of the sales process, as well as marketing education. Thus, the program needed to address two distinct needs. A focus group of "star sales performers" was held and the group was asked to structure the cards in a manner that reflected their own sales cycle for this particular product.

The 12 participants were divided into four groups of 3 participants each. Each of these subgroups worked to reach consensus on a sequencing of main program topics. The results of this process provided valuable information for the structuring of the course, as well as information on the topics to be covered. All four groups structured two paths through the program. They all felt that the material presented should be put together so that the marketing training path would incorporate all the topics, while a separate demonstration path would serve as marketing support.

Based on this type of sequencing, the groups added some additional topics for the training path. For example, they felt this path should include some hypothetical sales situations to help the marketing representatives more effectively learn to respond to customer's initial product questions, as well as be able to really see the features of the program in terms of user benefits.

In addition to the information gathered on sequencing and topics, the focus group also provided some information on the type of interactivity that should be considered for the individual paths and the program as a whole. For example, the group felt that the marketing path should not only be flexible enough for the marketing representative to show features and benefits but also actively use the program rather than letting the customers merely watch the videodisc material.

This type of feedback provided the developmental team with some initial design considerations. For example, the same video and computer material could be used on the training and demonstration paths, but with separate audio tracks that would provide a targeted message to each of the audiences. In addition, the user might be able to turn on and off the audio on the demonstration path, so the marketing representatives could "talk through" the visual material if they chose to.

Also, an extensive menu system might be considered to allow the marketing representative greater flexibility in the presentation of material. Thus, even at the early planning phase in the development process valuable information for structuring the program and forming the interactivity and design elements can be gathered.

Pre-Production Formative Evaluation

First-Generation Storyboard. During the design phase, a detailed examination of both content and treatment can begin when a first-generation storyboard is developed. The first-generation storyboard is a narrative document that provides an overview of what the learner would experience when going through the program, with some detail in terms of text, graphics, interactivity, audio, and video. The storyboard also contains a branching sequence that shows where a particular segment branched from and where it branches to. At this stage a number of pre-production formative evaluation issues can be examined.

• Comprehension: Is the method of presentation understandable and is it consistent with the information to be presented? Can the user follow the sequencing, structure, and flow of material from one segment to the next?

• Interactivity: Can learners understand how to get from where they are on the storyboard to where they would like to be? Is the apparent level of control and ability to move about the program sufficient for learners—too many options or too few?

• Appeal: Is the treatment of individual material appealing to the audience? Does the mix of media seem varied enough for them? Is the program treatment as a whole appealing and engaging?

At this still early stage in development, again it seems to be high level issues that are appropriate for formative evaluation; for example, looking at how the audience might respond to this rough "picture" of program content, structure, and treatment and how they work together.

To do this, the most appropriate methodology seems to be a careful one-on-one walk-through with an audience member and the evaluator. Prior to the evaluation, the evaluator might prepare a checklist of things to watch for as the walk-through progressed. This checklist might also be accompanied by the rough flowchart of the storyboard so problems and comments can be noted on the segment where it occurred. This allows for easy pattern recognition in analysis results as well. Combined, the checklist and flowchart allow the evaluator to reconstruct on paper what the subject did and said in the walk-through.

Tone is one of the most prominent issues that can be evaluated at this point, affecting both comprehension and appeal. Participants in a walk-through of the first-generation storyboard are given a rough idea of treatment and flow of the program. This provides them with a "feel" for what the program will be like, and they can center their feedback on areas such as characters used, level of detail of content presented, and whether they can move through the program as they would like to.

For example, an interactive program was designed to include a series of vignettes illustrating the right and wrong ways to perform a managerial communication skill. A preliminary walk-through with selected users showed that the examples were too simplistic and superficial. Thus, the design team changed the treatment to explore one example in more depth.

Final Storyboard. The format for the final storyboard varies from project to project based on client requirements, timeframe, and the type of authoring system or language required for program development. Often it is a complete paper storyboard, much like an advertising commercial storyboard with script and visualization screen by screen. A narrative description of motion and interactivity is included. Other times, especially if an authoring system is used, the final storyboard consists of a rough series of programmed screens with the basic linking and a final script of the videodisc-based components for the program. Again, at this stage the issues of comprehension, interactivity, and appeal can be examined but in greater detail, especially if some of the program has already been built on the computer because the actual delivery environment can be used in the evaluation.

• Comprehension: Is the information on the screens and the content presented in the script clear and can major points in the program be recalled? Are the learning objectives being met? What is the performance of the participant on the actual questions, exercises, and/or case studies? Are the instructions for the exercises, as well as moving through the program, clear to the participant?

• Interactivity: Are the participants able to move about in the program? How do they respond to the level of interactivity within the program?

• Appeal: Do the participants enjoy the program as a whole? Do they remain interested in the various components of the program? Are the exercises interesting and challenging? Does the appeal overshadow or aid the understanding and attainment of the learning objectives?

Again, we have found the most appropriate methodology to be a one-on-one walk-through. For this walk-through the participants will have more control of the process because the program will be in a more complete form. This is especially true if the computer elements have already been built, as the learner can work on the computer, with the formative evaluator providing the links not yet in the program, as well as "acting as the videodisc" using the script.

Even when still in a paper stage, valuable information can be gathered. In a walk-through of a training program on developing marketing observation skills, participants provided surprisingly detailed comments on the material and its presentation. Ten people from representatives of the target audience profile participated in the final storyboard formative evaluation. Each participant was walked through the program by the evaluator. The participants were asked to make selections and decisions at each branching point, as well as to respond to the exercises and testing included in the storyboard.

The evaluator provided the branching and added "life" to the program by describing in more detail settings and characters from the video material. The program length was approximately 1 hour and each participant spent about 2 hours with the evaluator. After walking through the storyboard with approximately six participants, patterns of response were fairly clear and consistent.

Initial responses centered on the on-paper treatment descriptions and the wording of the actual content material. Participants discussed different characters in the program treatment and provided feedback on whether they felt they could relate to the character, if the characters were realistic and reflected their understanding of the company's work environment.

Participants also commented on the language used by the characters in on-screen and voice-over sequencing, providing suggestions for rewording certain passages so they more accurately reflected this company. Thus, the most easily attained information was on comprehension, in terms of the language used, and appeal, in terms of the characters and tone of the program.

But, as each participant became more comfortable with the storyboard format and the evaluation process, they began to focus a great deal of attention on issues of interactivity. Although there was no "real" interactivity possible, participants, through their selections and interpretation of branching options, provided important input that was factored into the final design of the interactivity.

For example, most participants liked the interactive segments that allowed them to ask questions of a customer "on the screen" and get some immediate feedback from that person in response to their selection. One woman said, "I got the feeling of making a choice and then hearing and seeing what might happen. Even though the choices were limited, it did give you a chance to take a conclusive action in a reasonable amount of time."

The majority of participants liked the structure of the interactivity, in terms of making these choices and getting an immediate "customer" response. But, the participants also had some problems with the interactivity at this paper stage. For example, the branching structure did not allow the learner to go back and hear the consequences of other statements or questions that could have been put to the customer. One man said, "The material is such that there really isn't one right response. It's more a judgment based on certain circumstances and so it would be nice to see, given a specific situation, what the responses to other things would have been."

Another problem for participants was the use of a strategic hint option within the customer case studies. Participants liked the use of the hint option to gather more information on the particular situation to help the learner in making a decision. But 6 of the 10 mentioned some frustration that they could only see one hint at a time. They felt that it was unrealistic to be sent down one "path" and see only that path's strategic information. One participant explained, "In a real situation you would probably want to examine and collect 'hints' on different options before making a choice, not while in the middle of making it." Most felt that the ability to page through the strategic hints at the start of decision sections would be a more appropriate use of that feature.

Another area that participants began to comment on with great frequency, about mid-way through the validation, was the use and wording of the instructions. While instructions have not been a specific validation category thus far, the issue of instructions emerged as the focus for many of the comments, which of course has direct bearing on comprehension, ability to use the interactivity and program appeal.

Although there was a selection from the main course menu entitled Program Instructions, many of the participants did not select to go through this segment. But, mid-way through the program, when they could not understand some direction, they would ask if they could get back to the instructions. In an on-paper version this is not difficult, but the actual program might not be designed to allow such easy access to a review of instructions from somewhere in the middle of an exercise.

Those participants who did go through the instructions skimmed them rapidly, as the instruction segments consisted mostly of text screens that could be quickly paged through. These people also had a number of logistical difficulties that could have been avoided by paying closer attention to the instructions. After observing this several times, the development team discussed alternative treatments for the instructions to increase their appeal and encourage the learner to pay more careful attention to them.

For example, if providing instructions on how to go through a case study, a miniature trial version might serve as the method for presenting instructions. Thus, the user could learn the instructions as well as the strategic logistics of the exercise prior to moving into the case study.

Specific wording of instructions also was identified as a stumbling block to complete comprehension and effective use of the interactivity. This program asked the learner to use either the keyboard or touch screen to input responses at different points in the program. Often the participants found the directions unclear and were confused about which input device to use. Instructions such as "enter," which was to mean use the keyboard, or "select from the screen," which was to mean use the touch screen, were generically interpreted, and the learners had trouble making the fine distinctions the designers had intended. The need for clear and explicit instructions became an important factor in the last stages of development.

Thus, during the design phase, walk-throughs of the first and final storyboards can provide an abundance of information concerning learner comprehension, appeal, and interactivity. Revision decisions made in response to these formative evaluation data will increase the potential effectiveness of the videodisc program.

Production Formative Evaluation

Check Disc.   In the next phases of development the program is linked to the check disc, which is a low-cost short life-span videodisc, and taken through a preliminary debugging. At this point in development, two formative evaluations of the pilot disc or check disc will occur: one within the development facility with a sample audience brought in; the second at the actual end-user site where the program will be used under more typical conditions. Although information gathered during each of these evaluations could vary, in general they will examine the same primary elements.

- Comprehension: Is the program clear and is the learning, as defined and measured by the program's own structure and exercises, occurring to the specified degree?
- Interactivity: Are the participants able to interact with the system to learn the material? Is the interactivity built into the system responsive to the learner's needs and requests?
- Appeal: Does the learner enjoy, as well as learn from the program? Does it hold the interest and maintain a high degree of motivation to learn the material?

Also, at this stage in the development process, formative evaluation can examine some issues of attitude. These might include:

- Attitude toward this mode of training versus other training methodologies they have been exposed to.
- Attitude toward their role, as represented by the program. Are they anxious to go out and try the techniques; can they think of others they might use?

Several data collection methods might be used during the production formative evaluations. Comprehension and some of the interactivity issues can be looked at through the information collected by the computer as the participants go through the program. Observation might also be used to look at issues of appeal and interactivity—watching for such things as "getting stuck," "skipping something," and so forth.

Questionnaires or interviews before and after using the program can serve to gather information in all areas. In addition, the rough program map could be used by the participant (rather than the evaluator as in the storyboard testing) to map their own progression through the program and to make notes in appropriate areas on things that are striking to them.

During the production formative evaluation of a marketing observation skills program, two main types of evaluation results emerged. The first category of results consisted of modifications in instructions, sequencing, and formatting of screens. The second category of results centered on those things that were not easily corrected in the existing program, but that provided valuable information for subsequent development efforts. This category included issues of mix of media, use of colors within video sequences, and user-system interaction.

The formative evaluation of this marketing project was conducted with eight members of the target end-user audience. Each participant spent 1½ hours going through the program, with the evaluator observing and collecting comments as the participant talked through the course material. At the end of the program, the evaluator spent an additional 30 minutes with the participant discussing overall feelings and reactions to the program and the medium.

In the first category of results, those that were correctable within the time and budget, the majority of problems occurred with wording of instructions. Because the medium is new to most learner audiences, they need very clear explicit directions in order to feel comfortable interacting with the system.

Another issue that emerged in this category is the use of formats and what the learner assumes about their role based on the "look" of a screen. For example, this program included multiple-choice questions in which the learner was to select a single correct response and selection questions in which there were multiple correct answers. But both of these question types had the same visual format on a screen.

Through observation of the participants, it became obvious that there was a problem. By stopping and asking why there was a problem with understanding the directions, the evaluator found that the participants assumed a certain set of instructions based on the format; the format was used as "visual" instructions and the text instructions were ignored. As one participant commented, "when you see a page in a paper-standardized test, certain question types each look a certain way, and since that is how I am used to answering questions I guess the same assumptions carry over to this kind of program."

Although not always immediately valuable, the second category of information is of great importance as interactive videodisc continues to develop as an instructional medium. In commenting on this program, the most popular aspect was the constant mix of media used. "Whenever the media changed it drew my attention back in, and since it changed quite a few times it really kept my interest high during the program," one participant commented. This kind of information helps the development team in future efforts.

The difficulties are also useful to the next round of development efforts. For example, the touch screen was universally liked—but not without some difficulties for all the participants. For example, many of the participants were short and did not have a long reach. These people found it necessary to sit far forward to touch the screen, but then felt they were too close to comfortably watch the video. Again, observation helped to uncover this issue, as the evaluator noted that many of the participants had a tendency to move their chair forward and back— forward for interaction; back to watch video segments. Also, very bright colors, like oranges and bright yellows, seemed to be difficult to watch from within a comfortable reach of the screen for interaction.

CONCLUSION

The examples and techniques described in this chapter represent a beginning attempt to try to develop effective and appropriate formative evaluation methods for interactive videodisc development. Yet, this is not especially easy or straightforward. Ideally, it would be desirable to gather information on a program prior to the expense of production and disc mastering, but until all the program elements are in place and working together it is difficult to an evaluation participant to provide specific information on the interactive learning experience itself.

Therefore, for now, issues of comprehension, instructions, and basic appeal of ideas can be evaluated at earlier on-paper stages. But specific reactions to the interactive experience as a whole may be difficult to work into a revision of the program without great expense. This makes the information gathered in production stages of evaluation a valuable foundation for future development efforts.

Thus, in formative evaluation of interactive videodisc, it is important to gather evaluation during a program's development, but equally as important is building a bank of evaluation feedback and patterns across projects. As with any new media, the early years of its use are filled with experimentation and new approaches. Formative evaluation looks to be a valuable tool for helping this new medium to grow and reach its full potential.

8

In Search of a Methodology: Evaluating "SCOOP," the WGBH Teletext Magazine for High School Students

Valerie Crane
Linda Callahan
Research Communications, Ltd.

Shelley Isaacson*
ATEX Corp.

This chapter describes a formative evaluation of a teletext magazine entitled "SCOOP" that was produced by WGBH-TV for high school students. Teletext is a generic name for broadcast systems that transmit text and graphics in an unused portion of the regular broadcast signal called the *vertical blanking interval*. A broadcaster is able to transmit regular programming and teletext at the same time on a given channel. Teletext is a one-way system that permits the user to select desired pages of information that can be seen on television sets equipped with special decoding devices.

WGBH-TV in Boston, Massachusetts conducted a teletext demonstration project in order to gauge the production and technical requirements for broadcast teletext and to explore potential public service applications. WGBH was interested in providing a service consistent with its public television mission and serving the greatest number of people using a limited number of available decoders in a somewhat controlled environment. Public high schools not only met these guidelines but also offered the opportunity to work with a population not traditionally a public television audience, but likely to adapt to a new technology with relative ease. The project staff focused on producing a teletext magazine called "SCOOP" which consisted of 100 pages of materials targeted to high school students and designed to stimulate interest in a range of current events topics. The formative evaluation was conducted by Research Communications, Ltd., a company experienced in conducting

---

*At the time of drafting this chapter, Linda Callahan was Projects Manager at Research Communications and Shelley Isaacson was WGBH Teletext Project Director.

national media research studies. Harvard University and Boston University faculty served on a Research Advisory Committee that reviewed all research procedures and provided research assistants to collect data in the schools. This chapter describes the development of "SCOOP" and the formative evaluation activities carried out during its implementation in the schools.

IMPLEMENTATION FORMATIVE EVALUATION

Most formative evaluation for television usually occurs prior to broadcast; however, this formative research effort was designed to occur during the first broadcast season, as the magazine appeared in schools. Formative evaluation during the implementation phase of the project could be effective because broadcast teletext can be readily changed on a daily basis. The constant updating and changes in the magazine also proved to be a liability in the research. Although comprehensibility of television programming can be measured through the use of recall questions, no comparable test items could be developed for teletext because there was no assurance that the same stories would remain on the service from the design to the test phase.

The teletext experience differs from television in some other important respects. The availability of the magazine on a continuous basis is in sharp contrast to most television viewing experiences that are dictated by a broadcast schedule. This accessibility made the user's experience closer to that of a print magazine although there was an underlying assumption that teletext was a television, not a print magazine experience.

Differences between television and teletext affected the evaluation methodologies that could be used as well. For example, observation of television viewing has been effective in measuring eye contact and distraction from the set but has proven less effective in determining viewers' response to the program. In contrast, observation of teletext would reveal active selection of pages to be read.

Although these new features of teletext presented interesting opportunities, the technology itself also presented challenges for the research. Whereas technical difficulties with television are of almost no consequence to formative evaluation, "SCOOP" suffered from occasional system failures and technical difficulties. It was important for the research effort to figure these technical difficulties into the usage mix and also to plan for these system failures because there was neither videotape nor diskettes of the magazine available for test purposes.

Formative evaluation with television often provides producers with information about how well their product meets standards and expectations of quality. The expectation of quality for teletext derives from both broadcast experiences and exposure to other technologies such as computers. Because "SCOOP" used graphics as part of its package, expectations of quality were important to consider as the magazine was evaluated.

Another key challenge to the research derived from teletext being a novel technology. When conducting formative research on television programs, we have a large normative database on which to draw. In addition, we know a good deal about the television viewing experience. In contrast, there is no comparable database available on teletext use— particularly for use in public places or for the high school audience. One of the first challenges to the research effort was to determine how such a technology was used in order to understand how to tailor the magazine to meet the needs and interests of the high school students.

This chapter elaborates on the development of "SCOOP" and the implementation formative evaluation that was a part of its first broadcast season. The first of three sections recounts the development of the teletext magazine. The second section summarizes the formative evaluation activities, and the final section provides some insight into lessons learned from this experience of formative evaluation for teletext.

THE DEVELOPMENT OF "SCOOP"

WGBH-TV produced and transmitted "SCOOP" to six Boston area high schools using Antiope equipment (French standard) with alphamosaic graphics capability on sets loaned by Antiope and Telematics Corporation. The producers designed the magazine to be entertaining, informative, and educational but without a curriculum-based instructional focus that depended on teacher support. Teacher involvement was encouraged, but limited resources did not permit a system-wide instructional effort. During the summer prior to the fall broadcast, the small project staff (two page composers and a project manager) grappled with decisions concerning the right mix of content, updating, and editorial policy. During this time, the project manager also contacted Research Communications to conduct formative evaluation during implementation in the schools.

Aided by the experiences and research from other teletext services, the staff made basic format and design decisions at the outset. The number of colors and words per page, the use of color themes to designate sections of the magazine, page margins, and paragraphing were determined by project staff with the WGBH design department. The primary goal was to present this new medium in as clear, consistent, and appealing a format as possible to assist viewers coming to teletext for the first time.

The secondary goal was to define and implement a style for this particular application. To make "SCOOP" informative and entertaining, the magazine had to be visually appealing and written to capture attention. Out of this concern came the decision to use graphics where possible to add color and interest to the page; to use headlines as teasers to capture the viewer's attention; and to use special features like *flash* and *reveal*.

The *flash* command allowed a given element or elements within a page to flash on and off at a fixed rate of speed and was used as an enhancement and graphic illustration. The *reveal* feature allowed information to be hidden on a page and revealed only when the user requested it. In this way, limited interactivity was simulated. The reveal command was used within all areas of the magazine: news quizzes, sports quizzes, features, and others. "SCOOP" editors used it as an educational tool requiring the students to fill in the blanks, choose the correct answer, and so forth.

The WGBH design department and project staff created graphics and standard page formats. Graphics were used on approximately 75% of the magazine pages including the index pages of each of the seven magazine sections. The staff quickly learned not to overdo graphics or attempt images too complex for the system's resolution.

The following criteria defined the design of the various sections of "SCOOP":

• Availability of Information: Limited staff size necessitated utilizing acquired print and wire-service information with limited use of original material. Even so, "SCOOP" producers realized that their audience, design, and technology called for considerable print editing.

• Updating Requirements: Although the updating capability is one of the significant features of teletext, staff resources constrained the number of sections requiring frequent updating. A balance had to be struck in order to deliver a broad service. Although news stories were updated about three times a day, feature articles could remain on "SCOOP" for a few days without compromising the integrity of the magazine.

• Appeal: The "SCOOP" staff looked for stories and features that were local and teen-oriented wherever possible.

• Usefulness: "SCOOP" was also designed to be an information resource and many sections sought to deliver new information or to lead students to other resources.

Based on these criteria, "SCOOP" included the following magazine sections:

News Scoops. The first section of the magazine comprised world, national, and local news stories edited from Associated Press wire copy to lengths of 35 to 70 words and updated several times a day.

$$ and Sense. This section included daily updated news about consumer prices, unemployment, inflation, and the like. Features such as price comparison studies of record stores changed twice weekly.

Sportsbeat. Sports news, schedules, and scores were updated twice a day. This section also included several quizzes per day, often contributed by members of the high school audience. Twice weekly features reported on sports, recreation, and health issues.

Weather Vane. Today's weather, tomorrow's forecast, and an extended weather picture of the broadcast area were updated two or three times daily.

New Waves. This section provided current entertainment information such as TV tips, program information, radio highlights, Top 10 records, movie quizzes and reviews, local listings of performances, and a soap opera daily update.

Local Scene. This section included local events, profiles of local/high school personalities, listings of community/school activities, teen advice column, chess game, weekly free events, and letters to the editor.

Hot Bits. Usually two articles, running for 5 days each, presented topics that would not easily fit into the magazine's other categories or which needed multiple-page treatment. A glossary on the last page defined terms and concepts found elsewhere in the magazine.

Inside "SCOOP". The last section of "SCOOP" included answers to the questions: What is "SCOOP"? How do you use it? Where can you find it? Who is responsible for it?

Having made these early content and form decisions without the benefit of any formal research, WGBH recognized the need for a formative evaluation process to ensure that the demonstration project delivered on its promise to afford WGBH a learning experience. Formative evaluation of the magazine during implementation in the schools would provide feedback to the developers about its effectiveness and appeal, allowing revisions to be made.

RESEARCH QUESTIONS FOR EVALUATING "SCOOP"

The project and research teams formulated a wide range of questions. Because of limitations in the research budget, summative evaluation questions regarding the impact of teletext and extent of usage could not be addressed. After eliminating questions that could not be answered within the scope of this formative evaluation effort, the following remained to inform the research design.

1. *How do students approach the teletext experience on first use?* Because "SCOOP" was considered tangential to the school curriculum, the editorial staff anticipated that most students would be using "SCOOP" for the first time on their own—at least without direction from a teacher or other adult. Therefore, the team facilitated use of the magazine by providing instructions in the "SCOOP" magazine itself to supplement print directions kept next to the set. The research effort examined whether these instructions were used and met students' needs.

2. *What types of students use "SCOOP"?* The team wanted to know as much as possible about students who were using "SCOOP". Sex and age differences were considered particularly significant. The staff regarded current media usage as important also, particularly questions regarding general television viewing, television news viewing, and newspaper reading.

3. *How do students use "SCOOP"?* In order to design a magazine that was responsive to the audience, the team needed to learn how they approached and read the magazine. Did they start at the beginning of each section and use the index? Did they proceed through the section in order? Did they follow suggestions to go to other pages for further information? Did they use the flash feature? How long did they use the magazine? Did they work alone or in groups?

4. *Do the sections and stories in the magazine represent topics of interest to students?* The WGBH staff had chosen the initial magazine content without benefit of pre-production testing. Determining how students responded to the stories covered in the magazine and obtaining specific suggestions from students could help in the development of new stories.

5. *How can stories be structured to attract and hold the attention of high school students?* Both design elements and content factors that influenced the effectiveness of a page were of primary concern. A study conducted for the WETA teletext experiment (Champness & de Alberdi, 1981) suggested that the visual elements of the pages could appreciably affect how users responded to teletext. A challenge to the research effort was to develop instruments that would be sensitive to the relative effectiveness of pages. The design staff could use students' page-by-page reactions to revise the teletext format.

6. *How much information do students recall from their viewing experience?* Although measurement of long-term learning was not feasible in this formative evaluation, initial learning could be measured through post-viewing recall.

7. *How did the students respond in general to teletext as a new technology and specifically to some of the features in teletext?* The project team wanted to

learn how students would react to teletext. How unique was the teletext experience for high school students? This question would be difficult to answer, but research could provide students with an opportunity to talk about their perceptions and use of teletext.

LIMITATIONS TO BE CONSIDERED IN THE RESEARCH DESIGN

Early experiences with "SCOOP" indicated that technical difficulties could prove to be a substantial problem in two respects. First, researchers were assigned to collect data one day a week, on the average. If the system failed to operate in a school, the opportunity for feedback on that day was lost. Second, it might be difficult to distinguish dissatisfaction with the content contained in the magazine from frustration resulting from technical difficulties.

A second set of limitations were imposed by the one-way nature of the system. In order to obtain feedback on usage, observation or self-report would be options. As expected, observation proved very labor intensive for the project.

The placement of the sets posed another problem to be considered in the evaluation plan. In most schools, the set resided in the library; usage might then be a function of the flow of students through that part of the school. In fact, students who were in the library during their free periods were those most likely to use the set. The research design had to draw from a wide student base so that there was not a self-selective group of students directing the development of the magazine.

Although the high school administrators cooperated in accepting sets, they perceived "SCOOP" as tangential to the school curriculum and activities. This precluded a systematic selection of students to participate in a student survey that would determine how many students had used the system during the year.

With these research questions and limitations in mind, we developed a fairly ambitious research design.

FOUR METHODOLOGIES FOR EVALUATING "SCOOP"

The evaluation questions were translated into specific objectives for the research design. We employed a variety of methodologies to examine issues relating to use and design of the magazine. Four methodologies addressed these main issues. First, *focus groups* were conducted on a weekly basis throughout most of the school year to get specific feedback from students on individual sections of the magazine. Both ongoing and periodic reports were prepared for the production team in order to assist in making decisions about developing content. Second, *observations* of students using the sets provided data on how "SCOOP" was used by students. Third, after using "SCOOP," students completed a *survey* that appeared at the end of the teletext magazine. Fourth, researchers conducted *recall intercept interviews* in the spring to determine what students could recall of stories they had read.

Each of the methodologies contributed to the research objectives of the project as well as overall project goals. The relationship between these methodologies and the specific research objectives is outlined in Table 8.1. The following is a rationale for and description of each methodology and describes problems encountered and positive outcomes obtained.

TABLE 8.1
Design for Evaluating "SCOOP"

Research Objective	Focus Group	Methodology		
		Observation	Survey	Interview
To determine how students learned to use "SCOOP"	X			
To determine which students used "SCOOP" most frequently		X	X	
To examine how teletext was used by students		X	X	
To determine which topics were of most/least interest to students	X	X	X	
To determine how to structure stories to attract and hold the attention of student	X			
To determine what students could recall from stories they had read				X
To document students' reponse to teletext as a technology	X			

Method 1: Focus Groups

Because the technology allowed an opportunity for immediate experimentation with various approaches to "SCOOP," it was desirable to employ a research methodology that would provide ongoing feedback on student response to the magazine. Focus groups allowed the design and research teams to focus on each section individually and to make comparisons of appeal and comprehensibility across different sections of "SCOOP" over time. The focus group methodology provided input from students not only on what worked and what did not work, but why. This approach also collected general information on students' perceptions of "SCOOP" content, their news media usage, and first use of the teletext magazine.

Sample selection presented a problem with the focus groups. Random selection was not possible because accessibility to students was limited to those who were scheduled to be in the library for free periods. These tended to be the same students every week for the entire semester. Therefore, there was a danger of drawing from a very limited sample. Researchers were directed not to repeat students in their groups and to provide a mix of students who had experience using "SCOOP" and others who did not.

The focus group methodology combined quantitative and qualitative measures of the appeal and comprehensibility of certain sections and pages of "SCOOP." The specific measures used during the focus group are detailed here, but generally during the 1-hour sessions, small groups of five students each answered background questions on their sex, age, TV viewing habits, and use of news sources. Then, using Research Communications' scanning technique, students viewed and rated each page in the section being tested. For finer analysis of page design, a semantic differential was used. Finally, students completed a brief questionnaire and participated in a group interview. A total of 12–20 groups of five students evaluated each section.

Focus Group Scanning Technique. The scanning technique, developed and used by Research Communications in evaluating both television and print materials, helped to determine the relative appeal of individual pages of "SCOOP." The researcher showed the first page of the selected "SCOOP" section and students marked the corresponding box on their answer form if they found that page of teletext interesting. They were to leave the box blank if they found the page boring. The researcher proceeded to the next page of the section when all students looked up.

The scanning technique was useful as a diagnostic tool because it recorded the wide variability in appeal ratings for teletext pages. When the scanning data were paired with the focus group interview data, we were able to determine what pages worked best for students and why. For example, the patterns that emerged from the ratings and interviews revealed that pages presenting information that was new, entertaining, and useful resulted in high appeal ratings and those that provided information that was not useful or did not directly relate to students were rated much lower. The appeal ratings also showed consistently throughout the year that students came to expect stories limited to one page in length. When stories were continued on to a second page, appeal decreased markedly.

Although the scanning procedure represented an effective tool for determining the relative appeal of "SCOOP" pages, other research methods determined specifically why certain pages worked and others did not.

Focus Group Semantic Differential. In order to obtain reactions to specific design elements on a page, a semantic differential was utilized to determine appeal and comprehensibility of individual pages in the system. We modified a semantic differential that had successfully differentiated design elements of teletext pages in the WETA teletext experiment (Champness & de Alberdi, 1981). Because Research Communications had previously found semantic differentials effective in evaluating television program elements, it was hoped that it would also provide useful diagnostic information on teletext.

In an initial pilot test utilizing 12 bipolar adjectives, it became clear that students were confused on whether to rate pages for design or content. Therefore, we asked students first to look at the page before reading it and rate the page according to design. The design dimensions included: organized/chaotic; cheerful/gloomy; exciting/dull; bright/dark; warm/cold; and colorful/colorless. Then students were asked to read the page and analyze it for content. The content dimensions measured were: clear/unclear; meaningful/meaningless; useful/useless; easy/difficult; important/unimportant; and interesting/boring.

Despite this modification, we found the semantic differential to be an *ineffective* diagnostic tool. Although it provided interesting information on the general appeal of teletext design, comparisons across sections yielded few differences.

Focus Group Questionnaire. Because the content of each section of "SCOOP" was subject to constant update and change, it was not feasible to measure recall of each section. Therefore, a series of standardized questions included in the questionnaire each month assessed students' perceptions of the information contained in each section of "SCOOP." These items asked whether students found the information contained in the test section to be useful to them; whether it was new to them; and whether they had learned something. Although these items are limited by self-report bias, loyalty to television programming has been linked to viewers' perceptions that they have learned something from a program (Television Audience Assessment, 1983).

The stability of response to these items across sections was encouraging, however. For instance, most students found that there was something new in "SCOOP" and that "SCOOP" provided an opportunity for learning. Perceptions of usefulness varied from section to section and were directly related to appeal.

Focus Group Interview. At the end of each focus group session, a structured group interview was conducted. Although questionnaire data provided general information on what worked and did not work in "SCOOP," the interview schedules were developed to obtain specific in-depth response to "SCOOP" content, design, and special system features such as the reveal and flash features.

From the interviews we learned that students were apparently reluctant to reveal that anything about "SCOOP" was confusing to them. However, the interviews did show what students liked and disliked about "SCOOP" and provided specific suggestions for new material to be covered by "SCOOP."

Because the focus groups utilized small-group interviews, informal feedback from the on-site visits could be shared with the project team the same day the groups were conducted. Phone calls to the project director or staff would provide the team with some immediate concerns that could be remedied overnight. More formal feedback sessions were also scheduled after data from two sections had been compiled and included in print reports. At four different points throughout the school year, feedback sessions were held with all members of the project team and each section was analyzed in detail. In the formal feedback sessions, response to each page would be analyzed along with comments explaining why some pages worked better than others. For example, we learned early in the process that the entertainment section contained program listings from WGBH-TV and WGBH-FM but did not focus on some of the media selections that were of particular interest to students this age. Teenagers made a number of suggestions about what kinds of entertainment information were of interest including targeted television programs dealing with teen issues, movie reviews, and listings of local concerts of possible interest.

The formative evaluation process was particularly helpful in the confirmation of certain content and form decisions but also in the continuous reworking of the product to suit the interests and needs of the audience. Positive audience reaction to organization and format suggested that WGBH staff could concentrate on content and style considerations that received more criticism. Regular reports from the research team resulted in many changes within sections and several across sections such as increased updating and more use of the reveal feature. In addition, the research sessions had been useful in testing new concepts and ideas.

Method 2: Observations

Although the focus groups yielded data on the contents of "SCOOP," that methodology did not address questions of system usage. Observations were conducted in each of the high school sites to document use of "SCOOP" in an unstructured situation and to gather data on students who were not selective in responding to the "SCOOP" Survey. During the observation periods, researchers recorded the sex and number of "SCOOP" users; the length of use; and which sections, pages, and special features of the system were used. They also recorded the level of technical difficulty experienced during the period they observed use.

Although this methodology focused on who was using "SCOOP" and how it was used, it contained several limitations. First, it was extremely labor intensive requiring that researchers visit the schools and observe use for periods of 2 to 3 hours at a time. In that time, two to three observations would be completed. Hence, only 106 observations were completed across the year. The requirement that researchers position themselves near the teletext set also made the methodology obtrusive.

Because observations relied on subjective evaluation of student activity, they were subject to some degree of error. For example, in order to remain as unobtrusive as possible, length of use was not timed with a stop watch or similar device. Researchers used a watch or wall clock to record the beginning and end of their observations. Also, use of the teletext often involved coming and going of numerous students; researchers used their judgment in deciding when one observation ended and the next began. Observations also did not adequately quantify frequency or extent of use. Finally, because the sampling of observations was limited in number, no trends in use could be noted for the school year.

In spite of these limitations, observations did provide information on who used "SCOOP." For instance, findings showed that "SCOOP" was used most frequently as a group activity. Usage was heaviest among boys with most typical usage consisting of a group of two to three boys reading the sports scores and sports information. When boys and girls used the system together, the groups tended to be larger. This finding was shared informally with the project team and helped them to formulate pages with this group use in mind.

Observations also answered questions about how "SCOOP" was used by students. It was found, for example, that most students referred to the index page before proceeding to read through a section of "SCOOP" and that they read the section in sequence about half the time. This feedback suggested that the fundamental structure and format of the magazine was on target.

The observations also focused on the use of special features of "SCOOP." For example, the reveal button, which was used to answer quiz questions was used almost every time it was available; while the GO TO PAGE # reference that was used to expand a story, provide background information, or define words was used much less frequently by students.

Method 3: "SCOOP" Surveys

The project team wanted to take advantage of the technology itself in the research process and therefore included a user survey in the magazine. This additional data source might inform the team about use when the researchers were not present to conduct groups and observe.

A message placed in the index of the magazine encouraged students to complete the survey when they had finished using the set on their own. Next to the teletext set in each site was a box containing mark-sensitive answer cards and written instructions for responding to the "SCOOP" survey on the cards. The completed cards were collected on each visit to the site.

The "SCOOP" survey was designed to determine which sections of the magazine were used and which were favorites and least favorites. Students were also asked whether they used "SCOOP" alone or with one or more friends, how many sections they used, and how long they used "SCOOP."

The "SCOOP" survey sample was self-selective and small; only 141 were completed during the course of the school year. Also, the majority of students who completed the survey did not do so until they had used the system two or three times. Despite these limitations, most results correlated closely with findings from the focus groups and observations, reinforcing the reliability of the focus group research.

One contradiction was found between the observation data and the

"SCOOP" survey. Length of "SCOOP" use as documented by observations was much lower than that reported by students who completed the "SCOOP" survey. Although average self-reported use was 20–30 minutes, usage reported in observations was most frequently under 15 minutes. This discrepancy was probably a function of the amount of time students had available to them. It is likely that those who had less time available to use "SCOOP" would not have taken the time to complete the survey.

Method 4: Intercept Interviews

The constant changing and updating of "SCOOP" content limited opportunities to measure learning using the methodologies described thus far. Therefore, in order to collect some data on recall of "SCOOP," one interviewer visited two schools and conducted intercept interviews with 50 individual students immediately after using "SCOOP." They were interviewed to determine what sections they had reviewed and were then asked what they remembered about the stories they had read.

All students had read News Scoops and were asked to recall stories from that section. Then students were asked to select one other section they had read and to recall stories from that section. Demographic information was also recorded.

Although this methodology provided some information on learning from "SCOOP," it represents a measure of only one aspect of learning. Long-term retention of content was not determined. The desirability of the intercept interview is also limited because it is extremely labor intensive.

Slightly more than one third of the stories that had been read were recalled, on the average. Closer analysis revealed three to five stories were recalled by students, on the average, regardless of the total number of stories read in a section. This finding parallels results of another recall study of television news (Stauffer, Frost, & Rybolt, 1983) that found that a majority of adult viewers was able to recall three or four stories they had seen on the news.

The "SCOOP" experience also provided some interesting general findings about the technology itself. The high school students were not awed by the teletext technology and did not express much interest in how the magazine was delivered to them. Text services had already entered the marketplace via personal computers. "SCOOP" provided them with some interesting and useful information. However, they found successive pages of text visually monotonous as compared to a television experience. Early in the year, they found the brevity of news stories superficial as compared with newspapers although they developed expectations of headline-length material as the year progressed. The project team had been correct in their original assumption that the high school audience would adapt to the technology with relative ease.

LESSONS LEARNED: IN SEARCH OF A METHODOLOGY

A number of research methodologies were used in evaluating "SCOOP" for a variety of reasons. First, utilizing multiple research techniques provided an opportunity for checking both the validity and reliability of the research. If the scanning technique, questionnaire data, and interview responses agreed in their results, it was hard to ignore the findings. Second, little was known about teletext itself so we wanted to examine the process of usage as well as the product itself. This made the formative evaluation effort for "SCOOP" more ambitious than most. Third, we were not sure which methodologies would be most fruitful so a variety of techniques were implemented to search for the most effective.

Our discussion on formative evaluation for "SCOOP" would not be complete without considering which methods were most effective and which least effective. In formative evaluation, the most important criterion for effectiveness is the utility that it has for the production team. In this regard, the weekly focus groups were the most productive resource for shaping "SCOOP's" development because they provided specific and targeted responses to the magazine. The scanning technique pinpointed pages which were interesting and those which were not, while the interviews helped in explaining why. Although questionnaires have been very effective in evaluating television programming, they were less effective with teletext because of the daily changes in stories. The semantic differential, which has also been used successfully to discriminate between effective and ineffective television programming and talent, was less effective as a diagnostic tool for teletext. This is probably true because few production elements figure into developing teletext pages.

The observations met with mixed success. The labor intensiveness of these was of ongoing concern. The observations did not provide extensive quantitative data but proved helpful to the team in a qualitative sense because they revealed how the magazine was used. Group use was an unexpected outcome of the service and was best documented through the observations.

The "SCOOP" surveys were less effective than either the focus groups or the observations for a variety of reasons. First, the sample was highly biased with only a select few completing them. The survey data also reported longer than observed periods of use possibly because students who filled out the cards had more time at the set to do so. Originally, we hoped that we could track use and preferences across the year but found that too few were completed for this purpose. The general preferences questions (Which section did you like best and least?) were helpful in understanding satisfaction with a given section but not helpful to the producers in developing subsequent stories. In this regard, the focus groups were more targeted on a section and, hence, proved to be more effective for formative evaluation.

The intercept interviews were a compromise in obtaining some measure of what students learned from the magazine. This labor-intensive approach to research rendered little information that influenced the shaping of the magazine. The intercept interviews were undertaken as an experimental approach to address the problem of constantly changing text. The idea of holding some of the content constant was rejected since students complained when material was not updated.

The early 1980s will probably be remembered as the time during which many new technologies burst on the scene full of promise that our lives would dramatically change. However, this same short period of time also witnessed that few survived in the marketplace. These technologies often failed because the focus was on the technology and not on the users. Many tried to create a need for the technology rather than meet an existing need. They missed the fundamental message that they were in the business of serving an audience and not delivering a technology, and failed to realize that users do not care how a service is delivered to them but what is delivered to them. Projects that use formative evaluation avoid some of these pitfalls because it helps decision makers to make connections between the product and the audience. If the interests and needs of the audience are not met, the most well-endowed projects cannot, should not, and will not succeed.

REFERENCES

Champness, B. G., & de Alberdi, M. (1981). *Measuring subjective reactions to tele-text page design* (Research Report). New York: Alternate Media Center School of Arts.

Stauffer, J., Frost, R., & Rybolt, W. (1983). The attention factor in recalling network television news. *Journal of Communication, 33*(1), 29–37.

Television Audience Assessment. (1983). *The audience rates television* (Research Report). Cambridge, MA: Author.

III

THE METHODS

Planning Formative Evaluation

9

The authors of the previous five chapters acted as formative evaluators during the developmental stages of various electronic learning products. Each person carried out a variety of research tasks within a particular setting, but all had to answer the same general questions to define the parameters of their evaluation activities. The answers to these questions constitute their *formative evaluation plan:*

1. Which purposes will the evaluation serve and for whom?
2. What are the evaluation questions?
3. Which methods of inquiry are appropriate?
4. What measures will be used with whom under what conditions?

This chapter reflects on each of these questions in turn, examining the particular demands of formative evaluation within the broader field of educational evaluation. Drawing on the specifics of case studies in previous chapters, this chapter looks at the generic issues involved in planning formative research. The goal is to outline *how* to develop a formative evaluation plan for educational technologies.

WHICH PURPOSES WILL THE FORMATIVE EVALUATION SERVE AND FOR WHOM?

The first phase of an evaluation plan clarifies the purposes(s) of the research activities and identifies the recipient(s) of the information. For example, in the early stage of pre-production, our purposes might be to assess the accuracy of videodisc storyboard content or the appeal of various television cast members. The recipients of such information would be the production staff. In the later production phase, our purpose might be to measure effectiveness of a software prototype in achieving its learning objectives with students, thereby providing information for sponsors about the progress of the project.

Stufflebeam and Webster (1980) reviewed 13 different approaches to educational evaluation, each of which serves different purposes. Formative evaluation studies performed during curriculum development for electronic technologies fall mainly into four of these categories: connoisseur-based, decision-oriented, objectives-based, and public relations-inspired studies. Let us examine how each of these types is defined.

Connoisseur-Based Studies

The connoisseur-based study in educational evaluation requests that experts in a given field "describe critically, appraise, and illuminate the particular merits [and demerits] of a given object" (Stufflebeam & Webster, 1980, p. 14). Formative evaluators call upon experts (connoisseurs) to examine the developing materials from their particular vantage point. The purpose of these studies is to provide feedback on content, pedagogy, and media design from those who have devoted themselves to studying such issues. In most cases, experts contribute a type of information different from that obtainable from the target audience. For example, formative evaluators use experts to assess the accuracy of the program subject matter, while using learners to assess the effectiveness of the program in teaching that subject matter. In the connoisseur-based study, the program itself, not its effects, is appraised and examined for its content, objectives, instructional design, and media usage.

A variety of experts have been suggested as useful to formative endeavors (Markle, 1965; Stolovitch, 1975, 1982; Thiagarajan, 1978). The most common connoisseur-based studies in formative evaluation involve experts in subject matter, media, design, and utilization. The activities of these experts are described here.

Subject Matter Experts.   These experts review materials for content accuracy, significance, and sequencing as well as currency and comprehensiveness of the content. This approach is exemplified in chapter 7 where Jolliffe reports using experts in the planning phase of an interactive videodisc, which dealt with the process of selling a product. A focus group of "star sales performers" was given a stack of 3 × 5 notecards with content headings on them and asked to sequence the cards to reflect their own sales cycle for the product. The group also added topics to the original list, increasing the comprehensiveness of the content.

Media Experts.   Media experts assess the technical production quality and artistry of the materials. They examine the quality of the camera techniques, the appropriateness of the lighting, the sound quality, the efficiency of the computer programming, and so forth.

Design Experts.   Evaluating the materials against the criteria of good instructional design is the job of the design expert. Most often these experts draw on their experience and intuition; however, where appropriate, design experts apply instructional quality guidelines that are derived from research studies on effective instructional variables (Frase, DeGracie, & Poston, 1974; Golas, 1983; Montague, Ellis, & Wulfeck, 1983). For example, Burkholder (1982) used the Instructional Strategy Diagnostic Profile (Merrill, Richards, Schmidt, & Wood, 1977) to analyze and prescribe revisions in a self-instructional text on learning theory. When student groups were exposed either to the original text version or to the version revised according to the Profile prescriptions, the revised version produced significantly higher learning outcomes. Design guidelines have limited application but appear to be effective tools for revision within their defined boundaries.

Utilization Experts.   Those responsible for purchasing and using the program in its intended setting are utilization experts. This group includes the broadcaster who decides to air the television program, the administrator who purchases the computer software for the school system, and the teacher who chooses to use the videodisc in the classroom. Broadcasters may judge whether the program adds to their already full instructional schedule. Administrators may assess whether the software objectives and content fit in with their district's curriculum. Teachers may evaluate whether the videodisc presentation is suitable for their particular classroom environment. Of all the expert categories, utilization experts or teachers are reported to be used most frequently as expert reviewers for educational software (Truett, 1984; Truett & Ho, 1986).

As an illustration of connoisseur-based studies with utilization experts, Rockman (chapter 5) describes the use of experts in the formative evaluation of problem-solving software. Administrators and teachers read early design reports and computer scripts, responding to questionnaires about curriculum and technology fit, visibility of objectives, and classroom management issues. Rockman reports that the experts "give some guidance to the curriculum and to the nature of the computer program. They help fine-tune the goals and objectives. The major contribution has been to management issues and the need to incorporate management plans in each lesson" (chapter 5, p. 73).

In summary, connoisseur-based formative evaluation employs experts in subject matter, media, design, and utilization to provide critical analysis of program materials at various stages of development. Which experts one should consult—and when—depends on the project specifics, but some experts can contribute earlier in the process than others. For instance, subject matter experts can work effectively at the scripting stage, whereas a media expert might be brought in at the later production phases.

The weakness of connoisseur-based research is its dependency on the particular experiences, biases, and values of one's experts. The main advantage of connoisseur-based studies is that revisions based on expert appraisal will help insure that the program is valued, irrespective of its measured effects on learners. The content will be seen as accurate, comprehensive, and up to date; the technical quality will be high; the instructional design will be theoretically sound; and the program will be considered usable in its intended setting.

Evaluators should also measure the effects of a program on the target population. It is a misuse of experts to expect them to estimate the materials' effects on learners. Experts are not always able to predict the effectiveness of programs (Rosen, 1968; Rothkopf, 1963). For example, Weston (1987) found that instructional design experts evaluating a film-strip/audiotape program

> felt strongly that the objectives of the presentation had to be clarified and made explicit to the learner in order for the presentation to achieve its purpose. The learner data indicates that the learners understood the objectives of the program in spite of the fact that they were vague and not explicit. (p. 55)

The findings of Callison and Haycock (1988) also document the observation that teachers are not necessarily good predictors of student responses to materials. Over 3 years, 291 teachers and 2,308 students from Grades 3 through 12 evaluated 135 educational microcomputer programs. The students and teachers agreed more often about programs that were rated extremely low than they did about programs rated extremely high. Callison and Haycock (1988) found the following:

> a criterion which tended to have a strong association to high ratings given to software by teacher evaluators was "this program should arouse student

interest," but there was a weak correlation between the programs rated highly by teachers and the programs rated highly by students. (p. 26)

Thus, information on the *effects* of the electronic learning materials should come from students themselves through decision-oriented and objectives-based studies of the sort described here.

Decision-Oriented Studies

Decision-oriented studies in educational evaluation are "based on the idea that evaluation should help educators make and defend decisions that are in the best interest of meeting students' needs" (Stufflebeam & Webster, 1980, p. 12). The purpose of decision-oriented studies in formative evaluation is to gather information from the target users (both learners and program managers) to improve the design of a curriculum product. The usual recipients of such information are the production staff members.

Decision-oriented research occurs at any time during the design, production, and implementation stages of program development. Chapters 2 and 3 discuss in depth the decision-making process behind program development, so it is reviewed only briefly here. Design decisions are strategic, involving the planning of objectives, content, pedagogy, interactivity, and production formats. Production decisions are tactical, concentrating on the specifics of the program that carry out the earlier strategic decisions. Finally, implementation decisions involve program management and fine-tuning of the program in its intended setting. Examples of decision-oriented studies during each of the program development phases are presented here.

Design phase decisions benefit from knowledge about the existing competencies of the target audience and profit from responses of the target group to alternative television formats and interactive strategies. Schauble, in chapter 4, reports using decision-oriented studies during the design phase of software development. The project team for the preschool software program "Taxi" asked numerous design questions about the speed of the taxis, the shape and size of the streets, the presentation of directions, and the rate at which the game's difficulty would increase. To help with these design decisions, researchers watched children play with a special program prototype, while trying out different verbal instructions and adjusting various prototype parameters such as taxi speeds and street width. The researchers explored how comprehensible and accessible different versions of the prototype software were to the children. These data facilitated design decisions.

Decision-oriented research during the transition between the design and production phases uses the building blocks of a program (i.e., scripts, storyboards, flowcharts, program segments). These early materials are not usually complete enough for students to attain the intended outcome objectives, so in lieu of measuring learning achievement or attitude change, formative evaluation early in the production process measures audience or user engagement with the materials. This research approach is based on the debatable but commonsense assumption that engaging material—that which is appealing, accessible, comprehensible, and credible—provides a necessary foundation for the eventual achievement of the cognitive or affective objectives of the product.

Jolliffe, in chapter 7, gives an example of decision-oriented evaluation at the late design/early production phase of a videodisc. The evaluator *walked through* a paper version of the final storyboard and flowchart with individual respondents. The evaluator acted as the computer, branching respondents to different parts of the program. Users responded to the appeal and credibility of the characters, credibility of the language, comprehensibility of the instructions, accessibility of information, and appropriateness of the feedback mechanisms. These formative evaluation data guided revision decisions. A check disc or pilot disc was pressed and then tested with another user group. At such a point in the production phase, evaluators can effectively test for learning and attitude outcomes employing objectives-based studies described later.

During the early implementation phase of a program, decision-oriented studies are useful if program changes are still economically feasible. Crane, Callahan, and Isaacson (chapter 8) report that formative evaluation during the implementation of a teletext magazine in schools was effective because broadcast teletext is easily changed. Data about student usage, interest, and recall facilitated teletext revision decisions.

In summary, decision-oriented formative evaluation studies collect information on the effects of the developing program on learners, program managers (e.g., teachers), and other users. The kind of information necessary for making design and production decisions varies according to the specific project, and the research methods used range from observations and interviews to questionnaires and quasi-experimental designs.

The main advantage of decision-oriented studies is that program design and revisions in design can be in part empirically based. The observations of users and interviews with audience members provide insights into why a program is working or not working. Evaluators map out the program's strengths and weaknesses. Such data inform the decision-making process during the design, production, and implementation stages with the purpose of improving the program and maximizing its potential effectiveness.

The weakness of decision-oriented research is that it is not deterministic; it is not always clear what specific revisions are called for by the data. Experimental studies pitting one program variable against another program variable—and may the best one win—are not common in decision-oriented formative evaluation. Thus, if a viewing group rates a video character as lacking credibility and gives their reasons in an interview, the production staff is made aware of a credibility problem and receives some insight as to why; but there are no standard revision solutions. The experience and intuitions of the developer and producer come into play in the revisions along with deadlines, economics, and politics.

Objectives-Based Studies

Most well-developed curricula define a set of objectives to be attained by the target students. The objectives-based study determines to what extent the students achieve the stated program objectives (Tyler, 1942). Formative evaluators carry out objectives-based studies on pilot programs in the appropriate educational setting, measuring student performance on pretests and posttests.

The purpose of such studies is to provide developers with an estimate of how well the final implementation of the program will fare in achieving its goals and to provide project managers and sponsors with a quantitative assessment of progress. These studies may be considered formative evaluation to the extent that their data are timely and useful in making program changes. Failure to achieve on a posttest indicates problems with the prototype but may give few clues as to the specifics of those problems. If objectives-based studies are to be of use to program developers, they should be employed with decision-oriented studies that provide interpretative information to support revision decisions in the pilot or future programs.

The "Voyage of the Mimi" evaluation staff, as mentioned in chapter 3, carried out an objectives-based study on the computer software, "Whale Search" and "Treasure Hunt." The curriculum objectives involved learning to use various Logo programming commands. Students were tested through paper-and-pencil multiple-choice and fill-in-the-blank questions presented after exposure to the software. Results from a subset of the questions indicated that most students could interpret what would happen on the computer screen given a sequence of two Logo movement commands (e.g., RIGHT 180 FORWARD 100), but that younger students failed when the sequence was extended to three commands (Char, Hawkins, Wootten, Sheingold, & Roberts, 1983).

These outcome results interpreted alone might lead one to believe that the "Mimi" software programs were effectively teaching command combinations to the target users. However, observations in classrooms showed that when children played the computer games, they used single commands and only combined commands when explicitly assisted by another person. In this evaluation, the observation data helped with the interpretation of the objectives-based data to yield useful formative information for program revisions.

The main advantage of the objectives-based study is that it estimates whether the program can really achieve its goals. When carried out with a pilot program, the study's performance data help developers determine whether further revision is cost-effective. The weakness of objectives-based studies is that achievement data alone provide limited guidance for revisions; pretest–posttest results indicate learning problems but do not pinpoint what part of a program is weak in this regard. Decision-oriented studies that collect information during and about the learning process complement objectives-based studies. The latter identify lack of achievement while the former explore why students did not achieve.

Public Relations-Inspired Studies

The purpose of public relations-inspired studies is to collect data to obtain financial support or positive public opinion for a project. Such studies occasionally have been part of formative evaluation but do not really meet the definition used in this book of collecting data to improve the curriculum. Sometimes evaluators cooperate in the use of their data for public relations; other times they are "unwitting accomplices" (Stufflebeam & Webster, 1980, p.7).

The public relations-inspired study is included here to underline the need for the formative evaluator to identify the people who will use the evaluation information and to negotiate with them as to the purposes of the formative evaluation activities. Such negotiation is suggested not to put the evaluator in an adversarial position but rather to encourage the evaluation recipients to be partners in defining the evaluation plan. If program developers agree in advance of the formative studies about how research results will be used and what kind of information is considered credible, they will be more inclined to actually apply the information. If the program developer and evaluator are the same person, as in chapter 6 with the "Palenque" videodisc, there still must be explicit consideration of one's own values and goals in order to develop a useful formative evaluation plan.

When Not to Evaluate Formatively

"Evaluation as an applied research is committed to the principle of utility. If it is not going to have any effect on decisions, it is an exercise in futility" (Weiss, 1972, p.10). At an early point in the development of a formative evaluation plan, one should consider the possibility of not evaluating a particular product or at least one should clarify what is possible given the organizational politics and budget. There are three situations in which one might have second thoughts about initiating a formative evaluation.

First, if those in control of the project disagree with the philosophy of formative evaluation, then such effort is pointless. Evaluators do not usually have the power to act upon their information; they must rely upon others to consider the data in conjunction with other relevant facts (e.g., cost, deadlines, politics). Thus, support of project executives is critical to the impact of formative evaluation. Even when formative evaluation is supported, each organization will have different patterns of communication and utilization of the findings. For instance, in the WGBH teletext magazine project presented in chapter 8, out-of-house evaluators gave the magazine composers immediate verbal feedback on focus group results as well as later formal summary sessions and written reports. For the "Mimi" television pilot evaluation mentioned in chapter 3, the head writer participated as a research team member so the research findings impacted scriptwriting directly. A contrasting example of communication and utilization of formative evaluation is the case of the children's television program, "Freestyle." The executive producer translated for his writers the feedback from educators and researchers; direct contact between writers and researchers did not occur because of available time, budget, and writers' attitudes (Ettema, 1979). An understanding of the project team's attitude toward formative evaluation can help define the evaluation plan.

Second, it is difficult to plan an effective formative evaluation if the developers cannot agree on the goals of the program and the intended audience. The evaluator can define a personal interpretation of the goals and audience, but the developers can easily ignore the resulting research by claiming a different audience or goals. On occasion, the formative evaluation has been used to write the goals and define the audience of a program.

Finally, formative activities are wasted on a program in which there is no possibility for change. Sometimes evaluators become involved so late in the production cycle that the impact of formative information can be only minimal.

Summary

The formative evaluation plan begins with the establishment of the purposes of the evaluation activities and the designation of recipients of the information. We have reviewed four categories of studies that serve different purposes in the formative evaluation of educational technologies. The experts in connoisseur-based studies critically appraise the program materials, helping to insure that the program is esteemed, irrespective of its measured effects on learners. Decision-oriented and objectives-based studies collect information on the program's effects on target users. The former category gathers data relevant to making decisions about design and improvement of the program, whereas the latter category focuses on assessing the learner's achievement of program objectives. The final category of public relations-inspired studies has a purpose inappropriate to an effective formative evaluation plan. Ideally, the period of formative evaluation in product development involves application of each of the first three types of evaluation studies.

The next step in the formative evaluation plan delineates more specifically the research questions to be addressed by the connoisseur-based, decision-oriented, and objectives-based studies.

WHAT ARE THE EVALUATION QUESTIONS?

"The traditional formulation of the evaluation question is: To what extent is the program succeeding in reaching its goals" (Weiss, 1972, p.24). We need to recast this question for formative evaluation for several reasons.

Program Phases

First, formative evaluation functions at different phases in the development of materials, not just when a final program is available. Some preproduction formative work occurs without an audio or visual stimulus— as in chapter 2 when the "Sesame Street" researchers facilitated scriptwriting about Mr. Hooper's death with a review of preschoolers' understanding of death. The formative question at this time was "Given preschoolers' understanding of death, what messages should we communicate about Mr. Hooper?"

Additionally, some formative evaluation assesses stimuli of already existing programs that may have characteristics of interest to the developers. For example, Schauble in chapter 4 recounts an occasion when the software group wanted to use a computer format in which the user scrolled "off a main picture to a selection page where options could be 'picked up' with a cursor and brought back to the scene" (chapter 4, p. 59). A commercially available program with this design feature was tried out with the young target group. When the children quickly apprehended the format, the designers assumed that the format would be viable within their context as well.

Other formative research tries out not-final versions of the program such as scripts, storyboards and flowcharts, before evaluating the near-final pilots, prototypes, and check discs.

Thus, to meet the needs of formative evaluation, the traditional evaluation question—"To what extent is the program succeeding in reaching its goals?"—is revised. For formative evaluation questions, the particular development phase of the project replaces the word *program;* for example, "to what extent is the *pilot television program* succeeding in reaching its goals?"

Program Goals

We must also recast the traditional question in a second way. Because many formative evaluations employ not-final versions of a program, formative evaluation questions often focus not on terminal or end goals but on enabling goals. Enabling goals define student behaviors that are prerequisite to or enable the achievement of terminal goals. For example, interest in a program is not usually listed as a terminal goal but is an enabling goal. Many would agree that interest is a likely prerequisite behavior in reaching a terminal goal of retaining factual program information. Thus, in addition to rewording the traditional evaluation question to reflect the various stages of a program, we define *goals* as terminal or enabling. In the latter case, we reword the evaluation question to examine learner behaviors that are prerequisite to achieving end goals. Hence, "The Voyage of the Mimi" researchers asked the formative evaluation question in chapter 3—"To what extent does the pilot television program succeed in *attracting and maintaining interest?*"

Program Features

Although this evaluation question is now more appropriate for formative evaluation, it is too general to guide effectively the collection of data useful for facilitating revisions. We need to specify further the program features for investigation. There are many program features of the "Mimi" pilot show that could contribute to or detract from the program's appeal, but the evaluators and producers narrowed the field and concentrated on the appeal of the characters and the appeal of the storyline. Given these decisions, the formative evaluation question that guided data collection procedures was "To what extent do the *pilot program storyline and characters* succeed in attracting and maintaining interest?"

Target Population

In addition to specifying the program features and respondent behaviors to be investigated, note also the need to specify the population to be questioned. For instance, the "Mimi" evaluators had a valid interest in testing pilot appeal with broadcasters, teachers, and students. They chose to work with students using this final evaluation question to guide the formative inquiry: "To what extent do the pilot program storyline and characters succeed in attracting and maintaining interest of the *target students?*"

To review, formative evaluators define their research questions by specifying the program phase, program features, goals, and target population. Consider a question involving user friendliness, which encompasses the design features that function in the interface between the user and the machine. For the "Palenque" videodisc in chapter 6, researchers asked a user friendliness evaluation question: "To what extent can information in the check disc database be accessed by ten to twelve year olds manipulating a joystick?" The program phase was the check disc; the program feature of interest was the information on the disc; the enabling goal was the user's ability to access the information with a joystick; and the target population was the ten to twelve year old age group. Observations of target learners using the joystick to access sections of the videodisc guided revisions in the interface to improve user friendliness.

Unintended Outcomes

While formulating questions for expected goals, evaluators must also envision unintended outcomes. Recall that in chapter 2, the "Sesame Street" staff looked for planned effects but also asked—"To what extent did the segments about Mr. Hooper's death negatively affect the preschool viewers?" In this case, the unintended effects were anticipated with the research question, but most often these side effects become apparent only to a vigilant and observant evaluator. In fact, one of the most important goals of early tryouts should be to identify negative or unexpected outcomes.

Question Criteria

When we add the evaluation questions on unintended effects to those on anticipated consequences, the list of formative questions for a project can be extensive. The questions of evaluation must be pared down to a manageable number, but how? Weiss (1972) suggested three criteria: usability, practicality, and importance.

Usability. Which questions will yield information usable for decision making and specific enough to suggest revisions in the program? Measuring postviewing behavior may be important to some program objectives, but such data may not be easily interpreted for revisions to the program.

Practicality. Which questions can be answered within the time limits allowed by production and with the money available? Comprehensibility of various computer graphics techniques might provide usable information, but preparing alternative stimuli may take more time and money than such results are worth.

Importance. Which program attributes are really relevant to the objectives and the situation? Appeal of the host may not be significant in a noncompetitive training situation because in that case interest is engendered in the viewing situation by outside factors (e.g., promotion).

Uncertainty. To this list we need to add uncertainty as a fourth consideration for formative evaluations. The program development staff usually has some expectations about the answers to the formative evaluation questions. The more uncertain those expectations are, the more likely the questions should be investigated.

Usability, practicality, importance, and uncertainty are issues that must be weighed by the formative evaluator in conference with the production staff and/or the evaluation recipients. Evaluation questions acceptable under these criteria will guide data collection in connoisseur-based, decision-oriented, and objectives-based studies.

Summary

Questions guiding formative evaluation should specify the phase of program development, the program attributes and features to be investigated, the behaviors to be measured and the population to be tested. We can formulate evaluation questions for every stage of program development for a range of program attribute categories and design features and for a diversity of outcome behaviors. Evaluation questions meeting the criteria of usability, practicality, importance, and uncertainty will have the best chance of producing timely results that actually will be used to improve the program materials.

WHICH METHODS OF INQUIRY ARE APPROPRIATE?

How to answer the evaluation questions is the next step in the formative evaluation plan. Methods of disciplined inquiry as practiced by formative evaluators include both the hypothetico-deductive paradigm and the inductive paradigm. Let us examine what each of these paradigms entails with respect to formative research.

Hypothetico-Deductive Paradigm

The hypothetico-deductive paradigm presumes the deduction of a research hypothesis from theory or previous research and the testing of such hypothesis by means of an experiment, quasi-experiment, or ex post facto design (Campbell & Stanley, 1966).

As an illustration of this paradigm in action, consider the formative evaluation question posed by the producer of a dramatic television series for deaf teenagers—"To what extent does the positioning of text captions on the screen affect program comprehensibility for deaf viewers?" (Flagg, Carrozza, Fenton, & Jenkins, 1980). There is theoretical support for a *standard* captioning approach, that is, placing the caption consistently at the bottom of the television screen. There is also theoretical support for a *variable* positioning technique, placing the caption closest to the center of visual attention wherever it is (e.g., next to an image being described, or underneath the chin of a speaker). The null hypothesis to be tested statistically predicted that there would be no differences in story recall with captions in either standard placement or variable placement. A quasi-experimental design manipulating caption placement was employed to collect data to test the hypothesis. The null hypothesis was rejected: Variable placement of captions yielded significantly higher story comprehension than standard caption placement. Given these results, the producer felt confident in generalizing beyond the evaluation of one program by a small deaf sample and proceeded to caption the dramatic series with the variable placement technique.

The major advantage of the hypothetico-deductive paradigm for formative evaluation is to confirm or explore causal relationships between or among variables. However, the application of the paradigm to formative evaluation questions about electronic learning materials is infrequent for a number of reasons.

First, prior research or theory from which to deduce a research hypothesis is often not available. Second, producing comparison stimuli necessary for experiments that manipulate one or more variables (e.g., caption position) can be expensive in electronic learning programs, particularly for audiovisual materials. Third, experimental and quasi-experimental research designs recommended to test hypotheses to establish causality (Campbell & Stanley, 1966) tend to require more time and more control of subjects and the testing environment than is feasible in a typical formative evaluation project. For example, these research designs call for respondent groups to receive alternative treatments, which are not usually in a production budget, or to receive no treatment, which depletes the typically limited pool of subjects participating in a formative venture.

The hypothetico-deductive paradigm manifests itself in formative evaluation typically as a *one-group pretest–posttest design* (Cook & Campbell, 1979). The research hypothesis of such an objectives-based formative study predicts that students exposed to the program (in its early or later phases) will achieve the program objectives. Achievement is measured by "a criterion-referenced test which reveals one's mastery level of a given body of knowledge anchored to specific curricular objectives" of the program (Isaac & Michael, 1981, p.109).

An example of the one-group pretest–posttest design is the formative evaluation of Systems Impact's prototype videodisc lessons on fractions (Hofmeister, Engelmann, & Carnine, 1986). Teachers presented a series of daily lessons on fractions using videotapes and print materials to mimic the instructional design of the Level 1 videodisc.

Criterion-referenced tests[1] integrated into every fifth lesson and comprehensive pre- and posttests established the degree of mastery of the fraction concepts. These tests gave evidence as to what program content was or was not being successfully communicated.

Internal Validity. The major weakness of the one-group pretest–posttest design within the hypothetico-deductive paradigm is the absence of a second respondent group that received pretests and posttests but *no* program. Such a group controls for threats to internal validity of the research (Cook & Campbell, 1979). In our context, internal validity is

---

[1]Criterion-referenced measures assess a student's achievement of subject matter or a student's behaviors in relation to a criterion standard of performance, not in relation to the performance of other students on the same test.

the extent to which changes in learner behavior can be attributed to exposure to the program as opposed to other causes. The phrase *threats to internal validity* refers to the possibility that there are alternative plausible explanations to the hypothesis that the instructional program materials were the cause of, for instance, increased mastery of the content.

What might these alternative explanations or threats to internal validity be for the one-group pretest–posttest design?

- Maturation
- Mortality
- History
- Testing

These alternative explanations are defined in terms of our Systems Impact fractions videodisc example. Then we examine how each of these threats to internal validity can be ruled out by logical argument when program treatments are of short duration and tests are criterion-referenced.

Maturation refers to the possibility that pretest-to-posttest changes were caused by growth or changes in the respondents over time rather than exposure to the lessons on fractions. It is likely that students matured over the period of days during which the teachers taught fractions. The criterion-referenced tests, however, measured content mastery that was unlikely to have been affected by short-term maturational changes. The threat of maturation is even less in a formative evaluation where the program exposure is short, for example, one television program or one computer program session.

Mortality refers to the possibility that respondents dropping out of the test group differentially affected the results. Indeed, students in the fractions classes were probably absent from some sessions but likely for reasons unrelated to the program treatment. Moreover, the formative evaluator is interested usually in the performance of individuals and not in the average performance of the group, so drop-out that changes the group is less of a concern. Again with a short program exposure—for example, a 2-hour software session—mortality plays an infrequent role as an alternative explanation.

"*History* is a threat when an observed effect might be due to an event that takes place between the pretest and the posttest, when this event is not the treatment of research interest" (Cook & Campbell, 1979, p.51). The length of time over which the fractions lessons were given makes the study vulnerable to the history threat. One child might have received math tutoring in a different setting or another child might have watched a daily math television program at home. Again, a shorter pretest–posttest time interval limits the threat of an outside event affecting mastery of program content.

Testing prior to receiving the program treatment is the most serious threat to internal validity in the criterion-referenced testing case. The pretest provides practice on the test format which might inflate the posttest scores. Including a respondent group that does not receive the pretest provides some control for the testing threat.[2]

"In summary, the one-group pretest–posttest . . . design is most justified when extraneous factors can be estimated with a high degree of certainty or can be safely assumed to be nonexistent" (Borg & Gall, 1983, p.659). The one-group pretest–posttest formative design allows for reasonable causal inference when content mastery is measured by criterion-referenced tests with short pretest–posttest time intervals.

The pretest–posttest objectives-based study has limitations, however, in its utility for formative evaluation because it provides little insight as to *why* the program might be working or might not be working. In our previous example of the Systems Impact fractions videodisc, the evaluators generated hypotheses about learning problems noted in the criterion-referenced tests by analyzing "individual pupil performance on daily in-class assignments" that provided "information on the effectiveness of the specific instructional procedures used in daily lessons" (Hofmeister et al., 1986, p.6). Inducing hypotheses about the process of a program from particular respondent effects demonstrates the more common *inductive research paradigm* of formative evaluation that is discussed next.

Inductive Paradigm

The inductive paradigm does not begin with a predictive hypothesis as the hypothetico-deductive paradigm does but instead begins with the collection of qualitative and quantitative data directed by the evaluation question. Employing this bottom-up approach, the evaluator discerns patterns in the data and proposes working hypotheses to explain the effective and ineffective aspects of the program. The goal of the inductive paradigm is to explicate and understand the process of the instructional program (in its various phases) as it affects learner behaviors prerequisite to accomplishing its objectives.

Although some data collection measures are objective tests—for instance, the daily student worksheets of the Systems Impact formative

---

[2]For further discussion of threats to internal validity, see Cook and Campbell (1979).

evaluation, more often researchers themselves are data recorders through observations and interviews. For example, in developing the fractions videodisc, evaluators used classroom "observation data on 'teacher–child' interactions to help identify more successful instructional procedures for inclusion in revisions of the product" (Hofmeister et al., 1986, p.8).

Credibility.   Researchers answering an evaluation question through inductive analysis must be concerned with the truthfulness of their inferences, just as in the hypothetico-deductive paradigm. It has been argued elsewhere "that criteria for what counts as significant knowledge vary from paradigm to paradigm" (Lincoln & Guba, 1985, p.301). So whereas the hypothetico-deductive paradigm uses the criterion of internal validity, the inductive paradigm implements the criterion of *credibility*. In our context of formative evaluation, the task is "to carry out the inquiry in such a way that the probability that the findings will be found credible is enhanced" (Lincoln & Guba, 1985, p.296).

There are a number of techniques suggested to increase the likelihood of credible findings (Lincoln & Guba, 1985), but the one most practiced in formative evaluation of learning materials is *triangulation*. Triangulation refers to the use of multiple measures of the same phenomenon (Webb, Campbell, Schwartz, & Sechrest, 1966). Each single measure has inadequacies, so the use of multiple measures allows for cross-validation of results, and uncertainty in interpretation is reduced. As illustration of triangulation, reflect back on the formative evaluation plan of the WGBH teletext magazine in chapter 8. To determine the relative appeal to students of individual pages of "SCOOP," the evaluators employed multiple measures: an appeal rating technique, a semantic differential, structured group interviews, observation, and a survey in the teletext magazine itself. When comparable findings were obtained across measures, the triangulation of results increased the researchers' and producers' confidence in the inferences drawn.

Inductive Analysis.   In the hypothetico-deductive paradigm, statistical techniques have been developed to test the predictive capability of the research hypothesis. In contrast, in the inductive paradigm of formative evaluation, there are no well developed methods for guiding the inductive analysis of the specific findings and the generation of relational propositions or hypotheses to direct program revision. Although there are discussions of inductive data processing available (e.g., Glaser & Strauss, 1967; Goetz & LeCompte, 1984; Miles & Huberman, 1984), it is still more of an art than a science; and it is at this point that evaluator experience and intuition take over. Nonetheless, because of the iterative nature of formative testing, the effectiveness of data-based revisions in early program versions is verified by the testing of later program versions. This approach is apparent in the case of Systems Impact's fractions videodisc:

> In a typical field test, there will be two groups, approximately ten lessons apart, being field tested at the same time. As problems are encountered in the first group, alternative procedures are developed and tried out on the group that is ten lessons behind. Such a procedure allows for extensive product improvement in a limited time period. The field test and revision cycle is repeated until a version is developed that is consistently effective. Field test and revision cycles were repeated until 90% of the group had mastered the objectives. (Hofmeister et al., 1986, p.6)

Summary

Two inquiry paradigms are used to address formative evaluation questions. The hypothetico-deductive paradigm takes a top-down approach and tests a theory-based hypothesis; while the inductive paradigm employs a bottom-up approach and generates working hypotheses from the data gathered as guided by the evaluation question. Formative evaluation is not unidisciplinary; there is no consensus on a single inquiry method. The choice of evaluation design is that which will provide trustworthy evidence to address the evaluation question within the constraints of time, money, and politics of the formative evaluation environment.

WHAT MEASURES WILL BE USED WITH WHOM UNDER WHAT CONDITIONS?

Having established the evaluation questions and the inquiry paradigm of the formative evaluation plan, the final steps are to (a) develop measures for collection of the type of information needed to answer the evaluation questions and (b) identify respondents with whom these measures will be used.

Types of Methods

Formative evaluators employ a wide range of data collection measures, drawn mainly from four categories of methods: self-report, observation, tests, and records or documents.

Self-Report.   This is probably the most common data collection method. Respondents report their status with respect to a program presentation, for instance, by answering items on a questionnaire, responding to interview questions, or pressing buttons on a rating machine.

Observation.   Another popular method for collecting formative information is observation of student behaviors. For example, evaluators record viewers' attention to the television screen or observe learners' expressions of frustration and pleasure while using a computer program. Observation measures can be obtrusive as when a researcher walks through a videodisc paper flowchart/storyboard with a respondent or can be unobtrusive as when a researcher observes behavior through a one-way mirror. An example of mediated observation is a system whereby keyboard activity is recorded by computer while a user works with the program. This measurement technique renders an unobtrusive and objective record of product usability.

Tests.   Formative evaluators employ tests of achievement when assessment of cognitive gains or behavioral skills is desirable. If possible, existing tests are applied, but more often evaluators develop criterion-referenced tests based on the specific program content.

Records.   Finally, less frequently, formative researchers analyze records and documents, such as library records on the borrowing frequency of software and videocassettes to assess appeal of a program.

Within these four common method types, the formative evaluator develops measures that collect data needed to answer the previously defined evaluation questions. "Superiority or inferiority of a research method cannot be established as an inherent quality, but it can be established in terms of performance in answering the questions" (Mielke, 1973, p.35). The experience and ingenuity of the researcher comes into play in the choice and development of appropriate formative evaluation measures.

Quality of Measures

To provide acceptable and useful formative information, the evaluator must consider the quality of the information measures, whether they be paper-and-pencil tests or observation by the researcher. As much as possible, these measures should meet the conventional research criteria of *measurement validity and reliability.*

Validity. One can be confident of the *validity* of a measure to the extent "that the measure adequately reflects and represents the domain of interest and that it is not equally or more likely to be a measure of something else" (Anderson, Ball, Murphy, & Associates, 1976, p.458). For example, paper-and-pencil measures used with children to assess their program opinions or achievements may inadvertently measure their reading and writing ability as well. In that case, one's confidence in the validity of information collected would decrease.

Reliability. This term refers to the extent to which a measure repeatedly applied to the same person yields consistent and stable results. For instance, in formative evaluation of software, the researcher is often the recording instrument, keeping track of user behaviors. As the researcher misses behaviors or misdefines behaviors, the measurement procedure becomes more unreliable. It is important that an observer respond consistently to subject behaviors and that two or more observers respond in the same way to the same events. Methods of establishing high validity and reliability in measurement procedures are explained in most texts on research and evaluation.[3]

External Validity

Once data collection measures are valid and reliable to the extent possible, then formative evaluators plan their activities to maximize the possibility that the formative results can generalize beyond the specific study. When drawing inferences from their results, the project team members must ask themselves how much the findings are limited to their particular group of people studied, to the specific data collection setting and procedures, and to the program version tested. These are all issues of *external validity*, which refers to the generalizability of a study. Formative evaluators want to generalize results typically from the students studied to all program users, from the lab test site to the school setting, and from a script to the final program. Three issues of external validity (Smith & Glass, 1987) are described in more detail with respect to formative evaluation:

- population external validity;

---

[3]For further discussion of test validity and reliability, see American Psychological Association (1974).

- ecological external validity;
- external validity of operations.

Population External Validity. Every instructional product has a de-fined target audience or a target population. Because we cannot measure the effect of a program on the whole target population, we work with a subset or sample. Restrictions of time and money usually dictate that the samples for formative activities are made up of volunteers who are read-ily available to the researchers. Based on the responses of this kind of *nonrandom* sample, evaluators make inferences about responses of the rest of the population who were not observed or questioned.

Such inferences are supportable to the extent that the sample group is representative of the target population in its significant characteristics (i.e., age, gender, intellectual ability or knowledge, socioeconomic status, race, etc). Judgments of how similar a nonrandom sample is to the target population will determine the generalizability of the results. How far the findings of a study can generalize beyond the specific sample to other individuals is an issue of the *population external validity* of the study.

To illustrate, in chapter 6, Wilson and Tally report testing their early interactive videodisc designs with Bank Street School students in New York City. These students were experienced with open-ended discovery environments similar to that present in the "Palenque" videodisc. At issue was whether their responses could be generalized to students whose major school experience was in structured learning environments. Con-sequently, later samples included public school students; the main dif-ference observed between the two groups was the longer time it took the public school students to recognize and take advantage of the free dis-covery process available in the "Palenque" videodisc. Thus, evaluators considered results from earlier Bank Street samples generalizable, and product revisions based on those early findings about user friendliness and comprehensibility were validated.

Deliberate *sampling for heterogeneity* is a method for increasing external validity (Cook & Campbell, 1979). Such sampling is particularly appro-priate for formative evaluation because the goal is to develop a product that will function effectively for the whole range of individuals within the target population. Thus, a sample for formative evaluation of software would include those with and without computer experience; those at the high, middle, and low levels of content achievement, and so forth. The objective is to unveil the strengths and weaknesses of the program given differences among users within the intended population.

A study by Wager (1983) illustrates the effectiveness of heterogeneous sampling for formative evaluation. An illustrated text lesson was revised in three different ways based on one-to-one sessions with high aptitude students, low aptitude students, or a high—medium—low aptitude group. Wager found that materials revised according to feedback from the heterogeneous group were significantly more effective in achieving learning objectives than materials revised with data from the homogeneous groups. Thus, in this case, a heterogeneous sample yielded the most helpful feedback for revisions.

In addition to representative sampling and heterogeneous sampling, occasionally formative evaluators will test the product with *extreme samples*. The objective of employing respondents just outside the target population is to challenge the program design or to stress test it (Hofmeister et al., 1986). As a case in point, the Systems Impact fractions videodisc was field tested and performed well with two extreme samples—younger students with fewer entry skills and age-level students with learning disabilities.

The number of respondents in the sample also affects the population external validity. The sample size can be small if the variable being estimated is homogeneous within the population, that is, if the between-individual variability is low. Referring to testing television programs for unintended messages, Mielke (1973) argued that "if a [cultural] norm were truly universal (adhered to without exception) within a cultural category, it follows that even one representative audience member could indicate if a pretest TV program was offensive or subject to misinterpretation" (p.20).

Small samples are appropriate for feedback on user-machine issues that typically have low population variation. For instance, one might want to find out how preschoolers use a mouse as an input device for a software program. Because the population variation in physical requirements of mouse use is negligible across nonhandicapped preschoolers, a small sample of two or three students would be acceptable in order to generalize with confidence to the whole target group.

Small numbers of respondents may also be effective when the evaluator interacts with and monitors individual learners as they work through the program materials. This technique is variously called a one-to-one session, tutorial, or clinical session (Dick & Carey, 1978). Studies with text-based programmed instruction materials have shown that program revision based on feedback from one-to-one working sessions with three students was equally or significantly more effective than revision based on test feedback from 8 to 12 students, who worked through the materials without evaluator involvement or observation (Baghdadi, 1981; Kandaswamy, Stolovitch, & Thiagarajan, 1976; Wager, 1983).

Formative evaluators applying the inductive research paradigm sometimes use *serial selection* of sample subjects (Glaser & Strauss, 1967; Lin-

coln & Guba, 1985). As respondents provide information redundant
with that supplied by previous subjects, each successive respondent is
chosen to obtain possible contrasting information until the range of
variation has been sampled. Producers can then work from that range in
program responses, even though the evaluation has not provided a precise estimate of the frequency of responses in the population.

On the other hand, larger samples are more appropriate when the
population variation is estimated to be high; when analysis by subgroup
(age, gender, etc.) is desirable; or when hypotheses are to be tested
statistically. For instance, adults' opinions differ widely as to what characteristics make a good television host. Different age or gender groups may
also hold different opinions. Thus, when producers of an adult telecourse series wish to poll the target audience for their opinions on various host candidates, a large sample of respondents, stratified by age and
gender, yields increased confidence in generalizing the results.

The question of how large a sample a study requires to have satisfacto-
ry population external validity does not have a simple answer. Crane
(1985c) examined formative evaluation studies of television which utilized both

> focus group studies employing stratified samples of 50–100 viewers
> and . . . telephone surveys employing random samples of 200–400.
> Whether measuring viewing habits in the time slot or qualitative response
> to [TV] program elements, the data are appreciably the same from focus
> group to survey studies despite substantial variations in sample size. (p.18)

In the actual practice of software evaluation, wide variation in sample
size is reported. Of 40 companies who tested their software with students, about 18% reported using fewer than 20 students, 47% used 21–
50 students, 15% used 51–100, and 20% used more than 100 students
(Truett, 1984). In a second survey, Truett and Ho (1986) found that of
103 companies testing software, half used 50 or fewer students.

In deciding on the sample size, the evaluator must estimate the variability in the target population of the variable to be measured, must
consider whether the variable differs systematically according to population subgroup, and must decide also on the level of precision acceptable
to make decisions based on the data collected. Cost, time, and procedural
factors also control the sample size in formative evaluation.

In summary, for formative evaluation in which nonrandom conve-
nience samples are typical, "the only safe basis of generalizing is by
careful logical analysis about the similarities and differences between the
sample in the study" and the target audience or user group (Smith &
Glass, 1987, p.257). Population external validity is thus based on subjective judgment.

Ecological External Validity. A second issue of external validity that pertains to formative evaluation is how much the findings of a study can generalize beyond the specific study setting. This is called *ecological external validity* (Smith & Glass, 1987). Studies of early versions of learning materials are sometimes not conducted in settings in which the final materials will be implemented. Schauble (chapter 4) reports that CTW's computer software was initially tested in camps and in CTW offices and only later in the homes where it was to be used. The generalizability of results from the early settings to the final implementation settings, or ecologically natural settings, is sometimes uncertain.

Studying this issue of generalizability across settings, Crane (1985c) examined formative responses to television programming by focus groups in comparison with at-home viewers. "The focus group studies involved group testing while the telephone survey respondents were interviewed at home after viewing the program. The data show that when the same questions are asked in these two different settings, the results remain the same" (p.14). Similarly, in a later study, Crane (1985b) found that respondent ratings of educational audiotapes were consistent across home and group settings. Thus, apparently for some kinds of programs and subject reactions, setting differences do not limit generalization of the results.

On the other hand, a complete formative evaluation plan should include the eventual testing of materials in the intended usage environment to maximize ecological external validity. When the final setting can be defined and isolated, testing should occur there. For instance, TRW Inc. tests their industrial and military hardware/software prototypes "at special centers. These centers can simulate the user's actual workplace, including the noise level, lighting and decor" (Sims, 1986, p.D2). Conversely, when the exact setting is unknown as in the case of home-based or school-based programs, formative evaluators practice the concept of heterogeneous sampling (mentioned previously with respect to subject samples). For example, "evaluation field studies such as those conducted by AIT [Agency for Instructional Technology] use naturalistic classroom conditions in multiple sites and thus include a form of direct replication which provides confidence in reliability and the ability to generalize" (Rockman, 1980, p.7).

In summary, formative evaluators who test materials in settings other than the intended environment ought to be aware of possible limitations to the generalizability of their results.

External Validity of Operations. The formative evaluator must also pay heed to the *external validity of operations* (Smith & Glass, 1987). The operations are the specific procedures employed by the evaluator; the issue is whether slightly different techniques would yield a different pattern of results. For example, there are a variety of ways to measure the appeal of television programs "including appeal ratings, scaled items, semantic differentials, interview responses, and forced-choice items" (Crane, 1985c, p.9). External validity is increased if the different appeal measures produce similar results. In examining the appeal results from a variety of formative studies on television programming, Crane (1985c) noted "that variations in item format and even technique do not produce appreciably different responses to program elements" (p.9).

Another part of operations is the materials presented. In formative evaluation particularly, producers and researchers are concerned about the generalizability of results from early versions of program materials to later versions of a program. It is desirable that results from storyboard testing be generalizable to prototypes, and results from prototype testing be generalizable to final programs. For instance, Crane (1985a) reported the formative evaluation of a telecourse script treatment in which

> students commented that the program seemed to contain too many clips from archival film footage and that the pacing seemed very rapid to them. The production team believed that a complete program could overcome this difficulty by providing the students with a context in which they would be able to recognize events easily once they saw them. Hence, the density of filmclips was maintained from treatment to pilot. (p.10)

Respondents in the TV pilot testing confirmed the original findings in the treatment testing that the pace and density of film clips was overwhelming. Thus, in this case, the findings obtained from an early program version proved to be generalizable to a later program version.

A further consideration of the external validity of operations occurs when the evaluation plan calls for a pretest. The researcher must be cognizant that pretest activities may increase respondents' awareness of certain topics and may affect how learners work with and react to the program materials. "The pretest sensitization threat [to external validity of operations] means that the pretest and treatment acted in combination to produce an effect that cannot be generalized to similar, non-pretested treatments" (Smith & Glass, 1987, p.153).

Finally, experimenter (or teacher) effects can constrain the generalizability of results. When Systems Impact's fractions videodisc was introduced in a variety of classrooms, evaluators found that "some teachers implemented the program more effectively than others. While all students made significant gains in the pre-post analysis, there were differential effects across teachers" (Hasselbring, Sherwood, & Bransford, 1986, p.22). Thus, we must be cautious to separate experimenter/teacher effects from program effects to protect the external validity of the research.

In summary, the choices of specific procedures, materials, and experimenters affect the generalization of findings. Possibly the most critical concern in the external validity of operations for formative evaluation is generalizing from studies using early design materials. Although there is some research showing, for example, that appeal ratings are comparable for rough-cut and final television programs (Crane, 1985c), comparisons of early and later versions in other media for other program attributes are scarce.

Summary

The final steps in the planning of formative evaluation are to develop measures for gathering information relevant to the evaluation questions and to choose test respondents and procedures. In making these decisions, formative evaluators try to maximize validity, reliability, and generalizability, while minimizing cost, time, and administrative complexity.

CONCLUSION

This chapter has discussed the components constituting a formative evaluation plan for educational technologies. These components include:

1. purposes of the evaluation activities;
2. recipients of the evaluation information;
3. evaluation questions specifying the program phase, program attributes, respondent behaviors, and population to be investigated;
4. the inquiry paradigm;
5. data collection measures;
6. respondent samples; and
7. evaluation settings and procedures.

To illustrate these components, let us look at the formative evaluation plan of a teletext magazine. (The full evaluation of "SCOOP" is presented in chapter 8, this volume, by Crane, Callahan, and Isaacson.)

Purposes. Employing decision-oriented studies, the purpose of evaluating the teletext magazine is to "provide feedback to the developers about its effectiveness and appeal, allowing revisions to be made" (chapter 8, p. 117).

Recipients. The recipients of the evaluation will be the WGBH teletext development staff.

Evaluation Questions.   One of the evaluation questions, which meets the criteria of usability, practicality, importance, and uncertainty, is: To what extent do the story topics in the operational teletext magazine interest high school students?

Inquiry Paradigm.   A decision-oriented study will be implemented within the inductive paradigm. The evaluators will look for patterns in the quantitative and qualitative data and propose working hypotheses to explain the effective and ineffective aspects of the magazine topics. Credibility of findings will be established through triangulation of methods.

Data Collection Measures.   The data to answer the evaluation question will be gathered with multiple measures: self-report measures including questionnaires and interviews in weekly focus groups and a survey in the magazine itself; and observations of students using the system.

Samples.   The nonrandom respondent sample for focus groups will be drawn from students who have free library periods; some will have used the magazine before, some will not. The survey sample will be self-selective. Observations of self-selected users will be made daily for 2- to 3-hour periods.

Settings and Procedures.   An operational teletext will be evaluated in its final setting in six high schools.

By employing such a formative evaluation plan, the researchers can gather data that facilitate decisions in improving the learning materials. The better the validity, reliability, and generalizability of the evaluation, the more confidence one will have in basing decisions on the data. However, because of the demands of timeliness and utility, formative evaluation requires compromises of these research criteria. Evaluators, therefore, must have an understanding of the consequences of these tradeoffs when developing their plan and interpreting findings.

The final three chapters of this book focus on one portion of the formative evaluation plan, specifically, the data collection methods. For each method, we consider its purpose, its applicability to the various program phases, constraints on the sample and research setting, requirements for data analysis and reporting, and advantages and disadvantages for formative evaluation of electronic learning materials. The chapters lay out the characteristics of the many formative evaluation methods used to gather information about user friendliness (chapter 10), program reception (chapter 11), and outcome effectiveness (chapter 12). User friendliness involves the status of activities that occur in the interface between the user and the machine. Program reception refers to the initial effectiveness of the program in terms of respondent attention, appeal, and excitement. Outcome effectiveness involves learners' acquisition of motor skills, cognitive abilities, and attitudes as well as behaviors prerequisite to the target outcomes.

REFERENCES

American Psychological Association. (1974). *Standards for educational and psychological tests.* Washington, DC: Author.

Anderson, S. B., Ball, S., Murphy, R. T., & Associates (Eds.). (1976). *Encyclopedia of educational evaluation: Concepts and techniques for evaluating education and training programs.* San Francisco: Jossey-Bass.

Baghdadi, A. A. (1981). A comparison between two formative evaluation methods. *Dissertation Abstracts International, 41,* 3387-A.

Borg, W. R., & Gall, M. D. (1983). *Educational research: An introduction* (4th ed.). New York: Longman.

Burkholder, B. L. (1982). The effectiveness of using the instructional strategy diagnostic profile to prescribe improvements in self-instructional materials teaching abstract concepts. *Journal of Instructional Development, 5*(2), 2–9.

Callison, D., & Haycock, G. (1988). A methodology for student evaluation of educational microcomputer software. *Educational Technology, 28*(1), 25–32.

Campbell, D. T., & Stanley, J. C. (1966). *Experimental and quasi-experimental designs for research.* Chicago: Rand McNally.

Char, C., Hawkins, J., Wootten, J., Sheingold, K., & Roberts, T. (1983). *"The Voyage of the Mimi": Classroom case studies of software, video, and print materials* (Research Report). New York: Bank Street College of Education, Center for Children and Technology.

Cook, T. D., & Campbell, D. T. (1979). *Quasi-experimentation: Design and analysis issues for field settings.* Chicago: Rand McNally.

Crane, V. (1985a). *A study of formative research practices for the Annenberg/CPB projects: The first five years* (Research Report). Washington, DC: Corporation for Public Broadcasting.

Crane, V. (1985b). *An evaluation of three audiocourses* (Research Report). Madison, WI: WHA Madison.

Crane, V. (1985c, January). *Formative research for television: Believe it or not?* Paper presented at the meeting of the Association for Educational Communications and Technology, Anaheim, CA.

Dick, W., & Carey, L. (1978). *The systematic design of instruction.* Glenview, IL: Scott, Foresman.

Ettema, J. S. (1979). Working together: A study of cooperation among programmers, educators and researchers to produce educational television (Doctoral dissertation, University of Michigan, 1979). *Dissertation Abstracts International, 40*(10), p.5234-A.

Flagg, B. N., Carrozza, F. H., Fenton, T., & Jenkins, R. (1980). *Perception and comprehension of captioned television as a function of caption rate and placement* (Research Report). Boston: WGBH-TV Caption Center.

Frase, L. E., DeGracie, J. S., & Poston, W. K. (1974). Product validation: Pilot test or panel review? *Educational Technology, 14*(8), 32–35.

Glaser, B. G., & Strauss, A. L. (1967). *Discovery of grounded theory.* Chicago: Aldine.

Golas, K. C. (1983). Formative evaluation effectiveness and cost: Alternative models for evaluating printed instructional materials. *Performance & Instruction Journal, 22*(5), 17–19.

Goetz, J. P., & LeCompte, M. D. (1984). *Ethnography and qualitative design in educational research.* Orlando, FL: Academic Press.

Hasselbring, T., Sherwood, B., & Bransford, J. (1986). *An evaluation of the Mastering Fractions level-one instructional videodisc program* (Research Report). Nashville, TN: George Peabody College of Vanderbilt University, The Learning Technology Center.

Hofmeister, A. M., Engelmann, S., & Carnine, D. (1986). *The development and validation of an instructional videodisc program* (Research Report). Washington, DC: Systems Impact.

Isaac, S., & Michael, W. B. (1981). *Handbook in research and evaluation* (2nd ed.). San Diego: EDITS.

Kandaswamy, S., Stolovitch, H., & Thiagarajan, S. (1976). Learner verification and revision: An experimental comparison of two methods. *AV Communication Review, 24*(3), 316–328.

Lincoln, Y. S., & Guba, E. G. (1985). *Naturalistic inquiry.* Beverly Hills, CA: Sage.

Markle, S. M. (1965). The wastebasket reflex. A response to some exemplars of the art. *NSPI Journal, 4*(5), 8–11.

Merrill, M. D., Richards, R. E., Schmidt, R. V., & Wood, N. D. (1977). *The instructional strategy diagnostic profile: Training manual.* Orem, UT: Courseware, Inc.

Mielke, K. W. (1973). *Research and evaluation in educational television.* Bloomington, IN: Indiana University. (ERIC Document Reproduction Service No. ED 126 880)

Miles, M. B., & Huberman, A. M. (1984). *Analyzing qualitative data: A sourcebook of methods.* Beverly Hills, CA: Sage.

Montague, W. E., Ellis, J. A., & Wulfeck, W. H. (1983). Instructional quality inventory: A formative evaluation tool for instructional development. *Performance & Instruction Journal, 22*(5), 11–13.

Rockman, S. (1980, April). *What research has to say to the practitioner.* Paper presented at the meeting of the American Educational Research Association. Boston, MA.

Rosen, M. J. (1968). *An experimental design for comparing the effects of instructional media programming procedures: Subjective vs. objective revision procedures. Final report.* Palo Alto, CA: American Institutes for Research. (ERIC Document Reproduction Service No. ED 025 156)

Rothkopf, E. Z. (1963). Some observations on predicting instructional effectiveness by simple inspection. *Journal of Programmed Instruction, 2*(2), 19–20.

Sims, C. (1986, July 17). Technology: Personalizing software. *The New York Times,* p.D2.

Smith, M. L., & Glass, G. V. (1987). *Research and evaluation in education and the social sciences.* Englewood Cliffs, NJ: Prentice-Hall.

Stolovitch, H. D. (1975). Formative evaluation of instructional games. *Improving Human Performance Quarterly, 4*(3), 126–141.

Stolovitch, H. D. (1982). Applications of the intermediate technology of learner verification and revision (LVR) for adapting international instructional resources to meet local needs. *NSPI Journal, 21*(7), 16–22.

Stufflebeam, D. L., & Webster, W. J. (1980). An analysis of alternative approaches to evaluation. *Educational Evaluation and Policy Analysis, 3*(2), 5–19.

Thiagarajan, S. (1978). Instructional product verification and revision: 20 questions and 200 speculations. *Educational Communication and Technology Journal, 26*(2), 133–142.

Truett, C. (1984). Field testing educational software: Are publishers making the effort, *Educational Technology, 24*(5), 7–12.

Truett, C., & Ho, C. (1986). Is educational software fieldtested? *The Computing Teacher, 14*(2), 24–25.

Tyler, R. W. (1942). General statement on evaluation. *Journal of Educational Research, 35,* 492–501.

Wager, L. C. (1983). One-to-one and small group formative evaluation: An examination of two basic formative evaluation procedures. *Performance and Instruction Journal, 22*(5), 5–7.

Webb, E. J., Campbell, D. T., Schwartz, R. D., & Sechrest, L. (1966). *Unobtrusive measures.* Skokie, IL: Rand McNally.

Weiss, C. H. (1972). *Evaluation research: Methods for assessing program effectiveness.* Englewood Cliffs, NJ: Prentice-Hall.

Weston, C. B. (1987). The importance of involving experts and learners in formative evaluation. *Canadian Journal of Educational Communication, 16*(1), 45–58.

10

Issues of User Friendliness:
Does it Bite?

Television and radio rank as the most "friendly" of electronic learning devices. American preschoolers can turn on the tube, select a program, sit back and enjoy it. However, when the viewer becomes a user of computer-based courseware, then the learning device can quickly yield a less friendly experience. "Unfriendly" electronic learning materials evoke comments of the following sort from users:

What do I do?	Why is it taking so long?
Why doesn't it answer me?	It didn't do what I expected.
How do I undo what I just did?	Can I change the sequence?
How do I get out of here?	It's eaten my work!
Breaktime—can I mark my place?	How can I see that again?
Why am I wrong/right?	I'm lost—frustrated—angry!
Why did I end up here?	Help!!!!

A program that is confusing to operate can interfere with the learning process; however, a user-friendly program does not guarantee that learning will occur. Issues of measuring learning-outcome effectiveness are considered in a later chapter. This chapter describes the issues of user friendliness that formative evaluators might assess in an educational product and presents methods for collecting feedback data. For each method, we discuss its purpose and techniques, its applicability to various program phases, the nature of the participant's response, constraints on the sample and research setting, and requirements for data analysis and reporting.

WHAT IS USER FRIENDLINESS?

A user friendly program anticipates your needs, responds to your wishes, and remembers your behaviors. It has been suggested that a user friendly program needs "a sense of good service. A good role model would be the butler Hudson on the PBS television series of a few years ago, 'Upstairs, Downstairs'" (Hoekema, 1984, p. 39). To carry the "butler" analogy further, a good butler—and a user-friendly program—is accessible, responsive, flexible, and has a good memory. These components of user friendliness are elaborated here.

Accessibility

A good butler will help you into the house, around, and out; similarly, a good interactive program is easy to get into, easy to get around in, and easy to get out of. Program features that furnish users with information about how to operate the system, about where they are and where they have been, about what they can do next, about how to quit, and so forth, can be called features of program *accessibility*.

Students learn early in school how to access information in a book—using a table of contents, index, chapters, bookmarks, and so on—so books become user friendly learning materials due to early exposure and consistency in their structural conventions. In contrast, computer-based instructional design has not evolved and matured enough to have a large standard base of structural conventions that make interaction with the system transparently obvious to users. Thus, developers need to test the accessibility features of computer-based programs with target users to assure user friendliness.

Formative evaluators looking at program accessibility address questions such as the following:

- Can users find information easily? Is it clear which input device to use and how to use it to obtain one's goal?
- Do users understand how to begin, what to do next, and how to proceed through a decision-making process? Are the directions about where to go when and what options are available complete and appropriately worded?
- Are users anxious about where they have been or where they are going?

To illustrate an accessibility issue, let us consider Jolliffe's testing of a videodisc storyboard as presented in chapter 7:

> This program asked the learner to use either the keyboard or touch screen to input responses at different points in the program. Often the participants found the directions unclear and were confused about which input device to use. Instructions such as "enter," which was to mean use the keyboard, or "select from the screen," which was to mean use the touch screen, were generically interpreted, and the learners had trouble making the fine distinctions the designers had intended. (p. 109)

Generally then, accessibility features are those that allow the operation and use of the program.

Responsiveness

A good butler anticipates your every wish, responding to your requests with suitable and timely action. A valuable butler gives feedback when asked and sometimes initiates help to redirect your energies. Analogously, a user friendly program offers well-timed relevant feedback on users' inputs and directs users to appropriate program branches. Program *responsiveness* features are those that determine how the program reacts (or does not react) to users' input and users' needs.

When evaluators explore a program's responsiveness, they seek answers to these illustrative questions:

- Do users receive timely feedback appropriate to their needs?
- Is feedback complete, at the correct level and relevant to target users? Is the branching choice congruent with users' wishes and needs?
- Is the program responsive to users' wishes?
- Do users want other tools or features?

An example of a responsivity issue can be drawn again from Jolliffe's (chapter 7, this volume) evaluation of a videodisc training program on developing marketing observation skills:

> most participants liked the interactive segments that allowed them to ask questions of a customer on the screen and get some immediate feedback from that person in response to their selection. . . . [But] the branching structure did not allow the learner to go back and hear the consequences of other statements or questions that could have been put to the customer. One man said, "The material is such that there really isn't one right response. It's more a judgment based on certain circumstances and so it

would be nice to see, given a specific situation, what the responses to other things would have been." (p. 108)

Having users evaluate the responsiveness of a developing program highlights the strengths and weaknesses of the program's feedback procedures.

Flexibility

Good butlers are adaptable and flexible. Similarly, a user friendly program can be varied by users. Program *flexibility* comprises features that permit users to change the parameters in the program to suit their own needs. Flexibility refers to users' ability to control variables in the program and set them for their own learning needs or wishes. Some examples are altering the presentation rate of material, changing the number of examples provided, and deciding when to take a test. Evaluating a program while in development allows designers to respond to users' needs for flexibility in the particular application.

The flexibility issue was also examined in Jolliffe's (chapter 7) videodisc storyboard evaluation:

> Another problem for participants was the use of a strategic hint option within the customer case studies. Participants liked the use of the hint option to gather more information on the particular situation to help the learner in making a decision, but six of the ten mentioned some frustration that they could only see one hint at a time. . . . Most felt that the ability to page through the strategic hints at the start of decision sections would be a more appropriate use of that feature. (p. 108)

Thus, Jolliffe's users wanted flexibility of tool use built into the program. Then again, sometimes flexibility is programmed into a feature but rarely employed by users. Knowing where one can simplify is as important as knowing where one needs to add complexity.

Finally, one should note that even though flexibility may enhance the friendliness of a program, it can be used to the detriment of learning. Students do not necessarily know the best way to manage their own learning; for example, Clark (1982) asserted in a review of studies that students learn the least from the instructional method they say they prefer.

Memory

A good butler remembers your preferences and your behaviors and is able to report on these. A good program records and stores information about a user's performance and makes available such information to appropriate people. Formative evaluators can gather information from users as to what memory capabilities a specific program needs, thereby increasing the potential user friendliness of the final program. Evaluation questions might include, for example, how much should a program keep track of what users have done or where users are; who should have access to how much of that information; and should users be able to save their work, mark their place, and return later.

Summary

These four components—accessibility, responsiveness, flexibility, and memory—are behavioral qualities for both the butler and an interactive program. Formative evaluation serves to optimize these features in the user-machine interface. A user-friendly program permits students to concentrate on learning content rather than learning to operate the system.

WHEN TO ASSESS USER FRIENDLINESS

A program does not have to be totally operational to evaluate its user friendliness. In fact, the earlier in the design stage that feedback is obtained, the more amenable developers will be to changes because of lower costs. On the other hand, the closer the evaluation situation is to final form, the more confident the designers will feel in generalizing from formative findings.

Evaluators can use paper versions of software to judge user friendliness in the design phase, as Jolliffe did in the examples mentioned previously. Further, as the computer-based instruction industry grows, more rapid prototyping techniques of acceptable cost are being developed. Consider the following possibilities of using prototypes to obtain early formative evaluation data relevant to user friendliness features.

Pre-Production Formative Evaluation

Some design systems enable testing of prototype programs before they are operational and debugged. To illustrate, in a research method nicknamed the OZ paradigm, the researcher has the power to control the interface between the user and the unfinished computer program. The Oz appellation refers to the plot of the movie, *Wizard of Oz*, because the researcher functions like the wizard hidden behind a curtain controlling the action. Using this method, a user (Dorothy) feels that she is interacting with an operational program because the researcher/programmer (wizard) surreptitiously intervenes between the user and the program. The researcher translates the user's incomplete input statements into directions the program understands and supplies answers that the user expects in return (Hodges, 1985; Kelley, 1983). Thus, the researcher learns what is necessary to provide a smooth communication interface.

Kelley (1983) employed the OZ paradigm to derive empirically a set of natural language inputs for a personal calendar software program. Based on a task analysis with business professionals, Kelley defined the functions of the computerized calendar. Then, acting as the wizard, Kelley simulated the system while users communicated in everyday language, for example, "tommorow, call john at 7:30am" [sic](p.195). The resulting list of unconstrained user inputs formed the basis for programming a first-approximation language processor. The next step

> was the iterative design phase. Fifteen participants used the program and the "Wizard" intervened as necessary to keep the dialog flowing. As this step progressed, and as the dictionaries and functions were augmented, the experimenter was phased out of the communications loop. (p.193)

The OZ prototyping paradigm empowers designers at an early stage to obtain feedback from users within the natural computing environment. Mackay (1988) reported that Digital Equipment Corporation has used the Oz method "to help develop an automatic natural language generator, . . . to investigate effective tutoring strategies, ... [and] to explore alternative approaches to interactive video and computer-based instruction (p.339).

Also during the pre-production design stage, using a computer instead of paper to storyboard and flowchart can supply an early computer-controlled prototype for evaluation purposes (Harlow, 1985; Smith, 1985). On some videodisc projects where access speed is not critical, a videotape under computer control may simulate the content and branching activity for users (Fedale, 1985).

Production Formative Evaluation

During the production phase of an interactive videodisc, various prototypes may be developed for evaluation, prior to making a premastering videotape. For instance, some systems permit speedy compilation of different sets of analog video picture sequences, so branching and interactivity of a disc emphasizing motion video can be simulated for testing ("Adding creativity," 1984). For a curriculum project that deemphasizes motion video, on-line development, testing and revision of an interactive design can be performed on a desktop workstation that processes digitized video and audio using a hard disk drive. With this kind of system, users can play through several versions of a disk before it is premastered ("News feature," 1987).

Once the premastering videotape is available, evaluators can place it under computer control to test interactivity. However, because computer-controlled videotape has slow search times, often it makes sense to go one step further to make and evaluate a low cost, quickly produced check disc or Direct-Read-After-Write videodisc (DRAW) (Mark Heyer Associates, 1987; see Wilson & Tally, chapter 6, this volume).

Summary

Assessment of user friendliness should occur in the early design stages. New interactive design tools make it possible to rapidly build, evaluate, and revise program prototypes. These prototyping tools should be used for increasing the cost-effectiveness of formative evaluation. Testing early prototypes, however, does not obviate the need to evaluate a program in its final environment, whether it be the classroom or living room. Classrooms, in particular, present management requirements that may influence the design of the user-machine interface (Char, 1983).

Evaluators explore user friendliness of computer-based programs employing two common approaches: (a) connoisseur-based studies that call upon design experts and/or design guidelines; and (b) decision-oriented studies that collect information from target users. The remainder of this chapter discusses data-gathering techniques practiced within these two types of studies.

CONNOISSEUR-BASED STUDIES

Design Experts

Drawing on their own experience and intuition, design experts outside of the program team evaluate the user friendliness of materials. For example, in an evaluation of *Bank Street Writer III*, the head of a middle school computer science department pointed out the easy accessibility of dictionary options in this word processing program:

> the spelling checker and thesaurus . . . . offered by *Bank Street Writer III* are *resident*, which means you don't have to go through the awkward task of saving your document, quitting your word processor, booting up the spelling checker or thesaurus disk, then loading your document back into the computer to be checked. . . . (Schneider, 1987, p.14)

On the other hand, this expert reviewer identified the program's limits in flexibility and responsiveness:

> Tailored for easy learning and classroom use, the program does not incorporate such options as footnoting or margin flexibility within a document. Also, as with many other menu-based programs, the price paid for ease of use is a certain sacrifice in speed. (p.16)

Although the evaluation just discussed critiqued a finished program, one of several advantages of experts is their ability to evaluate materials at very early design stages, sometimes before target users (especially children) can respond effectively. Also experts bring to bear knowledge about alternative design possibilities. Finally, expert evaluation is usually faster and less expensive than evaluation with target users.

The disadvantage of experts is dependency on their particular experiences, biases, and values. Further, expert analysis is often at a general macrolevel, whereas target users can provide microanalysis that deals with the specifics of the application. For example, consider the case where experts evaluated Learningways' *Explore-A-Story* computer programs for children, 4 years old and older. Experts felt that using a mouse to choose from a menu bar would be no problem for the youngsters. Indeed, children who used the program learned quickly how to employ the input mechanism, but evaluators observed that 4- to 6-year-old users were frustrated because they often accessed an undesired choice with the mouse. When these youngsters clicked the mouse, they pushed so hard that they moved the mouse slightly forward, thus entering a different choice box on a menu bar. In this case, user information, not expert information, guided the designers' decision to widen vertically the menu area, making the program more accessible for 4- to 6-year olds.[1]

Design Guidelines

An alternative for or addition to the design expert is the internal review of programs using design checklists or style guidelines that are derived from research, theory, or practice with interactive materials. Such guidelines provide a set of questions, ratings, or principles by which to evaluate the effectiveness of the program, including its user friendliness.

Some guidelines propose *general principles* applying to any interactive

---

[1]This discussion is based on projects for a formative evaluation course taught by the author, Spring 1987. Students—S. Daver, G. Pretsfelder, J. Ratliff, and R. Umiker—worked in cooperation with Learningways' developer, Henry Olds.

materials. For instance, from human factors research, Simpson (1984) derived a styleguide for computer-based learning. Among the principles advocated are those related to program responsiveness; for example:

Provide Feedback

People need to know that an action they have taken has had an effect . . . . Feedback should be immediate and obvious. Show it on the screen in a place where it is expected. (pp. 132–133)

A second example is Jay's translation of research in cognitive psychology into general computer courseware guidelines, including directions about program responsiveness, for example, "inform the user when performance is being scored or evaluated" (1983, p. 25).

Other guidelines focus on *specific computer-based formats.* Rowe (1984) devised a 95-item checklist to contemplate in the design of a good simulation. Among these items are those that deal with program responsiveness to users' inputs. Consider these two examples that follow.

Check for User Mistakes on Input.

User mistakes on parameter values can include a lot of things. It's very important to check for them, however, because one badly mistaken value that slips through can easily ruin the whole simulation, and leave the naive user discouraged and muttering nasty things about "dumb computers." (p.183)

Make the Persistence of User Actions Clear.

Some simulations allow some kind of user control while they are running. If so, the exact effect of those actions must be clearly stated. (p.185)

Other interactive formats addressed by design guidelines include coaching environments (Burton & Brown, 1979), CAI lessons (McPherson-Turner, 1979), and dialogue-programming rules (Gaines, 1984; Gaines & Facey, 1975). For instance, a rule in dialogue programming proposed by Gaines (1984) on system responsiveness reads as follows:

*Make the State of the Dialogue Observable.*Give the user feedback as to the state of the dialogue by making an immediate unambiguous response to any of his inputs which may cause the dialogue to branch—the response should be sufficient to identify the type of activity taking place. (p.125)

A third type of guideline concentrates on *content areas.* Guidelines of varied complexity exist for a range of content areas including German (Cornick, 1983), reading comprehension (Bradley, 1984), science (Klopfer et al., 1984), and vocational education (Oregon State University, 1983).

Last, organizations have drawn up design guidelines for *specific instructional systems* including the TICCIT system (Bunderson, 1974), the Apple II (Minnesota Educational Computing Consortium, 1980), and the PLATO system (Seiler, 1981).

In spite of the variety of checklists or guidelines, those available may not encompass content, format, or hardware issues relevant to one's program or may serve a different set of target learners. Also, advances in hardware and software can render guidelines obsolete.

Summary

In conclusion, whether one evaluates with design experts or guidelines, no correct answers exist in design. As Norman (1983) pointed out, the application of a design principle "is apt to have its virtues along one dimension compensated by deficiencies along another. Each technique provides a set of tradeoffs" (p.4). For instance, a detailed computer display screen may provide help for a confused user, but more details require more time to display and more space on the program disk. To assess the specific values of design principle tradeoffs, we need to test them in the particular program context with the learners themselves. Formative evaluators do this within decision-oriented studies.

DECISION-ORIENTED STUDIES

Formative evaluation of computer-based teaching programs gathers from target users information relevant to design decisions about the user-machine interface. Three types of evaluation methods prevail in obtaining information about program user friendliness: observation, self-report, and tests.

Observation

Observation of learners and teachers using versions of a computer-based program is the most comprehensive yet most time-consuming and labor-intensive data collection method. Nevertheless, observation contributes valuable information about software user friendliness that connoisseur-based studies fail to obtain, as attested to by Owston and Wideman's research (1987). Their study collected teacher panel reviews of 36 final software packages using the York Educational Software Evaluation

Scales (Owston, 1987). These reviews were compared with teacher observations of students using the software in their classrooms for about 1 month. Although the panel reviews and observations agreed often about overall quality of software, the comparison suggested that classroom observation may

a) bring to light technical and design limitations that are not obvious to teacher reviewers; b) provide more accurate information on the ease of use of the software; c) suggest unique ways in which the software can be used in the classroom; and d) give a clearer indication of the suitability of software in meeting specialized student needs. (p.295)

Thus, observation of users yields unique data to facilitate revision decisions about user friendliness of computer-based curricula.

Formative evaluators of educational technologies practice both structured and unstructured observation approaches. In structured observation, the evaluator focuses on recording certain *selected* behaviors and events. In unstructured observation, the evaluator records *all* of the user's activities and the program status; thus, the observation is continuous and unselective during use of the program. In both approaches, observers may avoid an overload of data by limiting collection to certain time intervals (i.e., time sampling: for example, once every 5 minutes for 1 minute) or by sampling only when certain events occur (i.e., event sampling: for example, whenever the help mode is accessed).

A look at some actual observation data will help us explore the differences between unstructured and structured observation methods and reveal advantages and disadvantages of each. The following data were collected through observations during a field test of a teletext service in Massachusetts' welfare offices (Flagg, 1984). In the waiting areas of the welfare offices were placed televisions and instructions for using a keypad to change print information on the screen. Users could read on screen about job training, job openings, and employment center services. Researchers unobtrusively observed users in the waiting areas of the welfare offices for two 7-hour days per week for 4 weeks. Evaluation issues of interest included frequency of teletext use and procedural aspects of its use.

Structured Observation. Table 10.1 shows a portion of the structured observation schedule for one user of the employment teletext "magazine." The underlined sections indicate where observers recorded data as soon as a user approached the system. After observers described the user and any onlookers, they noted the occurrence of events predefined by the researchers. These events included keypad activities and the length

TABLE 10.1
Structured Observation Schedule for Teletext Users

Observation Begin Time	10 : 00 AM
Observation End Time	10 : 15 AM
Duration of Use (mins)	15
User Sex (1-Male, 2-Female)	2
Race (1-Wh, 2-Bl, 3-Hisp, 4-Asian, 5-Other)	1
Age (1-Adult, 2-Child)	1
Other Adult Observers (#)	
Reason for Initiation of Use	1
(0-Reason not obvious; 1-Job interest;	
2-Intro by staff; 3-Reads poster directions;	
4-Imitation of previous user)	
Keypad Usage:	Frequency tallies
Holds keypad without use	
Reads poster directions	
Asks for help, info	////
Keypad directional difficulty	//
Cannot obtain pages (presses repeatedly)	/
Pressess TV key	
Presses NEXT key	////////
Presses ENTER with page #	//
Presses INDEX key	/

of time the user worked with the teletext. Observers also recorded other predefined behaviors that are not shown in Table 10.1, such as questions voiced by users to themselves or others.

Structured observation schedules define specifically, before observation begins, the behaviors and situations thought to be relevant to the evaluation issues. Some behaviors are *descriptive,* for instance in Table 10.1, "reads poster directions" or "presses INDEX key". Other behaviors are *inferential* requiring some conclusions on the part of the observer; for example, in Table 10.1, from verbal or nonverbal behavior the observer infers the reason for initiating use of the system. The structured observation record entails *frequency counts,* how often behaviors occur, and *duration recording,* how long behaviors occur.

Unstructured Observation. Table 10.2 portrays the unstructured observation of the same teletext user as was recorded in Table 10.1 (Flagg, 1984). The evaluator narrated sequentially the user's verbal and nonverbal behaviors and the teletext status.

The purpose of the unstructured observation is to furnish an unselective, detailed, continuous description of the interaction between the user

TABLE 10.2
Unstructured Observation of Teletext User

Recording Shorthand: W = White, F = female, R = receptionist, : = quotaton,
// = teletext page description.
Time: 10 : 00 AM. Only R and self in waiting room. Teletext shows // Title
screen. WF with infant enters, appoaches screen, reads screen, looks down on
keypad on shelf, touches tentatively, presses keypad (still on shelf). WF to R: Do
you know how to control this? R: What did you want to see? WF: Just curious.
Are there jobs for this area? R shows WF how to point keypad at TV, how to
enter # for jobs pages. WF presses <40 Enter> // The Job Shop appears.
WF: Boy; I'll be a plumber for $11.30 an hour. Presses <Next>. //Job descrip.
WF reads. Presses <Next>. //Job page appears with video interference. WF: Oh,
look I put holes in the picture! Presses <Next>. Page doesn't appear. WF to R:
Why didn't it change? R reminds about keypad direction. Presses <Next> quickly
- 5 times. WF to R: Why aren't the pages changing now? This thing is completely
useless. Just like this place. R explains about slow speed of system. R: Be patient.
WF waits until page 48 appears. // Clerk position. WF writes down phone # to
call. WF to R: What else is on here? R explains Index key. WF presses <Index>.
WF: Oh, "Hot tips". That sounds good. Presses <34 Enter>. // Hot tips. WF:
Boring. WF called away by staff. Time: 10 : 15 AM.

---

and the content and machine. The advantages in evaluating user friendliness issues with this technique are numerous. The frequency of use of
functions and the length of time the system was used can be calculated
from the record, just as from the structured observation. Even more, the
unstructured record adds a richness to the evaluation that is missing
from the structured approach. To illustrate, from the continuous narrative of the unstructured observation, we can draw conclusions about
the sequential relationships among system features; for instance, in
Table 10.2, the user chose to access the job section first, then the index,
then the hot tips section. From the comprehensive record of verbal comments, we can link behavior with the situation and infer the user's attitude toward the system's responsiveness and flexibility, and we can see
changes in the user's attitude over the duration of use. From the user's
dialogue with the receptionist, we can pinpoint accessibility problems
that occurred for the user.

In addition, unintended effects of the system are best detected
through unstructured observation. In the running commentary of Table
10.2, we learn that the user felt responsible for the video interference
appearing in the teletext picture (i.e., "Oh, look. I put holes in the
picture").

Eventually, for analysis and interpretation, the unstructured observation record is coded in categories and tallied in a manner similar to the
structured observation, yet the rich qualitative observations are still avail-

able to help interpret the quantitative summary statistics. Because the unstructured approach lets the observer be open to diverse phenomena, the categories resulting from this method might be different from those defined a priori in the structured observation schedule. Moreover, one can go back into an unstructured narrative to study questions that might not have occurred to the evaluators earlier.

The main disadvantage of the unstructured technique for formative evaluation is the time and labor required to collect and analyze sets of extensive observations. Moreover, training is needed so that observers are recording similar data in an unbiased manner. Sometimes unstructured observations on a small sample are used to define the behaviors for a larger scale structured observation study.

Reliability and Validity. Reliability and validity are as significant for observational recording as for any other data-gathering measure.[2] The fact that the observer is more often human rather than a mechanical device highlights the importance of recording reliability. Human observers may have biasing expectations and their recording methods may change over time due to fatigue or practice. Structured observation with a coding scheme is typically more reliable than unstructured observation, but training of observers is critical to both approaches. Observation is obtrusive to the extent that the observer interacts with or is obvious to the user. Being able to record unobtrusively the natural activity of the user in a natural setting improves the ecological external validity of the evaluation, that is, one's ability to generalize the findings to other settings. Because of the time and human labor involved in conducting observation, samples are often of small to medium size, perhaps limiting population external validity, that is, one's ability to generalize beyond the sample observed.

Observation Using Prototypes. Observation is least obtrusive when a program is fully operational and the observer does not have to intervene to make the interface work. However, because formative evaluation is most cost effective when performed early in the development of a product, evaluators observe usage of design phase materials also. These materials may be paper storyboards and flowcharts or prototype computer programs, but they all require intervention by the evaluator in the user-material interaction.

Rockman and Jolliffe (chapters 5 and 7, this volume) report testing first-generation storyboards and flowcharts that lay out on paper all the media presentations and branching directions of the program. The eval-

---

[2]See chapter 9, this volume, for discussion of validity and reliability.

uator acts as the computer for the users and leads them through the paper program. During this one-on-one walk-through or paper proof procedure, the evaluator (or a different observer) records user responses.

Schauble (chapter 4) depicts the use of a research prototype in testing childrens' ability to drive a taxi character on computer screen roads. As users interacted with the prototype, the evaluator adjusted design parameters of speed, road width, and so forth, in order to observe how the variations affected users' responses. Again, the feedback came from observation, but the observer intervened in the interface with users in order to test the effects of a variety of program attributes.

Mediated Observation Techniques.   Evaluators have long utilized audio and videotaping as mechanical devices for observation. For computer-based instruction, evaluators take advantage of the computer to record and store information about users' interactions with software programs. "Online monitoring is the process of capturing characteristics of the human-computer interaction automatically, in real time, from an operating system" (Borgman, 1986, p.110). Online monitoring goes by various names including keystroke records, audit trails, and logging data.

As part of the BARN project, schools implemented a series of interactive computer programs to provide adolescents with health information and behavior change strategies (Hawkins, Bosworth, Chewning, Day, & Gustafson, 1985). Evaluators assessed system usage with student surveys and intermittent computer collection of data on the age, sex, number of users, and topics viewed. The researchers found that online monitoring of topics viewed was "most useful in discovering which program segments were or not [*sic*] being used heavily (and adjusting new versions accordingly)" (p.235).

The previous example restricted computerized data collection to a limited set of variables. Yet a computer-collected data trail grows to enormous size when it records all transactional and temporal data (Chen, Liberman, & Paisley, 1985). Transactional data refer to the interactions between the user and the system; for example, what segments of the program were accessed in what sequence, which commands and features were used, what decisions were made in response to program queries, what performance was achieved in task and test situations, which error messages appeared, what kind of assistance was requested. Temporal data supply the time and duration of transactions. From temporal data, one comprehends the pacing of the user-program transactions by examining frequency of commands chosen, time spent on program segments and help facilities, and time to task completion or learning criterion. Evaluators analyze such continuous objective data to assess accessibility, responsiveness, and flexibility of computer-based programs.

Although mechanical recording devices postpone the coding and analysis process required of all observation data, they have advantages of being relatively unobtrusive, decreasing the number of observers necessary, increasing observational reliability, and providing a permanent record for alternative analyses. Further, the mechanical record (particularly audio and videotapes) can play a critical role in communicating results to the production staff.

The cost of audio, video, and computer recording equipment is the main drawback of mediated observation. Another disadvantage is the inherent limitation in what each technique can observe. The audiotape records only verbal comments with no contextual information; the videotape has a restricted field of view; the computer stores only user activities as they impact on the machine itself. To increase the completeness of the observational data, these methods can be used together or in conjunction with a human observer.

A combination of mediated observation techniques is the basis for a methodology called "Playback," developed by Neal and Simons (1984) for evaluating user friendliness of software. During the time that the user works on the prototype system being tested, each keystroke is time-stamped and recorded by a second computer. In a different room, an observer monitors the output of two television cameras; one camera focuses on the user's workstation, while the other records closeups of printed material available to the user. The observer also views a screen that repeats what the user is currently seeing on the program display. The observer types into the time data record observations and comments about the user's behavior. In addition, the user has a function key to request special assistance from the observer.

During analysis, the evaluator can playback the display that the user saw during the test session while simultaneously viewing the user's keystroke activity and the observer's comments. With the combination of methods in the "Playback" technique "an eight-hour day of user activity can usually be analyzed in an hour or two . . . . much less analysis time than would be required to review an equivalent amount of user activity had it been recorded on video tape only" (Neal & Simons, 1984, p.95).

Neal and Simons recounted an application of the "Playback" methodology to test the training material for a word processing machine:

> The number and severity of user problems were the primary data item collected, along with training time, test completion time, and frequency of calls for assistance. Four interactions of this test were conducted, with modifications being made in the training material as a result of the findings of each interaction of the test. The process resulted in very worthwhile improvements in the training, as reflected in several of the performance measures. (p.93)

The "Playback" methodology is a highly sophisticated, objective observation technique used in a laboratory-like setting. Those unable to apply this method might benefit still by recording at least keystrokes whenever the software and hardware configuration permits it. Such mediated observation nicely complements human observation.

Summary. During design and production phases, observation techniques may be structured or unstructured, restricted in sampling to certain times or events, and mediated by mechanical recording devices. The methods vary in their advantages and disadvantages but all yield valuable information relevant to the accessibility, responsiveness, and flexibility of computer-based educational programs.

Self-Report

Self-report data collection methods require users to report on their own response to the program. Traditional self-report methods of diaries, questionnaires, and interviews can be applied to interactive program evaluation. More recently developed methods appropriate to measuring user friendliness with interactive programs include the thinkaloud technique, escorted trial, and the use of confederates.

Common to all of these self-report methods is the advantage of obtaining users' own perceptions of the strengths and weaknesses of the program. In some of the techniques, the researcher intervenes and questions users about their experience with the program; no inferences need be made by an observer. The main disadvantage of self-report measures is response effect, that is the tendency of a respondent to give inaccurate information. Response effect refers to situations when users give conventional answers, answer thoughtlessly, respond in a manner intended to please, or evade response with "I don't know" answers (Fiske, 1971; Sudman & Bradburn, 1974; Weiss, 1975). Pretesting of measures and using multiple measures help avoid some of these response sets.

Let us define and differentiate the individual self-report techniques by looking at how each could be applied to issues of user friendliness. The computer software used as a case example in this section is "Robin Hood's Challenge: A Fraction Fortune Fantasy" developed by Massachusetts Educational Television for Agency for Instructional Technology.[3] This software uses a game format to provide practice in five fraction topics including recognizing fractional parts of wholes and com-

---

[3]This discussion is based on projects for a formative evaluation course taught by the author, Spring 1986. Students—S. Chase, D. Cheong, S. Mulley, D. Oberoi, and M. Palmquist—worked in cooperation with Anne Davis of Technology Training Associates.

paring fractions with like and unlike denominators. The user's goal is to collect as many gold coins as possible to prove to Robin Hood that the player is worthy of being a member of his gang. Players earn coins by correctly answering fraction word problems, with problem difficulty determining the number of coins earned. After spinning a computer spinner, the user moves forward or backward on a computer screen gameboard. Upon landing, each board space dissolves into a new screen that presents the fraction problem to be solved.

Thinkaloud.   The thinkaloud or talkaloud technique asks the participant to reflect out loud on what he or she is doing or wants to do while using the software. Occasionally, the evaluator may intervene to ask for clarification of user comments or to provide help if the program is an early prototype. Most often, an audiotape of the monologue is accompanied by unstructured observation or videotape of user activity. A fourth-grade girl contributed the following thinkaloud report while playing the "Robin Hood" game:

> "Ok, now I'll spin." Presses ⟨s⟩. Spinner shows 1.
>
> "And I'm going to move forward." Presses ⟨F⟩. Her marker moves forward 1 space. "It's a blank space. What's that mean? Maybe I should go forward again?" Presses ⟨F⟩. Nothing happens. "Do I go again?" Presses ⟨s⟩. Spinner shows 2.

This thinkaloud example shows that the meaning of a blank space on the game board was not clear to the user. Nor did she notice a highlighted menu at the bottom of the screen instructing her to spin again. In fact, half of the students in the sample expressed some confusion about what to do after landing on a blank space. Although the initial game directions described the function of the menu highlighting, many students did not comprehend or recall this as they played the game. In this case, students' experience with blank spaces on real-life board games did not necessarily transfer to the use of the computer board game.

Thus, the purpose of the thinkaloud technique is to obtain information from users about their moment-to-moment processing of the program while they are using it. The thinkaloud techniques used in evaluation derive from psychological research methods that are designed to reveal intermediate stages in cognitive processing (Duncker, 1926; Ericsson & Simon, 1984). Formative evaluators typically ask the subject to "think aloud as you work" and may use a warm-up task to elicit the desired behavior (particularly with children). Instructions also vary in their request for completeness ("say everything you think about even if it seems irrelevant"), for explanation ("explain every step as you go along"), and for content ("tell me what you are doing, what you are perceiving") (Ericsson & Simon, 1984).

Most thinkaloud methods include unstructured observation, so we reap the advantages of that method, encompassing information on the frequency, duration, and sequence of use of various program features. From those data, evaluators formulate conclusions about where, when, and under what conditions users encounter difficulties. The thinkaloud technique presents us with the additional advantage of being able to ascertain why users perceive problems in the accessibility, responsiveness, flexibility and memory qualities of the program.

Knowledge about users' reasoning processes can help guide revision decisions. In our "Robin Hood" example, we might have guessed at the accessibility problem of blank spaces from observation of the keyboard inputs alone; however, listening to the users' thought processes identifies the problem more directly and more reliably. Furthermore, the biases of human observation are in part balanced by the users' own interpretations of what is going on in their interaction with the program. Another advantage of the thinkaloud technique appears in the reporting stage of the evaluation. Hearing about a user friendliness problem from users themselves via audio or videotape provides face-valid evidence to convince developers that changes are needed.

The thinkaloud technique carries with it the disadvantages of observation methods and adds unique problems to that list. Ecological external validity is threatened by the obtrusiveness of the researcher and by the fact that users are asked to perform the unusual activity of reflecting on and verbalizing their thinking. However, in a review of studies comparing verbalizing subjects with nonverbalizing subjects, Ericsson and Simon (1984) concluded that "there appears to be little reason to anticipate differential effects of verbalizing. . . . the observable structure of cognitive processes is not affected significantly by the instruction to think aloud . . ." (p.89).

Another disadvantage of the thinkaloud technique is the fact that samples are usually small and restricted to verbally able subjects. For 8- and 9-year-olds, for example, evaluators frequently must encourage talking by prompting with questions like "What are you thinking about?" or "What do you want to do next?" Using pairs of respondents collaborating in using the program elicits more data because they will more readily discuss the program with each other than alone. Also, if users find the cognitive and/or performance demands of the program taxing, they will sometimes stop verbalizing their thoughts to concentrate energy on the task. For instance, in the "Robin Hood" game evaluation, the concept of fractions is so difficult for many fourth graders that when presented with a hard problem they could not tell the evaluators what they did not understand about its directions. (See Schauble, chapter 4, this volume, for other examples of thinkaloud reports.)

Escorted Trial. The thinkaloud technique is useful with near-final programs and early prototypes because the evaluator is present to smooth over operational problems. On the other hand, developers may desire self-report feedback on user friendliness at an even earlier design stage; this requires a slightly different data collection technique. Rockman (chapter 5, this volume) describes the escorted trial method in which the evaluator verbally guides a small group of students or teachers through a computer program script, eliciting their comments on the way. This technique is related to the one-on-one walk-through observation method discussed earlier in this chapter, but in the escorted trial method, a thinkaloud component is added.

For example, if the "Robin Hood" program had been presented to students in the script phase with the escorted trial technique, evaluators would have found that fourth graders had a great deal of difficulty reading through the initial pages providing directions on how to play. Problems with vocabulary, comprehension of the directions, and recall overload would have been apparent while the students read aloud and commented on the pages representing the computer screens. Instead, these problems were not revealed until the prototype was programmed and tested. At this later stage, time and money limited the revisions that were needed to make the directions more accessible and memorable.

The purpose of the escorted trial method, therefore, is to obtain potential users' reflections on the accessibility, responsiveness, and flexibility of a program as it is designed on paper. The escorted trial technique has the advantages and disadvantages of the thinkaloud method, with two further advantages. First, small groups of respondents rather than individuals can be handled in the escorted trial method. Second, being able to assess user friendliness features prior to actual programming could save considerable money and energy put into making revisions later. Assessing such features as speed of feedback and clarity of print has to wait for an operational prototype, but other user friendliness features may be examined using a paper version through the escorted trial method.

Diary or Log. Users also can report their own responses to a program in a diary or log. In this method, students or teachers keep a record of their activity with the program and write open-ended comments on their use and understanding of the program.

To illustrate, fifth-grade users were given a sketch of the "Robin Hood" game board and asked to record on it while playing the game.

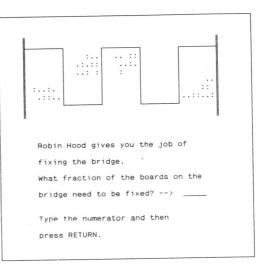

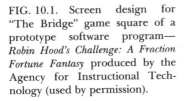

FIG. 10.1. Screen design for "The Bridge" game square of a prototype software program— *Robin Hood's Challenge: A Fraction Fortune Fantasy* produced by the Agency for Instructional Technology (used by permission).

They marked whether their answer was right or wrong and described any trouble they had following directions or understanding the picture and words of the problem. For instance, Fig. 10.1 shows a fraction problem that states "Robin Hood gives you the job of fixing the bridge. What fraction of the boards on the bridge need to be fixed? Type the numerator and then press Return." An accompanying graphic shows five boards of which four have cracks drawn on them. Some of those students who got this problem wrong wrote the following on their game board logs: "can't tell which boards are broken"; "I wanted to change my top number after I pressed return. Why can't you go back?" Although not all students kept reliable records or commented at all, this inexpensive data collection method indicated a broad range of problems to be addressed in revisions.

The purpose of the diary or log, then, is to collect a large sample of unbiased responses to computer-based programs in cases where observation and thinkaloud techniques are logistically difficult, expensive or time-consuming. Diaries function well with programs meant for home usage: Schauble (chapter 4) describes how parents and children kept usage logs on software that was available for days or weeks in their homes. Diaries are also an inexpensive method to gather feedback on programs intermittently used like grammar checkers or databases. Finally, diaries can capture subtleties of change in repeat uses of a program over a substantial time period. On the other hand, the disadvantages of logs are numerous. Respondents need to be able and willing to cooperate and to write legibly and coherently; reliability of the data is sometimes suspect; and recording may interfere with the natural flow of using the program. Further, the program must be sufficiently finished so as to function without outside help, thus diaries are utilized most often during the implementation stage. When combined with more intensive information gathering techniques that provide depth of data, logs can provide breadth of data from a large sample.

The three self-report methods described so far—thinkaloud, escorted trial, and diary—are implemented during use of the program. These methods ask for immediate and continual comments from users and thus are sometimes called *continuous reaction measures*. In cases where a program is operational and evaluators can wait until after use to gather friendliness feedback, diaries can be applied, and other suitable methods such as confederates, questionnaires, and interviews are discussed here.

Confederates.   In this method, a user who has experienced the program explains to a peer or researcher confederate how to use the program. In the case of our "Robin Hood" example, child participants were asked to describe to the next participant from their class how to play the "Robin Hood" game:

> Experienced User: "This game's about joining Robin Hood's band. So you want to join it, right? And Robin Hood says you have to go collecting gold to prove if you would be, you know."
>
> New User: "able to get in?"
>
> Experienced User: "And so you press ⟨s⟩ to spin and you get a number and you can press ⟨f⟩ for forward or ⟨b⟩ to go backwards and everything. When you get enough gold, you have to go all the way back to the forest where Robin Hood is and ask him if he'll accept you. I lost. Do you know all you need to know?"
>
> New User: "Uh-huh."

The purpose of the confederate technique is not really to teach new users how to use the program. As an evaluation method, the use of confederates reveals at least two dimensions of users' understanding of a program: (a) which operations are perceived as significant to the working of the program, and (b) which operations may be misunderstood. Of six important issues to be covered in a complete presentation of the "Robin Hood" game directions, only the two reviewed in the dialogue just presented were mentioned by fourth graders (i.e., spinning the spinner and moving around the board by going forward or backward). The omitted operational facts included: solving problems correctly earned points or gold, solving more difficult problems earned more points, using the back arrow erases a mistake, and finishing with the most coins wins the game. These omissions do not necessarily mean that the experienced users were unaware of these rules; only direct questioning of users would tell us that. For example, when asked how to win the game, 63% of experienced users said that the player with the most coins or points wins, whereas 37% responded that the one who got to Robin Hood first would win.

Evaluators employ the confederate method after each participant uses an operational prototype or final program. Users contribute unbiased and spontaneous interpretations of the program's operation. This unobtrusive method avoids the possibly biased prompting of questionnaires and interviews and the reading and writing requirements of questionnaires and diaries. Unfortunately, the time and labor required for data collection usually limits the sample size. Moreover, the drawback of the method for children is that they may mention only operations necessary to start using the program without meeting the complete information needs of the naive player. A combination of data-gathering methods is needed to obtain a complete picture of a program's user friendliness.

Questionnaires. Written questions asking respondents to report their experience or opinion of a program's user friendliness constitute a questionnaire. Respondents usually answer questions after completing the program, but occasionally questionnaires are presented during the use of the materials. Questionnaires include open-ended questions that need written responses.For example:

1. Which instructions of the Robin Hood game were hard to understand? _____.

Questionnaires also present closed-ended questions that entail choosing an answer. These may vary in format, as in the following two examples:

2. Which of the following activities in the Robin Hood game were hard to learn how to do? (You can check more than one)
   _____ How to begin to play
   _____ How to spin the spinner
   _____ How to move forward
   _____ How to move backward
   _____ How to know the score
3. The Robin Hood game instructions were easy to follow.
   _____ Yes
   _____ Sometimes
   _____ No

The critical task in developing a questionnaire is deciding which question format and wording will elicit information relevant to the evaluation issues. What words will motivate a response? What words will facilitate a reliable and valid answer? Occasionally, experimental research is available to guide questionnaire design; for instance, Root and Draper (1983) compared two question formats that asked users to evaluate the interface of a screen-oriented editor. Users responded to checklists and specific questions, and both formats produced similar results.

Empirical research is not available to help guide all decisions of questionnaire design, so pretesting questions with some of the target audience and revising them is suggested procedure. Pretesting can clear up situations where evaluators and respondents differ in their interpretations of the meaning of particular questions.

Cross-checking questionnaire results with other data helps establish validity and consistency of findings. Sometimes the questionnaire incorporates cross-check questions. To illustrate, after pairs of students played the "Robin Hood" game, both students responded to the following question:

4. Did your partner have problems following the instructions on how to play the Robin Hood game?
    _____ Yes, a lot of problems
    _____ Yes, some problems
    _____ Not many problems
    _____ No problems

Then, these responses were compared to each partner's own self-reported difficulty level.

Many texts discuss the art and science of designing questions and questionnaires. In addition to following general rules of good design, it is important for the formative evaluator to consider the needs of the development team. For each question, the evaluator must ask: *What kind of information will I receive from this question and how will it help producers revise their materials?*

It is possible to develop valid and reliable questions that are useless in providing information on which to base revision decisions. Look at Question 3, which asks about the user friendliness issue of accessibility. If the majority of users answer "yes" to Question 3, then producers can feel comfortable that the instructions were accessible to the sample. If the majority answer "sometimes" or "no," what action should producers take to improve accessibility? We might be able to decide on actions based on other data collected such as observations or interview responses, but let us assume the questionnaire is our only measure. Results from Question

3 can pinpoint a general weakness in game instructions but give no direction for revisions. Which instructions should change and how?

Through the open-ended and checklist formats of Questions 1 and 2, we can draw a more detailed picture about confusions students may have relevant to specific game instructions. With these data, software producers have more information with which to revise the game instructions.

Formative evaluators must design questions carefully so that the results will facilitate revisions in interface features. Sensitivity to question wording, format, and sequence is important for any questionnaire to be reliable and valid. However, formative researchers, in particular, must be aware of how producers can use the results of a question to effectively revise curriculum materials. If evaluators use general questions such as Question 3 to establish usage statistics for the sample, then data from other methods should contribute guidance for revisions of usage features.

The purpose of the questionnaire, then, is to gather participants' thoughts on the friendliness of a near-final or final program. Evaluators employ questionnaires because they are easily administered and analyzed for a large sample. This permits broader generalization of findings and faster turnaround time from receiving test materials to producing a research report. Further, questionnaires provide a standardized presentation and anonymity for respondents that may yield more accurate and more critical evaluation data than other self-report measures.

On the other hand, questionnaires assessing user friendliness have disadvantages, in addition to those characterizing all self-report measures. First, the advantage of standardized questions is also a disadvantage in that the intended meaning of questions cannot be clarified for respondents and follow-up probing in a questionnaire is limited to predefined directions.

Second, when filling out the questionnaire after using the program, respondents may not clearly remember their specific difficulties with respect to user-machine interactions, especially if they adapted their behavior to cope with the difficulty. For example, Stevens (1986) evaluated a chemistry interactive videodisc in laboratory classrooms using observations, achievement tests, and postuse questionnaires. The questionnaire data yielded high ratings of the user friendliness of the disc, implying that no revisions were needed. Contrary to this conclusion, analysis of the observations showed that most students had difficulty at the beginning of the disc lesson. Stevens (1986) explained as follows:

> They had no problems operating the equipment; however, when faced with the content options, they had no idea what to do. For some unex-

plained reason, very few used the Help or the Definition sections. After they learned some of the material, the different options became clearer, thus contributing to positive evaluations [on the post-use questionnaire]. (p.70)

Finally, questionnaires may not be sensitive to unintended effects of the program unless open-ended questions are used. Also a sample of respondents may be interviewed about their program experiences. The interview method is suitable when alternative answers to questions are not readily apparent, or in-depth explanatory information is desirable, or the respondents cannot read or write.

Interviews.   In an interview, the formative evaluator tries to obtain accurate information and opinions from respondents by asking questions verbally. The interview can be *structured* as if one were presenting an oral questionnaire; for example, the Robin Hood questions mentioned earlier could be asked by the interviewer in lieu of a paper–pencil presentation. In a *semi-structured* interview, the evaluator begins with closed- and open-ended questions and then probes for further explanation depending on the answers given. *Unstructured* interviews in which the interviewer has a general plan of action but not specific questions are typically not productive for assessing user friendliness, because feedback needs to be tied to program features in order to be useful to producers.

Sometimes evaluators show a program section again during an interview in order to elicit opinions and prompt recall of operational difficulties. The following interview was recorded when a student reviewed the "Robin Hood" game square called "The Bridge" (see Fig. 10.1):

Interviewer: (pointing to screen) What does a player do at this square?

Student: Find how many boards need fixing.

Interviewer: Did you have any trouble with this square?

Student: I think I counted the wrong ones.

Interviewer: Which ones did you count?

Student: See these (pointing to dotted lines)? I just thought they were marks—not broken boards, but they must mean those boards are broken.

Interviewer: Did you have any other difficulty here?

Student: No.

Evaluators conduct interviews with groups or individuals. Group interviews avoid the extra time and labor of individual interviews, but are also more difficult to control. All participants must be encouraged to talk, respondents may influence each other, and irrelevant topics can intrude. A group interview process that has proved useful for formative evaluation is to use the same group of respondents repeatedly throughout the development phase. For example, Schauble (chapter 4, this volume) describes a "computer club" of children who played regularly with programs in progress and provided feedback to designers.

Thus, the purpose of interviews as a method of evaluating user friendliness is to obtain a clear understanding of users' problems with a program and the possible reasons behind those problems. The main advantage of an interview is its adaptability. The interviewer (unless giving an oral questionnaire) follows up on users' responses with questions leading to further clarification and more depth of information.

The flexibility of an interview is also its main disadvantage. As the interviewer probes, question wording, tone of voice, and nonverbal movement may reflect a bias that interferes with the collection of valid data. Obtaining rapport with respondents, particularly young children, is critical to the success of the interview technique. Training of interviewers minimizes some of these problems. Further, interviewed subject samples are usually smaller than those responding to questionnaires so generalization is more restricted. Finally, interview data are more difficult to categorize, analyze, and summarize quickly and efficiently. On the other hand, quotes from users can be very convincing evidence to encourage producers to make program changes.

Summary.   Self-report methods contribute the users' own perceptions of a program's user friendliness. Some methods operate during program use—thinkaloud, escorted trial, diary—whereas others typically function after use—confederates, questionnaire, and interview. The methods vary in their requirements of time, labor, sample size, subject ability, and administrative setting. They differ also in their characteristics of structure, obtrusiveness, and ease of analysis. Consideration of the methods' different qualities in conjunction with the program's attributes and the developer's information needs dictates which self-report method to use in a formative evaluation of user friendliness.

Tests

Another way of looking at the user friendliness of a program is to measure students' knowledge of program features after use with written or oral test questions. As an illustration of testing program feature knowledge, the following are alternative test-question formats for assessing students' understanding of one of the "Robin Hood" game rules:

5. You win the Robin Hood Game by _____.
6. How does one win the Robin Hood Game? (Check one)
   _____ Collect the most gold coins
   _____ Reach Robin Hood first
   _____ Get the most problems correct
   _____ I don't know
7. One wins the Robin Hood Game by collecting the most gold coins.
   _____ True
   _____ False

Formative evaluators attempt to frame test questions so that the data will give guidance for revision. Note that if Question 7 is used, we can learn which specific rule is difficult to understand, but we do not obtain information to guide revisions. In contrast, the results of the open-ended and multiple-choice formats of Questions 5 and 6 will reveal possible misconceptions that students have about winning the game.

The purpose of tests is to assess users' knowledge of particular program interface features. Tests have the advantages of standardized administration, large samples, respondent anonymity, and easy analysis. The main disadvantage of tests for formative evaluation purposes is that by themselves they give limited direction as to what revisions to make if users do not understand program features. In formative evaluation, tests are best used in conjunction with other measures that furnish data for revision guidance.

CONCLUSION

The friendliness of the user-machine interface in computer-based educational programs is important. Although a user-friendly program does not guarantee learning, it can interfere with achievement of outcomes and frequently facilitate those outcomes. Designers can try to maximize user friendliness by employing a variety of formative evaluation techniques that gather feedback from experts and users about program accessibility, responsiveness, flexibility, and memory. These techniques include connoisseur-based studies that call on design experts and/or design guidelines as well as decision-oriented studies that use observation, self-report, and tests to gather feedback from target users and program managers. The choice of methods depends on the evaluation questions asked, and because each method has its own strengths and weaknesses, use of multiple measures is recommended.

REFERENCES

Adding creativity to editing with "montage." (1984). *E-ITV, 16*(5), 47–48.

Borgman, C. L. (1986). Human-computer interaction with information retrieval systems: Understanding complex communication behavior. In B. Dervin & J. Voight (Eds.), *Progress in communication sciences* (Vol. 7, pp. 91–122). Norwood, NJ: Ablex.

Bradley, V. N. (1984). The surface features of four microcomputer reading programs. *Journal of Educational Technology Systems, 12*(3), 221–232.

Bunderson, C. V. (1974). The design and production of learner controlled courseware for the TICCIT system: A progress report. *International Journal of Man-Machine Studies, 6*(4), 479–491.

Burton, R. R., & Brown, J. S. (1979). An investigation of computer coaching for informal learning activities. *International Journal of Man-Machine Studies, 11*, 5–24.

Char, C. A. (1983, October). *Evaluating educational software designed for children: Developing methodology to address classroom learning contexts and computer design features.* Paper presented at the meeting of the Evaluation Network and the Evaluation Research Society, Chicago, IL.

Chen, M., Liberman, D., & Paisley, W. (1985). Microworlds of research. In M. Chen & W. Paisley (Eds.), *Children and computers* (pp.276–296). Beverly Hills, CA: Sage.

Clark, R. E. (1982). Antagonism between achievement and enjoyment in ATI studies. *Educational Psychologist, 17*(2), 92–101.

Cornick, L. (1983). *Microcomputer software for teaching German: An evaluation.* Syracuse University. (ERIC Document Reproduction Service No. ED 234 752)

Duncker, K. A. (1926). A qualitative (experimental and theoretical) study of productive thinking (solving of comprehensible problems). *Pedagogical Seminary, 33*, 642–708.

Ericsson, K. A., & Simon, H. A. (1984). *Protocol analysis: Verbal reports as data.* Cambridge, MA: MIT Press.

Fedale, S. V. (1985). A videotape template for pretesting the design of an interactive video program. *Educational Technology, 25*(8), 30–31.

Fiske, D. W. (1971). *Measuring the concepts of personality.* Chicago: Aldine.

Flagg, B. N. (1984). [Teletext for a special interest group: The Employment Network]. Unpublished raw data. Harvard University, Cambridge, MA.

Gaines, B. R. (1984). The technology of interaction-dialogue programming rules. In D. F. Walker & R. D. Hess (Eds.), *Instructional software: Principles and perspectives for design and use* (pp.115–129). Belmont, CA: Wadsworth Publishing.

Gaines, B. R., & Facey, P. V. (1975). Some experience in interactive system development and application. *Proceedings IEEE, 63*, 155–169.

Harlow, R. B. (1985). A personal computer program for storyboarding. *E-ITV, 17*(1), 34–36.

Hawkins, R. P., Bosworth, K., Chewning, B., Day, P. M., & Gustafson, D.

H. (1985). Adolescents' use of computer-based health information. In M. Chen & W. Paisley (Eds.), *Children and computers* (pp.228–245). Beverly Hills, CA: Sage.

Hodges, M. E. (January, 1985). *Wizard of Oz: A formative tool for interactive technologies*. Paper presented at the meeting of the Association for Educational Communications and Technology, Anaheim, CA.

Hoekema, J. (1984). A few principles of interactive videodisc design. In R. Daynes & B. Butler (Eds.), *The videodisc book: A guide and directory* (pp.35–44). New York: Wiley.

Jay, T. B. (1983). The cognitive approach to computer courseware design and evaluation. *Educational Technology, 23*(1), 22–26.

Kelley, J. F. (1983). An empirical methology for writing user-friendly natural language computer applications. In A. Janda (Ed.), *Human factors in computing systems* (pp.193–196). Boston: Association for Computing Machinery.

Klopfer, L. E., Abegg, G. L., Batoff, M. E., Doyle, J., Finley, F. N., Horak, W., Keane, J., Luncsford, D., & Lunetta, V. N. (1984). Microcomputer software evaluation instrument version 1983. *Science Teacher, 51*(1), 95–98.

Mackay, W. E. (1988). Tutoring, information databases, and interative design. In D. H. Jonassen (Ed.), *Instructional designs for microcomputer courseware* (pp.327–346). Hillsdale, NJ: Lawrence Erlbaum Associates.

Mark Heyer Associates. (1987). *The "fast track" to videodisc success* (Product brochure). Greenwich, CT: Author.

McPherson-Turner, C. (1979). CAI readiness checklist: Formative author-evaluation of CAI lessons. *Journal of Computer-Based Instruction, 6*(2), 47–49.

Minnesota Educational Computing Consortium (MECC). (1980). *A guide to developing instructional software for the Apple II microcomputer*. MECC Publication No. M(AP)-2. St. Paul, MI: Author.

Neal, A. S., & Simons, R. M. (1984). Playback: A method for evaluating the usability of software and its documentation. *IBM Systems Journal, 23*(1), 82–96.

News feature: Cost benefits, New technologies highlighted at SALT IX show. (1987). *E-ITV, 19*(10), 13.

Norman, D. A. (1983). Design principles for human-computer interfaces. In A. Janda (Ed.), *Human factors in computing systems* (pp. 1–10). Boston: Association for Computing Machinery.

Oregon State University Vocational-Technical Education Department. (1983). *The development of an evaluation instrument for computer programs with application in vocational education* (Final report). Corvallis, OR: Author. (ERIC Document Reproduction Service No. ED 233 160)

Owston, R. D. (1987). *Software evaluation: A criterion-based approach*. Scarborough, Ontario: Prentice-Hall.

Owston, R. D., & Wideman, H. H. (1987). The value of supplementing panel software reviews with field observations. *Canadian Journal of Educational Communication, 16*(4), 295–308.

Root, R. W., & Draper, S. (1983). Questionnaires as a software evaluation tool. In A. Janda (Ed.), *Human factors in computing systems* (pp. 83–87). Boston: Association for Computing Machinery.

Rowe, N. C. (1984). Some rules for good simulations. In D. F. Walker & R. D. Hess (Eds.), *Instructional software: Principles and perspectives for design and use* (pp.181–186). Belmont, CA: Wadsworth.

Schneider, R. (1987). Bank Street Writer III. *Classroom Computer Learning, 8*(1), 14, 16.

Seiler, B. A. (1981). *Guidelines for designing Plato lessons* (Tech. Rep.). Newark, DE: University of Delaware, Office of Computer-based Instruction.

Simpson, H. (1984). A human-factors style guide for program design. In D. F. Walker & R. D. Hess (Eds.), *Instructional software: Principles and perspectives for design and use* (pp.130–142). Belmont, CA: Wadsworth Publishing.

Smith, R. C. (1985). From script to screen by computer for interactive videodiscs. *E-ITV, 17*(1), 31–33.

Stevens, D. (1986). Results of implementing and evaluating classroom applications of an interactive videodisc high school science project. In W. Sybouts & D. Stevens (Eds.), *Proceedings of the National Videodisc Symposium for Education: A National Agenda* (pp. 67–72). Lincoln, NE: University of Nebraska–Lincoln.

Sudman, S., & Bradburn, N. M. (1974). *Response effects in surveys*. Chicago: Aldine.

Weiss, C. H. (1975). Interviewing in evaluation research. In E. L. Struening & M. Guttentag (Eds.), *Handbook of evaluation research* (Vol. 1, pp.355–395). Beverly Hills, CA: Sage.

11

Issues of Reception:
Does it Appeal?

Mr. Scranton records his family's daily television viewing in a diary—he is part of a Nielsen family. Mrs. Glomer turns on the television and then punches a code number into a "peoplemeter" device—she is part of an Arbitron family. When Jimmy turns on the TV, he presses buttons on a machine, sees his name on the screen and knows that a heat sensor is scanning the room for his presence—he is part of a Percy family. Each of these family members is participating in the collection of data to answer the question of which TV programs are being received (and presumably viewed) in their homes.

Nielsen ratings are a familiar method of measuring the reception of broadcast television programs, but a measure of audience size is useless for formative evaluation because it lacks diagnostic information on the strengths and weaknesses of a program's appeal. This chapter defines the issues of a program's initial effectiveness or reception and discusses formative evaluation methods appropriate for measuring reception of television and computer-based educational programs. For each method, we give examples of the technique, define its purpose, and explore its advantages and disadvantages for formative evaluation.

For the purposes of discussion in this chapter, reception is divided into three components: *attention, appeal,* and *excitement.* Attention refers to the viewer's behavior of looking and listening and is typically measured by observation. Appeal consists of viewers' self-report of their attraction to and interest in a program or production features. Excitement is indicated by overt participation or physiological arousal in response to a program or its elements. On occasion evaluators define reception as including immediate recall; in this book, recall is subsumed under the rubric of comprehension in the next chapter.

Developers of educational and training curricula concentrate less on the entertainment quality of a program because typical program goals are to increase knowledge or skills and change attitudes. Yet the first step in the comprehension or persuasion process is to attract and maintain the learner's attention and interest (Gagné, Briggs, & Wager, 1988; McGuire, 1969). In order to address its teaching objectives, the program must compete with other stimuli to be positively received by the learner. Knowing how learners receive a program gives meaningful diagnostic information for the production staff.

It should be clear, however, as in the horse-to-water saying, that reception of a program is a necessary but not sufficient condition of learning. Evaluators supplement reception indices with measures of comprehensibility, recall, retention, and so forth, in order to obtain a complete picture of how the learner is processing and integrating the material. These latter behaviors are discussed in the next chapter.

MEASURING ATTENTION

Factors that affect attentional responses include environmental distractors, reasons for using the program, characteristics of the individual, and properties of the program itself. The latter factor is the only one over which the program producer really has any control. The developer of an educational television segment or computer screen wants to present information and can use a wide variety of instructional designs and production techniques to communicate that content. Formative evaluation supplies feedback as to how viewers attend to television program segments and computer screens. The general evaluation question at issue here is when and how does the program elicit, maintain, guide, or discourage looking and listening behavior?

This formative evaluation question is of particular importance to the medium of television because television lacks the participatory qualities of computer-based programs to hold the target audience. Television competes with other environmental variables and other TV shows for the attention of the learner, particularly in a home environment. But even for the captive school audience, high program attention is critical:

> If a student is not attending to the program, he or she is likely to be doing something else—and that something else is likely to be disruptive to the rest of the class. . . . Normal classroom patterns are disrupted by bringing a television into the classroom. If further breaks from the instructional

norm or with traditional decorum occur while viewing, teachers will relegate the TV sets to the closet. (Rockman, 1983, p.304)

Evaluators less frequently measure visual and auditory attention for a computer-based instructional system because the system will not operate if the user does not attend. An exception to this is when a computer-based program is designed for whole classroom use where the teacher is the operator. In this case, assessing patterns of wandering student attention facilitates program revision.

Aural Attention

Attention is a covert mental activity but researchers infer its occurrence from observation of participant behaviors. Listening has been difficult to measure because the activity of this sensory system is not easily observed. Those who have tried to study aural attention to television have required viewers to turn a switch to improve the quality of an intermittently degraded auditory presentation (Bohannon & Friedlander, 1973; Friedlander & Wetstone, 1974; Rolandelli, Wright, & Huston, 1982). This technique is obtrusive and unnatural for the viewer but still measures aural attention during the viewing. Otherwise, one must infer aural attention by testing, after viewing, recall of content presented only in the auditory modality or content presented when the viewer was not looking at the program. One future task of formative evaluators will be to develop an unobtrusive technique to study listening behavior.

Nevertheless, research findings suggest a close relationship between listening behavior and looking behavior in young children. Recall of auditory information in television presentations is related to visual attention for viewers through 10 years of age (Field, 1983; Lorch, Anderson, & Levin, 1979; Rolandelli et al., 1982; Zuckerman, Ziegler, & Stevenson, 1978). Thus, many evaluators feel comfortable measuring only the more easily observable visual attention for young viewers and then generalizing from those data.

Visual Attention

What strikes the casual observer most about young TV viewers is that their eyes are glued to the set one minute and they're off playing with a toy the next minute. Thus, the most common measure of visual attention is the gross orientation of the head and eyes toward or away from the program display. The observable behavior of eyes looking toward a TV screen is a valid indicator of visual attention for children under 8 or 9.

This measure decreases in validity for older children and adults because they can monitor the TV program with less frequent visual orientation, using the audio track and knowledge of the medium to guide their monitoring. To assess program reception with older children and adults, we move toward measuring opinions, that is, measuring appeal, rather than measuring behavior such as attention.

A less common measure of visual attention is to record eye movements to determine exactly where a viewer or user is looking on a television screen or computer screen and keyboard. With state-of-the-art equipment, point-of-gaze information can be recorded from any age learner in response to any kind of visual stimulus. These two measures of attention, gross visual orientation and eye movements, are elaborated here.

Gross Visual Orientation

The Children's Television Workshop led the way in using visual orientation data in formative evaluation. Both in-house researchers and commissioned evaluators have analyzed the effects on viewer attention of production design attributes in "Sesame Street" (Anderson & Levin, 1976; Bernstein, 1978; CTW, 1974; Lasker, 1974; Reeves, 1971; Rust, 1971a; Watt & Krull, 1976) and in "The Electric Company" (CTW, 1973; Fowles, 1971; Rust, 1971b).

Early in their work, "Sesame Street" evaluators realized that a preschooler in a room alone viewing television would give the program almost complete attention. To increase the variability of attention, they introduced a controlled distractor in the laboratory-viewing situation (Palmer, 1974). The Palmer distractor technique consists of recording when the individual viewer is watching or not watching the television, while age-appropriate slides are projected on a screen to the side of the television set at a 45 degree angle from the viewer. The observer instructs the viewer to watch whatever he or she wishes. Then the observer, seated so as to see the child's eyes, estimates visual attention to the TV screen for every 7.5-second interval (the duration of slide exposure). The observer scores whether the child's eyes were fixed on the TV for the whole period, more than half the period, less than half, or not at all. When possible, event-recording equipment is used permitting observers to press a button whenever the child's eyes look away from the program, thus producing a continuous record of viewing (Reeves, 1971).

The purpose of the Palmer distractor technique is to measure visual orientation under conditions in which distraction is controlled and to relate those attention patterns to the program features of the televised display. "This method presumes that the appeal of a televised segment is

TABLE 11.1
Variations on the Distractor Method to Measure Gross Visual
Orientation toward Television

Type of Distraction	Sampling Time & Sample Size	Recorder	Program Series	Example Reference
1) Slides	Sum attn every 7.5 sec interval or continous, for $N = 1$	Observer in room	"Sesame Street" "The Electic Company"	Palmer, 1974
2) Small grp of peers	Sum attn every prog. segment, for $N = 3-5$	Observer in room	"Sesame Street" "The Electric Company"	Bernstein, 1977
3) Living rm, toys, bks & mother	Continuous, for $N = 1$	Observer behind mirror	"Sesame Street"	Anderson & Levin, 1976
4) Soundless colorcd animation & mother	Continuous, for $N = 1$	Videotape of child's face and setting	"Watch with Mother" (Japanese)	Kikuta, Muto, Uchida, Shirai, & Sakamoto, 1987
5) Two peers	Continuous, for $N = 2$	Videotape behind mirror	"Today's Special" (Canadian)	Parsons, Duggan, & Karam, 1981
6) Large grp of peers	At end of prog segments, for $N = 5$	Observers in room	"Reading Rainbow"	Dwyer, 1982
7) Classroom of peers	At every 10 secs, for $N = 5$	Observers in room	Most elementary series from Agency for Instructional Technology	Rockman & Auh, 1976

inversely related to a child's distractibility while watching that segment. That is, a child watching an unappealing segment will be more susceptible to having his attention distracted by other stimuli than will a child watching an attractive segment" (Schauble, 1976, p. 1).

Table 11.1 displays the range of variations practiced for the distractor method. Formative evaluators have modified the distractor method in terms of (a) type of distraction to permit variability in attention, (b) how frequently data are recorded, (c) the size of the sample observed for each program presentation, and (d) the obtrusiveness of the recording technique.

For example, the Agency for Instructional Technology (AIT; see Table 11.1, Row 7) tests each of their pilot television programs in actual elementary classrooms using an Attention Profile System:

> To measure attention to a program, 2 observers watch separate groups of students to see if their eyes are on the television screen. Every 10 seconds, 5 students are observed; observers alternate the student samples as well as 10-second periods. . . . Although the observers could watch as many as 20 different students in each class, for any single data point only 5 students would be included. (Rockman & Auh, 1976, p.25)

Then the AIT evaluator combines observations from classes and plots the percentage of students viewing at every 10th second against a description of program events. Figure 11.1 presents the attention profile of 26 classrooms who watched a rough cut of the program, "Pressure Makes Perfect" from AIT's series, "Self Incorporated" (Rockman & Auh, 1976). Visual attention is high overall with two clearly indicated low points.

The advantage of all of the distractor techniques is in producing a highly reliable continuous record of visual orientation fluctuations that can be related to program events. The procedures vary in their ecological validity, in their observer obtrusiveness, in their ability to control the kind and level of distraction, and in their sampling frequency.

On the other hand, numerous disadvantages of the distractor methods exist. The beginning of the viewing record is less reliable as the child adjusts to the novelty of the distractors. Children may commit to distractors (especially toys) early in the session and ignore the program altogether. Small samples observed with each program presentation mean that much time and labor is consumed obtaining a large enough sample from which to generalize comfortably. Finally, noncomputer recording dictates a long data analysis period.

Do these different distractor conditions affect the attention results? Several studies have compared the results of various viewing conditions. Epstein (1976) looked into the relationship between "Sesame Street" attention scores obtained for individuals viewing with a slide distractor and for a small group of peers viewing without slides (see Rows 1 and 2 in Table 11.1). After eliminating the less reliable data at the beginning of the session, Epstein calculated a correlation of + .51 between the slide distractor and peer distractor scores. Lorch et al. (1979) compared atten-

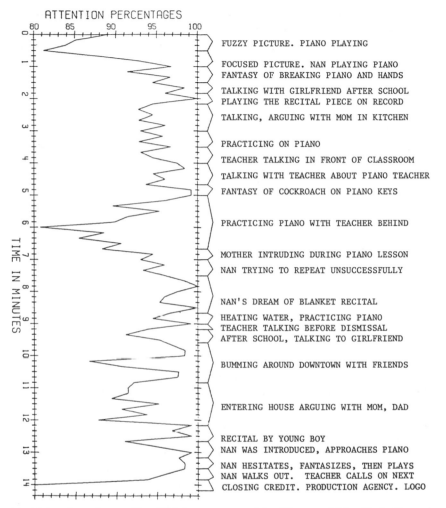

FIG. 11.1. Attention profile of 26 classrooms watching "Pressure Makes Perfect" rough-cut from the TV series, "Self Incorporated," produced by the Agency for Instructional Technology (used by permission).

tional responses of "Sesame Street" viewers who had access to toys with those who did not. Although having toys reduced overall attention, no significant differences were found between the groups in their program knowledge.

Additionally, Bernstein (1978) measured visual attention to "Sesame Street" for four different viewing conditions: (a) single child with slide distractor; (b) child and parent; (c) child, parent, and toys; and (d) small groups of three or four peers. He discovered some differences in the sets of production features that predicted attention variance for the four groups. For example, "kind of storyline" accounted for much variance for his first three viewing conditions but not for the small-group viewing situation. "Repetitive content" was an important predictor of attention for his group viewing situation but not for the conditions with single children.

The differential effect of viewing conditions on viewer attention is still an open research question. Nonetheless, in order to maximize external validity, the viewing conditions should match those under which the final program will be viewed.

After collecting visual orientation data, evaluators and producers scrutinize the onscreen/offscreen patterns of viewing as they relate to content and production features. Unless experimentally manipulated materials are presented as stimuli, evaluators follow an inductive hypothesis generating process to analyze and interpret the attention data.

Look at the attention profile in Fig. 11.1. During the first low point of attention, the program employed a fisheye lens and rack focus to move in and out of the scene before becoming a focused picture. The evaluators' analysis and interpretation for this section of the data follow:

> Through the first 90 seconds, significant portions of the class still have not focused completely on the screen. While this period of orientation is occurring, several fantasy sequences take place [on screen]. Student comprehension data . . . indicate that students do not fully distinguish these as fantasy scenes. The lack of initial picture focus and the slow movement toward picture focus do not grab attention at once; only gradually do the students figure out what the first scene is actually presenting and this causes comprehension problems. . . . One would think that a fuzzy visual opening would stimulate the viewer and cause him to watch intently to figure out what was happening. The attention data suggest that the opposite is true. Viewers seem to ignore the opening moments and wait for the picture to become sharper before paying close attention. In addition, this slow opening and its associated inattention may well interact with the initial fantasy sequence; it is the most ambiguous of the several that appear. (Rockman & Auh, 1976, pp. 75, 90)

This case illustrates the importance of collecting attention data to confirm or question intuitive choices of how to present content. "The more innovative the message design in its exploitation of production factors, the greater the need for trial and revision through formative research" (Mielke, 1983, p.234). This example also demonstrates the significance of gathering more than one type of viewer response (e.g., comprehension data) to support inferences from the attention results.

Attribute Analysis. As in the example just given, most evaluations interpreting visual orientation data investigate viewers' responses to program-specific features in order to facilitate revisions in that particular program. Evaluators qualify their generalization of these findings. However, for the production of a series of programs, it may be worthwhile to use visual orientation data from a number of programs or segments to determine generalizable principles of design for development of future programs.

The Children's Television Workshop again led the field in systematically analyzing which production attributes of televised materials relate to children's patterns of visual attention. The formal attributes of television programming encompass basic program formats such as documentary, situation comedy, and game show, as well as specific within-program attributes. Within-program features range from microlevel audiovisual production and editing techniques (e.g., dialogue, sound effects, color, movement, cuts and fades) to combinations of microlevel features (e.g., pace and complexity) to macrolevel attributes (e.g., repetition, humor, visual format, audiovisual synchrony). Two analytic methods have evolved for relating attention data and program attributes.

One method entails a post hoc analysis, reasoning from the outcome behavior back to the medium characteristics. For example, Rust, (1971a, 1971b) in his attribute analyses of "Sesame Street" and "The Electric Company" presented programs to children and recorded their visual orientation toward and away from the television screen. Rust grouped together those program segments obtaining the extreme highest attention scores and those obtaining the extreme lowest scores and then examined each group for production attributes that were present across all of one group but absent in the other. This post hoc attribute analysis identified the following, for instance, as effective attention-grabbing characteristics in "Sesame Street": "Show and Tell" segments in which concrete objects or activities are discussed, labeled, and/or counted; and "Catch/Get Caught" segments that present a theme of chasing, fleeing, catching, or getting caught (Rust, 1971a).

A number of methodological concerns arise with this approach to defining significant attributes related to attention outcome behavior. The first is generalization of attribute definitions. The restricted number of program segments shown and the analysis of only those receiving extremely high or low attentional response limits the extent to which identified attributes can be generalized. Second, broad macrolevel features, such as those Rust developed, need to be succinctly defined in language that producers and writers can understand and reliably translate into new production of the same genre. Third, there is the problem of establishing external validity—Can the attributes be used to predict viewers' attention to new program presentations? Unfortunately, Rust's attributes did not stand a test of external validity. Levin (1974) found that predictions of preschoolers' visual attention to "Sesame Street" were less accurate using Rust's attributes than using a particular researcher's intuitions. Despite these drawbacks, this inductive method generates interesting macrolevel attributes that subsequently can be refined and tested.

A second method of identifying attributes significant to viewer attention involves developing an a priori taxonomy or classification of program features (Bernstein, 1978; Lasker, 1974; Levin & Anderson, 1976). Suggestions for such a taxonomy come from various sources: (a) attributes suggested by writers and producers as being significant and consciously manipulated in their program development; (b) attributes drawn from previous television research such as that of Rust (1971a, 1971b); and (c) attributes derived from psychological research on non-television stimulus characteristics that have demonstrated a relationship to attention (e.g., complexity, novelty; Berlyne, 1960; Lema-Stern, 1980).

With the a priori attribute taxonomy in hand, researchers rate the television program for the presence or absence of the various attributes. Specificity of attribute definitions and interrater reliability is crucial at this stage. The onset and offset of viewer attention in response to the coded program material is then related to the presence or absence of attributes. For example, Bernstein (1978) measured preschoolers' visual attention to "Sesame Street" that had been coded for presence of 43 production attributes, such as special visual effects, degree of visual action and movement, music type and pace, complexity of language, and kind of storyline. The kind of storyline used in "Sesame Street" segments predicted visual attention best.

In comparison with the post hoc method, the a priori taxonomy method of television attribute analysis has similar but less serious problems of generalization, specificity of definition, and validity. Since a priori attributes are defined independently of viewer response behavior, they are less subject to variations of stimulus material and potentially more universal in application. However, both methods focus on attributes as independent of content, thus assuming that the impact of a production attribute on the particular audience remains consistent regardless of variations in content. A priori attributes are typically better operationally defined for reliable usage by evaluators and producers; nonetheless, such taxonomies often avoid the more difficult to handle qualitative and interactive aspects of production features that the post hoc method considers.

Most attribute analyses simply relate the presence or absence of an attribute with the presence or absence of gross visual orientation. This approach does not answer the more interesting questions of whether a production feature attracts attention to the screen, holds that attention, or terminates it. To speak to these questions, Anderson and his colleagues applied a time-locked analysis of attributes and attentional patterns (Alwitt, Anderson, Lorch, & Levin, 1980). An example of their findings is that the occurrence of the feature "sound effects" in children's programming elicited the attention of children who were not attending to the television and maintained the attention of those already watching. The termination of "sound effects" was associated also with both eliciting and maintaining attention.

The attributes chosen for analysis and the statistical procedures used to establish the relationship between television features and attention are critically related to the conclusions drawn. Much of the attribute analysis research treats stimulus attributes as isolated entities, testing the positive or negative effect of each feature separately (e.g., Anderson & Levin, 1976). However, producers do not treat production techniques individually but think of them in relation to each other as well as in relation to the program's content. Examining independent effects of attributes yields comprehensible results but is sometimes misleading because attributes are not necessarily independent but often correlated with the presence or absence of one or more other attributes. As an illustration of this problem, Anderson and his colleagues report that the attribute "puppets" significantly increased attention of preschoolers (Alwitt et al., 1980); yet the "puppets" attribute was moderately correlated with two other attributes, "peculiar voices" and "children's voices." Calculations removing the overlap with these two latter features found the "puppets" attribute alone no longer significantly influencing attention.

Researchers (going beyond what formative evaluators usually have time and money to do) have used factor analysis techniques to assess the relationships and patterns of association within a set of production attributes and to combine correlated individual features into superordinate categories (Alwitt et al., 1980; Wartella & Ettema, 1974; Watt & Krull, 1974). If we look at the Alwitt et al. study again, a puppet factor was identified that accounted for 7.2% of the variance in attention. The puppet factor included the individual attributes of "puppets," "peculiar voices," "inactive stationary characters," "absence of adult male voices," and "absence of animation." Attention was significantly elicited and maintained in the presence of the puppet factor attributes.

Thus, the purpose of attribute analysis is to use visual orientation data from a corpus of programs to determine which program attributes likely contribute to viewing patterns for a particular target audience. The goal of attribute analyses is not to "substitute research rules and guidelines for production creativity and artistry. . . . not to replace production intuition and experience. Rather their function is to make these intuitions explicit, and to test their generality" (Bernstein, 1978, pp.172–173).

Eye Movements

From time to time you will overhear program developers voice program concerns: "I want the audience to notice the change in this picture"; "I hope they can follow the action"; "I'm worried that this screen is too busy." The recording of a viewer's eye movement patterns offers a unique opportunity to investigate the actual distribution of visual attention while the viewer is watching the program material. Eye movement patterns are rapid, continuous indicators of the viewer's allocation of attention and processing within a display. Moreover, eye movements are less under conscious control of the viewer than gross visual orientation. Thus, eye movement monitoring is a valuable, objective, and reliable tool to analyze the effectiveness of program design in directing viewers' attention.

To illustrate the use of eye movement data in formative evaluation, let us consider the problem that faced the producers of a college-level telecourse on introductory statistics (Falk & Flagg, 1988). They were uncertain as to how to present on television the tables of many numbers common in statistics instruction. In particular, the production staff debated how much numerical material could be presented on screen at one time without overwhelming the student. Two alternate forms of graphics to explain the table of z values were developed. Version A showed a wide angle view of the z table (13 rows down and 5 columns across) and used highlighting to direct students' attention to relevant numbers. Version B showed smaller sections of the table (often one column or row at a time) and used close ups and pans in addition to the highlighting to direct students' attention. Both versions presented the identical audio track.

In response to a questionnaire, more than three quarters of the student respondents reported that Version A (wide view) taught the z table best, was clearer, and was more appealing than Version B. But what the producers found most helpful, in guiding their decisions as to how to present numerical tables, was looking at a dynamic visual representation of viewers' eye movement patterns superimposed on the video displays of the z table. These data provided insight as to the process by which viewers actually used the table presentations. Viewers of Version A (wide angle) tended to practice several times the skill of searching the columns and rows for a specified z value and reported feeling more skillful at reading the z table than students who saw Version B. Visual scanning of

Version B was limited to following the speed of the camera pan, and the visual search pattern was performed only once. Version A allowed viewers the freedom to gaze repeatedly down columns and across rows, whereas Version B restricted attention and closely controlled visual scanning of the z table.

The purpose of eye movement monitoring to assess visual attention is to discover how the target audience responds to program design features once viewers are visually oriented toward the screen. Visual distractors can be set up in the viewing environment to measure elicitation of attention with eye movement data, but the strength of this method is in illuminating direction and allocation of attention within the stimulus display. The technique is most applicable to programs in which comprehension of visual material is critical to the teaching goals. As with gross visual orientation data, large sample sizes take time to amass and measurement of other responses such as comprehension aids interpretation of eye movement data.

Collecting eye movement data for formative evaluation of dynamic displays once required high capital investment in equipment and obtrusive uncomfortable recording situations (Flagg, 1982; O'Bryan & Silverman, 1972). However, Applied Science Laboratories of Waltham, Massachusetts currently offers a data collection service to evaluators of instructional materials. To unobtrusively record eye movement data, an individual viewer sits in a comfortable lounge chair up to 7 feet from the TV screen. No equipment is attached to viewers and no equipment, other than the TV screen, is visible to them. The recording unit "looks" at the viewer through a 3-inch red hole visible in the wall below the TV screen. Eye movement data are summarized into group results. Moving white spots, representing the point-of-gaze of viewers, are superimposed onto the video stimulus, so that producers see simultaneously a visual of what was shown to viewers and how respondents attended to it. Further computerized analysis determines what elements of the program were looked at, by whom, for how long, and in what sequence.

Eye movement monitoring is also possible for computer-based instructional systems, including videodisc and teletext. A different data collection method is more appropriate for computer-based presentations that vary in their stimulus displays dependent on the actions of the user. In such cases, the respondent wears a headband mounted with eye tracker optics and a camera that records the changing scene at which the viewer is looking. This system weighs less than 6 oz., permits normal user activity, and is portable to allow data collection in a natural setting (Applied Science Laboratories, 1987).

Summary

Formative evaluators collect gross visual orientation data to provide feedback on how effective a program is in eliciting and maintaining attention. Eye movement monitoring offers guidance on the effectiveness of program design in directing viewer's attention.

MEASURING APPEAL

Appeal refers to respondents' opinions about the attractiveness of a program, its content, and any of its elements (e.g., characters, situations, screen displays, icons, etc.). If a program is to teach knowledge and skills and affect attitudes, then it helps to be attractive to learners. But appeal is not a simple construct; typically formative evaluators measure a number of characteristics that come under the general heading of appeal, including likableness, interest, personal relevance, familiarity, credibility, and acceptability. These variables overlap, and a few may arguably belong in the next chapter's general category of comprehension, but as we see here each offers a slightly different perspective of the general issue of appeal.

Appeal Variables

Likableness. Liking or disliking is a basic dichotomy for measuring appeal. The more users like the content and cast of a videodisc simulation program, for instance, the more effort they are likely to put into the decision-making requirements of the program's tasks. The more viewers like or admire a character, the more likely they are to move their attitude toward the character's position—thus, the practice of using celebrities in commercials.

Interest. Interest is a different slice of the pie of appeal, embodying feelings of curiosity, fascination, and engagement. Producers work to maximize interest and to minimize boredom. Low interest signals the need to contemplate program changes; however, interpretation of appeal data is sometimes facilitated by other knowledge about the learner group. For example, Honey (1987) tested a prototype for *Maya Calculator,* a software tool that used the Maya base 20-number system. Fourth through sixth graders were not interested in the prototype calculator for a variety of reasons. One group of students simply did not have a clear understanding of place value and needed a motivating game to lead them into use of the tool. The second group understood the concepts but lost interest in using the calculator in its prototype format; this group needed challenging activities to provide a richer environment in which to use the tool.

Personal Relevance. Viewers who identify with characters and situations will be more interested in the program and more likely to recall and imitate the program behaviors, attitudes, and messages. When a pilot television program of "The Voyage of the Mimi" was tested, the majority of the characters appealed to the audience; however, girl viewers preferred female characters, boys preferred males, and younger viewers preferred the younger cast members (Char, Roberts, Vibbert, & Hendrick, 1982).

Familiarity. When content, characters, or presentation features like screen icons are familiar to respondents, their messages are attended to more effectively. Because novel formats and production techniques run against tradition and expectations, they require careful testing to determine their true appeal.

Credibility. Those characters and scenes that are seen as believable and realistic are enjoyed more by viewers. For example, to explain their dislike of a television pilot targeted for older Americans, "most viewers said that the characterization of older people was at the root of their criticism. . . . characters were atypical. . . . stereotyped. . . . feeble and powerless beyond their years" (Corporation for Public Broadcasting, 1981, p. 41). Lack of character credibility decreased program appeal.

Acceptability. Material that matches one's expectations works well but that which is surprising, offensive, or somehow unacceptable will need special handling to reach its audience. For instance, Baggaley (1987) reported researching the appeal of a film to teach seal hunters how to improve their techniques. At one point in the film when a seal is killed, high school viewers showed disapproval. The analyses revealed that children from sealing families were most disapproving "for fear that their fathers would be viewed in a barbarous light. Rather than connoting a distaste for the seal hunt, therefore, the . . . data were eventually interpreted as revealing disapproval of the film at that particular point, borne of a distinctly pro-sealing attitude" (p. 232).

Evaluators measure one or more of these six appeal variables for presentation techniques, content, and characters, using a variety of self-report methods including continuous reaction measures, within-program questions, choice situations, questionnaires, and interviews. Each of these self-report methods is discussed here.

Self-Report Methods

Continuous Reaction Measures

Theater actors have the applause and boos of the audience, rock groups have the screams and tomatoes of the crowd, but television and computers—the "cool" media—receive little in the way of overt viewer response. Thus, continuous reaction measures play an important role in formative evaluation because they permit learners to report on their changing opinion of appeal during viewing or use of the program. Some of the methods gather spontaneous reports, whereas others elicit specific evaluation responses from the learner. Some methods record rich verbal reports; others, restricted nonverbal feedback. The purpose of all the methods is to relate the appeal data directly to specific points in the program, similar to the visual attention analyses presented previously.

Thinkaloud. The thinkaloud technique is the one continuous reaction measure applicable to interactive programs. The evaluator asks the learner while using a software program to reflect out loud on the appeal of the program: What parts do they like or dislike? Where is the content particularly interesting or boring? Do they identify with the characters? Are there sections where a simulation is unrealistic? Keeping questions like these in mind, the user supplies a stream of consciousness report on the appeal of the program as he or she is operating it.

For example, while using a videodisc simulating a real estate negotiation, two professionals commented on the credibility of the video presentation (Parker, 1988):

1. "So we have a deal guy and a lawyer. Why are they negotiating together?"
2. "I don't know."
1. "That is one thing that never happens by the way. Deal people never negotiate directly with attorneys. It is very atypical. Attorneys negotiate with attorneys and business people negotiate with business people, . . . do you agree with that?"
2. "Yes. Business people reach fundamental agreements and then tell the lawyers to put that into legaleese."

The thinkaloud technique obtains users' immediate assessment of program appeal. Unfortunately, the evaluator is at the mercy of users, because users choose when to comment. Some users may have felt the same way about the credibility of the videodisc as the professionals in the example just given but simply failed to mention it. If an issue is important enough to want everyone's immediate opinion, then evaluators can interrupt program use with a question about appeal. This technique of within-program questions is elaborated later in the chapter.

Program Evaluation Analysis Computer. In the late 1970s, the Children's Television Workshop (CTW) and the Ontario Educational Communications Authority (now TV Ontario) developed a recording instrument that permitted viewers to respond continuously to the appeal of a television program while watching it. Continuous response instruments had been used earlier in formative evaluation (Cambre, 1981), but the new device was made portable, computerized, and easy to use. This device, the Program Evaluation Analysis Computer (PEAC), is now commercially available through PEAC Media Research Inc. in Toronto, Canada.

Using the PEAC system, viewers press buttons on a hand-held calculator-like keyboard indicating whether the program is "interesting," "fun," "boring," and so forth (Nickerson, 1979). The battery-powered keyboard unit stores responses to be fed later into a personal computer for analysis. Viewers' opinions are anonymous and can change from moment to moment.

The PEAC system conveniently monitors opinions of large groups of viewers in one setting. However, because the data collection units are relatively expensive, most evaluators resort to many small groups to accumulate a large sample. Viewers at home also can register their vote on the portable unit. Researchers employ the system reliably with children as young as 4 years (Baggaley, 1985a) but most often with older children and adults who are capable of continually monitoring and registering their opinion toward a program.

Evaluators use various labels for the response buttons on the PEAC keyboard. Preschoolers responded to antismoking promotions using "smile" and "frown" buttons (Baggaley, 1985b). With elementary school children, TV Ontario specified three buttons, "like a lot," "okay," and "do not like" (Teachman, 1980). Adults can manage four-button interval scales, including "very realistic to unrealistic" (Baggaley, 1982), "very interesting to very boring" (Corporation for Public Broadcasting, 1981), and "good to poor" (Baggaley, 1987).

CTW practiced the following PEAC procedure for 8- to 12-year-olds during development of "3-2-1 Contact," a TV series on science:

Half of each test group received only a positive response option: "Whenever the program is interesting to you or fun to watch, hold this button down; if you're not sure, don't press the button at all." For the other half, only a negative response option was offered: "Whenever the program is boring or not fun to watch, hold this button down; if you're not sure, don't press the button at all." (Mielke & Chen, 1980, p. 11)

These instructions enable the viewer to concentrate on one criteria only, and they control children's tendency to give only positive responses by granting permission for negative feedback. Moreover, the two groups validate each other's data, that is, high positives should match low negatives (Mielke & Chen, 1980).

The response-button labels reflect whatever quality is important to the producers. However, an on-the-spot evaluation is difficult for respondents to furnish for some qualities, like stereotyping. For instance, shown a program about older Americans, adults pressed their PEAC button when they saw instances of negative stereotyping (Corporation for Public Broadcasting, 1981). Button pressing for stereotyping was surprisingly infrequent compared with postviewing discussion results in which viewers sharply criticized the program's stereotyping. Apparently, evaluating stereotyping in the immediate fashion required by the PEAC system is different than having time to reflect on instances in postviewing interviews.

In addition, certain program formats lend themselves better to PEAC analysis than others. PEAC ratings are easier with informational programs or segmented formats. Viewers of dramatic narratives, however, seem to prefer to judge a program in its entirety than "to make moment-by-moment judgements of scenes whose full interpretation rests on the final denouement (Mielke & Chen, 1980, p. 12).

The fact that the PEAC response is nonverbal and private is an advantage with young children, illiterates, and non-native speakers. A disadvantage of the response mode is that evaluation criteria are limited to one or a few fixed variables. One obtains a picture of the fluctuations in appeal at specific points in the program, but explanations as to why these fluctuations occur necessitates collection of interview or questionnaire data. Additionally, the mental and physical capabilities of viewers restricts the range of responses. Evaluators can ask viewers to respond on graduated scales for one or more variables, but reliability can be questionable even with adult groups (Baggaley & Smith, 1982).

A question of measurement validity arises with self-report data—does the PEAC really measure appeal or is it, for instance, measuring what viewers think the evaluators want? One method of controlling for positive response bias was previously mentioned in CTW's procedure, namely, having half the viewers rate the positive—"it's interesting"—and the other half rate the negative—"it's boring." Also postviewing results that correlate with the continuous reaction data help in establishing validity; for example, "3-2-1 Contact" evaluators found that viewers' interview choices of best-liked and least-liked segments after viewing were very consistent with PEAC data (Myerson Katz, 1980).

One should be concerned also that the evaluation activity is not changing the viewing process in some way. This issue is addressed in a pair of studies that showed preschoolers a televised antismoking promotion. One study observed visual orientation of preschool viewers (Caron, Caron, & Michaud, 1985), whereas the other study asked preschoolers to press "smile" and "frown" buttons on the PEAC units (Baggaley, 1985b). Those production factors that elicited high visual orientation matched those that elicited more "smile" responses from the preschoolers. Similar results were found for elementary classes viewing a program on coping with stress. Half of the sample were observed for visual orientation and the other half responded with the PEAC system. The high and low points in the test program were the same for the attention and appeal measures (Rockman & Storey, 1980).

The PEAC is powerful in a formative evaluation environment because it provides almost immediate computerized numerical and graphic feedback. Data memories from each response unit are automatically transferred into a personal computer. The evaluation responses of the sample or subsamples are printed across time on line graphs that can be related to program events (see Fig. 11.2 for example output). In addition, producers quickly apprehend viewer appeal responses with real-time visual feedback displays, as graphic data are displayed on one TV screen in synchronization with the test program shown on a second adjacent screen. Nonetheless, as we have noted before, inferences from continuous reaction measures are made more reliably when data from other measures are available also.

Baggaley (1986) reported an excellent example of the data output of the PEAC system and how it can be used to effect changes in a program. Adults from rural Newfoundland and Quebec viewed a short rough-cut film on skin cancer prevention, evaluating it using four PEAC buttons: "good," "fairly good," "not very good," and "poor" (see Fig. 11.2). Specific moments in the film elicited strong negative reactions from viewers; pretest and posttest information helped interpret these reactions for the producer. Baggaley (1986) recounted that

> The producer responded by shortening various segments, by changing the voiceover to strengthen character identification, adding montage and graphic sequences to emphasize some of the educational points, repeating certain sequences in order to create relief, and adding music to heighten mood and structure. (p.37)

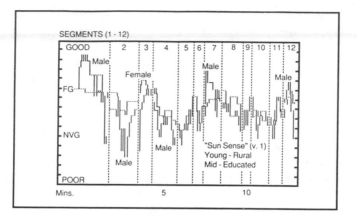

FIG. 11.2.   Data output of PEAC system for rough-cut film. Figure features the responses of a representative subgroup of viewers: rural 18–25 years old, with high school education; $n = 18$. (Reproduced with permission from Baggaley, 1986.)

Rural Canadian adults similarly evaluated the final film with the PEAC system, as seen in Fig. 11.3. Comparing Fig. 11.2 and 11.3, we can see that the producer's changes elicited a higher approval rating of the film's segments. Baggaley (1986) pointed out that the "relatively negative response to the first of these segments—set in a doctor's surgery—is eliminated altogether" (p.39). Thus, PEAC data help producers become aware of weak areas in a television program.

As with the visual orientation data, the PEAC system applied to a corpus of programs can yield general production guidelines for a television series. To illustrate, "3-2-1 Contact" researchers, using the PEAC system to study effects of program attributes on appeal, found that for 8- to 12-year-olds "unusual or action-filled pictures of phenomena were of high interest, such as those of the world's largest pizza or a massive oil spill. Material with static visuals, which relied heavily on the audio track to carry the informational load were unappealing" (Mielke & Chen, 1980, p.13).

Paper-and-Pencil Viewing Response Measurement.   Those who cannot afford an instrument-mediated continuous reaction method like the PEAC system may substitute a paper-and-pencil technique. In this method, the evaluator calls out a series of numbers while the television program plays. At each number, viewers immediately evaluate the program since the last number and mark their response sheet. Numbers can designate time intervals (e.g., every 3 minutes) or relate to prespecified segments that production is interested in. Evaluators and producers define the response dimension, just as for the PEAC system.

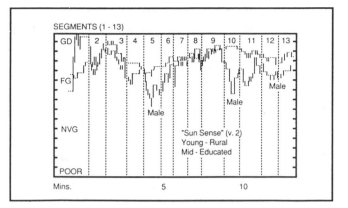

FIG. 11.3.   Data output of PEAC system for final film. Figure features
the responses of a representative sub group of viewers; rural 18–25 years
old, with high school education; $n = 19$. (Reproduced with permission
from Baggaley, 1986.)

The PEAC method and paper-and-pencil method are fairly comparable, except the paper-and-pencil data need more processing time and are
not immediately available for interpretation. Further, the paper-and-
pencil technique deals with discrete points of measurement rather than
continuous measurement, but it still furnishes real-time evaluations of
specific program segments. Evaluators of "The Voyage of the Mimi"
television pilot compared paper-and-pencil interest data with PEAC data
and concluded that the latter, "though broken down into much finer
episode segments, largely correspond with the appeal profile . . . based
on the paper and pencil measure" (Char et al., 1982, p. 8).

To recapitulate, the continuous reaction methods enable the learner
to evaluate the appeal of a program during viewing or usage. In the case
of the thinkaloud technique, the evaluation of interactive programs is
verbal, open-ended and spontaneous. In the case of the PEAC and paper-and-pencil response methods, opinions about television programs
are nonverbal, close-ended, and elicited frequently.

Within-Program Questions

Pause for a moment in your reading to answer the following question:
What, if anything, have you found enjoyable to learn about so far in this
chapter? Explain why. You have just experienced a within-program
question. (I look forward to receiving your replies.) The purpose of
within-program questions is to obtain a richer understanding of how
learners feel about a program midstream. Compared to postprogram
questioning, this method captures opinions at their point of formation,
with experience of the program still fresh.

The spontaneous nature of the thinkaloud technique is a drawback if one wants to obtain everyone's opinion about a particular program feature, and the close-ended nature of the PEAC and paper-and-pencil methods is a drawback if one wants to know the reason behind a learner's opinion. One solution to these limitations is to stop the program at a prespecified point and ask for an opinion and a reason. This procedure, if performed orally, is particularly applicable to young children who have difficulty with the mental and physical demands of the continuous reaction methods.

If a program is of considerable length, then within-program questions become more significant for collecting valid and useful opinion data. Formative evaluators of Great Britain's Open University multimedia higher education courses have applied successfully the within-program questioning technique (Nathenson & Henderson, 1980). They found that within-program questions yielded higher quality data for revision purposes than did postprogram questions.

Within-program questioning has its disadvantages also. The technique breaks the pace of the learning experience and can frustrate television viewers and computer users. Certain kinds of questions can influence the learner to look at or use the succeeding material in a different way. Moreover, sample sizes are small if learners must be questioned orally.

In summary, within-program questions give learners opportunities to comment on a program unit while the experience is still memorable.

Choice Situations

We discussed earlier, in the visual orientation studies, the distractor technique that granted viewers a choice of watching either the test program or various distractors. Appeal measurement has an analogous method in which learners experience several programs, pieces of programs, or program elements and choose which is most interesting, least interesting, and so forth. "Such procedures elicit a process of discrimination from the viewer, and legitimize the negative response by specifically asking for it" (Mielke & Chen, 1980, p. 11).

Choice situations are especially useful for assessing character appeal, relatively independent of program content and production features. Viewers look at photographs and hear or read character descriptions, or they may view videotapes of potential cast members. For example, to help guide the decision of who should host a college telecourse on statistics, videotapes of auditions of nine statisticians were tested (Flagg & Falk, 1987). Each host teacher read a short piece of script and then using provided props presented an extemporaneous lesson on the making of and meaning of an histogram. After rating each host individually on several qualities, student viewers chose their top three hosts and explained their choices.

During a project's design phase, formative evaluators are often asked to determine which program format or program elements are most appealing to target learners so that the developers can maximize use of those features. For instance, to gain feedback about content and production techniques at the early development stage, evaluators for "3-2-1 Contact" showed children "one-minute program excerpts in sets of three. Each 'triplet' featured a snipet on an outer space, animal, or microorganism topic. After viewing each triplet, children chose their most- and least-liked segments" (Myerson Katz, 1980, p.28).

In addition, using a choice situation with prototype material, producers can estimate how their program will play against competition. For television programs, learners view excerpts from several programs including the pilot piece; for computer software, users play for a short time with several programs including the prototype. Learners then choose which program they would like to continue to see or play with and which one they liked least. Probing for reasons behind student decisions is important also.

Evaluating prototype materials in choice situations can save producers from making costly mistakes. Graphics, for instance, are expensive to use in electronic text transmissions so understanding when users prefer graphics is helpful to designers. To assist decision making for a videotext project, Carey and Dozier (1985) showed three pairs of electronic text screens to college students. One screen of each pair presented text alone, whereas the other included the same material with graphic enhancement. Viewers preferred graphics that communicated information not available in the text; they did not prefer decorative graphics. Similar findings about graphics resulted when final videotext versions were field tested. Thus, in this case, results from experimental screens in a choice situation generalized to the final product in its usage setting.

Another choice situation simulates the channel selection available in a home environment. An individual viewer is given a channel selector and told he or she can watch whatever he or she wishes. The channels present test material and alternative programming. The evaluator is interested in which programs are watched for how long. Wakshlag, Day, and Zillmann (1981) used a channel-selection task to assess the effect of humor on viewers' selection of television programming. Elementary school children were allowed to switch back and forth among three short programs. One program contained humorous segments, unrelated to program content, which were inserted at a particular frequency (slow, intermediate, or fast). The children chose to view for significantly longer

durations those programs with humor and particularly those with segments inserted at an intermediate and fast pace as opposed to slower
paced inserts. Although channel choice is a natural nonverbal activity, it
is limited to individual testing and occasionally young viewers will commit to a show without seeing the alternatives.

To summarize, the purpose of choice situations is to force the learner
to make comparisons among program materials. This method is unique
in that it enables producers to obtain appeal feedback at early decision
points and to assess appeal of their designs in competition with other
materials. Testing is quick, easy to interpret, and feasible with large
samples. One concern with this method is the validity of generalizing
findings from early materials to the final product. The little research we
have to address this issue is positive: Carey and Dozier (1985), as noted
previously, found that electronic text screen testing in a choice situation
obtained results similar to testing the final product in the field. Also
Flagg and Falk (1988) observed that appeal of the program host in final
programs was equivalent to appeal in host audition tapes assessed in an
earlier choice situation.

Questionnaires

Evaluators commonly employ questionnaires alone or in conjunction
with other appeal methods. Questionnaires are popular because they
collect a large amount of data in an easily interpretable form in a short
amount of time. Moreover, questionnaires function at all stages of the
program development from the early conceptual stage through prototypes to final versions. Computer-based systems can include a questionnaire in the software itself.

Postviewing questions are often close-ended (i.e., asking learners to
rate a software segment or feature on a graduated scale or obtaining
agreement or disagreement with a series of statements). Open-ended
questions gather information about why situations are realistic or not,
why content is acceptable or not, why icons are likable or not, why an
activity is interesting or not. These questions contribute qualitative information that will guide revisions.

Question format and wording should be pilot tested to assure a motivating, reliable, and valid instrument. CTW has tackled effectively the
task of obtaining valid and reliable questionnaire data from children, as
indicated in this description of their methods:

> Written instruments . . . were kept extremely simple, always designed to
> require minimal reading ability and adult supervision, and to maximize the
> individuality of children's responses. For example, researchers found it
> quite useful to make the response sheets in the form of closed "booklets,"

encouraging children to cover their selections as if they were "secret ballots." It was easy for children to mark a favorite response by circling it, and to note a least favorite by actually crossing it out. Cartoons and photographs were also added to response sheets whenever possible, to denote specific program segments or characters, to distinguish among possible responses. (Myerson Katz, 1980, p.28)

Question formats that work well in one setting may not transfer easily to another program or technology. For example, Crane, Callahan, and Isaacson (this volume) recount that the semantic differential, which is a mainstay of television appeal research, failed as a diagnostic instrument when applied to teletext screens. "While it provided interesting information on the general appeal of teletext design, comparisons across sections yielded few differences" (p. 122).

The guiding principle to keep in mind when developing formative evaluation questionnaires is how the question responses will facilitate decision making for program design and revision. Are the questions dealing with attributes that can realistically be changed? For instance, if there is no possibility that a videodisc will be mastered again, then concentrate evaluation energies on appeal of more easily changed computer features and activities. Do the questions elicit information specific enough to suggest direction for changes? A typical written response of "I don't like it because it's boring" leaves the producers with a problem and no hints as to a solution. Are the uncertainties of the producers addressed? Consultation and feedback from the production staff during questionnaire design are critical to collecting evaluation data that are actually utilized.

Interviews

Interviews and discussion groups provide insights into responses on continuous reaction measures and closed-ended questions. Interviewers explore and clarify the "whys" of learner reactions. Moreover, the openness of semistructured and unstructured interviews enables the emergence of opinions that have not been anticipated by the evaluators or producers in a questionnaire. On the other hand, a group-interview situation may inhibit a willingness to give one's true views because answers are public and opinions of others may dominate.

Interviews grant the flexibility to delve into respondents' reasoning about the program. The appeal issues of personal relevance, credibility, and acceptability sometimes require longer answers and more clarification than questionnaires allow. For example, Rockman and Storey (1980) presented a questionnaire to teenagers following a television program called "Coping with Stress." "The subject was treated in a humorous manner, whereby characters and situations were exaggerated and a voice-over narrator commented sarcastically throughout the program, with a humorous intent" (p.11). Multiple-choice questions established that teens could relate to the topic of stress and the situations shown and also that female viewers felt that the characters were not typical of teens they knew. The interview (or class discussion in this case) revealed the range and depth of feeling toward the program:

> this program was *not* perceived by teenager viewers as a successful comedy or farce. Rather, the humor and exaggeration in the program worked against the program's appeal, realism, and teenagers' identification of characters and situations. . . . In addition, when humor was identified, it was thought to be in poor taste and/or to detract from the educational intent of the program. (p.11)

The producers made major revisions in the program, taking their direction from the interview results.

Interviewing is a challenging technique for evaluators, requiring training so as not to bias responses and demanding hours of content analysis, coding, and summarization. Yet the rewards are in discovering the range and complexity of the strengths and weaknesses of the program. Further, quotations from interviews bring quantitative data to life for producers who are not versed in reading numbers and graphs in research reports.

Summary

Formative evaluators draw from a large repertoire of methods to assess program appeal, including methods for use during the program (i.e., continuous reaction measures, within-program questions) and after the program (i.e., choice situations, questionnaires, and interviews). The general evaluation question is when is the program appealing or unappealing? More specifically, when is it likable, interesting, relevant, familiar, credible, and acceptable? Thus, armed with a diagnostic profile, producers and programmers make decisions and revisions.

MEASURING EXCITEMENT

Learner excitement as used in this chapter encompasses overt participation and physiological arousal in response to a program or its elements. Here we are looking at behaviors that indicate some sort of involvement beyond simple attention. The data collection method is observation by the evaluator, videotape, or mediating instruments (in the case of arousal).

Overt Participation

Overt participation is defined loosely to include motoric participation such as dancing to music, nodding, and pointing, and oral participation such as laughter, singing, and verbal commentary. Overt participation is expected from young children but is also illuminating when observed in older audiences. For example, during televised showings of "Coping with Stress" (mentioned previously), the narrator posed questions like "What should Brad do?" to which teen viewers called out responses like "Study!" and "Cheat!" (Rockman & Storey, 1980). It is important also to observe activity unrelated to the program; for instance, Rockman and Storey noted that half of one class preferred concentrating on their homework rather than viewing the television program.

A more complex observational technique that has been used with television, but not as a formative evaluation method, entails videotaping the facial behavior of viewers and inferring emotional responses based on specific muscle movements (Ekman et al., 1972). However, it is not clear that the benefits of this analysis for formative evaluation merit the expense of expert coders and coding time.

Physiological Arousal

Academic researchers have employed numerous measures of physiological arousal with television viewers: heart rate, skin conductance or sweating, pupil dilation, and brain activity. These nonverbal involuntary responses yield an objective continuous measure of private reactions to a program. From measures of arousal, specific emotions are inferred.

So far, none of these methods have been used effectively in a formative evaluation context for several reasons. First, most of the measures necessitate expensive equipment and trained operators and analysts; however, there are commercial and academic groups available to collect and interpret such data. Second, with the exception of pupillometry, the measurement techniques are intrusive; recording equipment must be attached to one respondent at a time in a laboratory situation. Accumulating a large enough sample for acceptable external validity is time consuming.

In addition, physiological responses, other than pupil dilation, have a delayed reaction so it is difficult to relate a response directly to a specific part of a program. One can use the methods to obtain comparative measures of general arousal; for example, comparing responses to segments with and without certain features in order to discriminate which elements are contributing to audience responses (Fletcher, 1984).

Finally, physiological responses reflect intensity of attitude without any indication of its direction or meaning. For example, pupil dilation has been interpreted to mean both attraction and aversion (Hinton, 1982; Janisse, 1974). Data from other methods would be necessary to help interpret and validate physiological data for formative purposes.

Thus, overt participation is a commonly used measure of learner excitement, whereas physiological responses are still in the experimental stage in their application to formative evaluation.

CONCLUSION

The initial reception of an educational program helps define its potential for affecting learner knowledge and attitudes. An attractive program puts the learner one step ahead on the road to achieving program objectives. This chapter characterized three major components of reception—attention, appeal, excitement—and presented analyses of methods that measure learner reception of electronic learning materials. Choice of a method or combination of methods depends upon one's formative evaluation question, the program, target audience, and usage setting.

REFERENCES

Alwitt, L. F., Anderson, D. R., Lorch, E. P., & Levin, S. R. (1980). Preschool children's visual attention to attributes of television. *Human Communication Research, 7*(1), 52–67.

Anderson, D. R., & Levin, S. (1976). Young children's attention to "Sesame Street." *Child Development, 47,* 806–811.

Applied Science Laboratories. (1987). *Series 3000 eye view monitors.* Waltham, MA: Author.

Baggaley, J. (1982). *The electronic analysis of communication technique* (Research Bulletin No. 82-007). Newfoundland, Canada: Memorial University, Institute for Research in Human Abilities.

Baggaley, J. (1985a). Design of a TV character with visual appeal for preschool children. *Journal of Educational Television, 11,* 41–48.

Baggaley, J. (1985b). *Formative evaluation of a televised anti-smoking promotion for preschool children: Part I: Audience responsiveness during viewing* (Report to the National Film Board of Canada). Montreal, Canada: Concordia University, Department of Education.

Baggaley, J. (1986). Formative evaluation of educational television. *Canadian Journal of Educational Communication, 15*(1), 29–44.

Baggaley, J. (1987). Continual response measurement: Design and validation. *Canadian Journal of Educational Communication, 16*(3), 217–238.

Baggaley, J., & Smith, K. (1982). Formative research in rural education. *Media in Education & Development, 15,* 173–176.

Berlyne, D. E. (1960). *Conflict, arousal, and curiosity.* New York: McGraw-Hill.

Bernstein, L. J. (1977). *Measuring the appeal of children's television: A review of research methods and findings.* Unpublished manuscript, Children's Television Workshop, New York.

Bernstein, L. J. (1978). *Design attributes of "Sesame Street" and the visual attention of preschool children.* Unpublished doctoral dissertation, Columbia University, New York.

Bohannon, J. N., & Friedlander, B. Z. (1973). The effect of intonation on syntax recognition in elementary school children. *Child Development, 44,* 675–677.

Cambre, M. (1981). Historical overview of formative evaluation of instructional media products. *Educational Communication & Technology Journal, 29*(1), 3–25.

Carey, J., & Dozier, D. (1985). *Assessing electronic text for higher education: Evaluation results from laboratory and field tests* (Research Report). San Diego, CA: San Diego State University, Electronic Text Consortium.

Caron, A. H., Caron, L. R., & Michaud, C. (1985). *Formative evaluation of a televised anti-smoking promotion for preschool children: Part II: Audience comprehension after viewing* (Report to the National Film Board of Canada). Montreal, Canada: University of Montreal, Department of Communication.

Char, C., Roberts, T., Vibbert, M., & Hendrick, D. (1982). *The Voyage of the Mimi project in science and mathematics education: Pilot show evaluation.* (Research Report). New York: Bank Street College of Education, Center for Children and Technology.

Children's Television Workshop, *Sesame Street* Research Staff. (1974, March 26). *Group observation report on several selected bits* (Research Report). New York: Children's Television Workshop.

Children's Television Workshop, *The Electric Company* Research Staff. (1973, March 15). *Character and format study* (Research Report). New York: Children's Television Workshop.

Corporation for Public Broadcasting. (1981). *A comparison of three research methodologies for pilot testing new television programs.* Washington, DC: Author.

Dywer, M. C. (1982). *Evaluation of "Reading Rainbow"* (Research Report). Hampton, NH: RMC Research Corp.

Ekman, P., Liebert, R. M., Friesen, W. V., Harrison, R., Zlatchin, C., Malmstron, E. J., & Baron, R. A. (1972). Facial expressions of emotion while watching televised violence as predictors of subsequent aggression. In G. A. Comstock, E. A. Rubinstein, & J. P. Murray (Eds.), *Television and social behavior: Vol. 5: Television's effects: Further explorations* (pp.22–58). Washington, DC: U.S. Government Printing Office.

Epstein, S. L. (1976). *A comparison of two methods for measuring children's attention to television program material* (Research Report). New York: Children's Television Workshop.

Falk, J. K., & Flagg, B. N. (1988). *Formative evaluation of graphic presentations of a statistical table* (Research Rep. No. 88-002). Cambridge, MA: Harvard University, Laboratory of Human Development.

Field, D. E. (1983). *Children's television viewing strategies*. Paper presented at the meeting of the Society for Research in Child Development, Detroit, MI.

Flagg, B. N. (1982). Formative evaluation of "Sesame Street" using eye movement photography. In J. Baggaley (Ed.), *Experimental research in televised instruction* (Vol. 5, pp.15–27). Montreal, Canada: Concordia University.

Flagg, B. N., & Falk, J. (1987). *STATMAP host teacher formative evaluation* (Research Rep. Nos. 87-001 & 002). Cambridge, MA: Harvard University, Laboratory of Human Development.

Flagg, B. N., & Falk, J. (1988). *Formative evaluation of "Against All Odds" programs #104 and #113* (Research Rep. No. 88-003). Cambridge, MA: Harvard University, Human Development and Psychology.

Fletcher, J. E. (1984, July). *The application of electrodermal measurement to the evaluation of television advertising*. Paper presented at the meeting of the International Organization of Psychophysiology, London.

Fowles, B. (1971). *Appeal research up to date*. Unpublished manuscript, Children's Television Workshop, New York.

Friedlander, B. Z., & Wetstone, H. S. (1974). *Effects of informational and cartoon program format, musical distractors, and age on children listening to television soundtracks*. Unpublished manuscript, University of Hartford, Hartford, CT.

Gagné, R. M., Briggs, L. J., & Wager, W. W. (1988). *Principles of instructional design* (3rd ed.). New York: Holt, Rinehart & Winston.

Hinton, J. W. (1982). Ocular responses to meaningful visual stimuli and their psychological significance. In R. Groner & P. Fraisse (Eds.), *Cognition and eye movements* (pp.204–212). New York: Elsevier North-Holland.

Honey, M. A. (1987, October). *The role of formative research in the design of educational computer software*. Paper presented at the meeting of the American Evaluation Association, Boston, MA.

Janisse, M. P. (1974). Pupil size and affect: A critical review of the literature since 1960. *The Canadian Psychologist, 10,* 311–329.

Kikuta, R., Muto, T., Uchida, N., Shirai, T., & Sakamoto, T. (1987). *Formative research on television programs, "Word Game", of language acquisition for young children in Japan*. Unpublished manuscript, NHK, Media Research Group for the Study of Two-Year-Olds, Tokoyo, Japan.

Lasker, H. (1974). *The Jamaican project: final report*. New York: Children's Television Workshop. (ERIC Document Reproduction Service No. ED 126 865)

Lema-Stern, S. (1980, September). *Children's visual attention: Effects of color, complexity, movement and incongruity*. Paper presented at the meeting of the American Psychological Association, Montreal.

Levin, S. (1974). *Stimulus determinants of children's attention to "Sesame Street."* Unpublished master's thesis, University of Massachusetts, Amherst, MA.

Levin, S., & Anderson, D. R. (1976). The development of attention. *Journal of Communication, 26,* 105–107.

Lorch, E. P., Anderson, D. R., & Levin, S. R. (1979). The relationship of visual attention to children's comprehension of television. *Child Development, 50,* 722–727.

McGuire, W. J. (1969). The nature of attitudes and attitude change. In G. Lindzey & E. Aronson (Eds.), *The handbook of social psychology: Vol. 3. The individual in a social context* (pp.136–314). Reading, MA: Addison-Wesley.

Mielke, K. W. (1983). The educational use of production variables and formative research in programming. In M. Meyer (Ed.), *Children and the formal features of television* (pp.233–252). New York: K. G. Saur.

Mielke, K. W., & Chen, M. (1980). Making contact: Formative research in touch with children. *CTW International Research Notes, 3*, 9–14.

Myerson Katz, B. (1980). CTW's new science series: The role of formative research. *Televisions, 7*, 24–31.

Nathenson, M. B., & Henderson, E. S. (1980). *Using student feedback to improve learning materials*. London: Croom Helm.

Nickerson, R. (1979, March). *Program evaluation using the program evaluation analysis computer (PEAC)*. Paper presented at the meeting of the Association for Educational Communications and Technology, New Orleans, LA.

O'Bryan, K. G., & Silverman, H. (1972). *Report on children's television viewing strategies*. New York: Children's Television Workshop. (ERIC Document Reproduction Service No. ED 126 871)

Palmer, E. L. (1974). Formative research in the production of television for children. In D. Olson (Ed.), *Media and symbols: The forms of expression, communication, and education* (pp.303–329). Chicago: University of Chicago Press.

Parker, P. (1988). [*Hawkins Negotiation* videodisc evaluation]. Unpublished raw data. Cambridge, MA: Harvard University.

Parsons, P., Duggan, K., & Karam, B. (1981). *"Today's Special": Formative evaluation of two pilot programs* (Report No. 5-1981). Toronto, Ontario, Canada: Ontario Educational Communications Authority.

Reeves, B. F. (1971) *The responses of children in six small viewing groups to "Sesame Street" shows 261–274*. New York: Children's Television Workshop. (ERIC Document Reproduction Service No. ED 122 823)

Rockman, S. (1983). Formative research and evaluation of instructional programs. In M. Meyer (Ed.), *Children and the formal features of television* (pp.279–309). New York: K. G. Saur.

Rockman, S., & Auh, T. (1976). *Formative evaluation of "Self Incorporated" programs* (Rep. No. 30). Bloomington, IN: Agency for Instructional Television.

Rockman, S., & Storey, K. (1980). *"On the Level": Formative evaluation: Coping with Stress* (Research Rep. No. 72). Bloomington, IN: Agency for Instructional Television.

Rolandelli, D. R., Wright, J. C., & Huston, A. C. (1982, April). *Auditory attention to television: A new methodology*. Paper presented at the meeting of the Southwestern Society for Research in Human Development, Galveston, TX.

Rust, L. (1971a). *Attributes of "Sesame Street" that influence preschoolers' attention to the TV screen* (Research Report). New York: Children's Television Workshop.

Rust, L. (1971b). *Attributes of "The Electric Company" pilot shows that produced high and low visual attention in second and third graders*. New York: Children's Television Workshop. (ERIC Document Reproduction Service No. ED 126 872)

Schauble, L. (1976). *The "Sesame Street" distractor method for measuring visual attention*. Unpublished manuscript, Children's Television Workshop, New York.

Teachman, G. (1980). *The role of formative evaluation in the production process: A case study* (Research Rep. No. 26, 1979). Toronto, Ontario, Canada: Ontario Educational Communications Authority.

Wartella, E., & Ettema, J. S. (1974). A cognitive-developmental study of children's attention to television commercials. *Communication Research, 1,* 69–88.

Wakshlag, J. J., Day, K. D., & Zillmann, D. (1981). Selective exposure to educational television programs as a function of differently paced humorous inserts. *Journal of Educational Psychology, 73*(1), 27–32.

Watt, J., & Krull, R. (1974). An information theory measure for television programming. *Communications Research, 1*(1), 44–69.

Watt, J., & Krull, R. (1976). *Form complexity and children's physiological responses, attention, and recall: A final report* (Research Report). New York: Children's Television Workshop.

Zuckerman, P., Ziegler, M., & Stevenson, H. W. (1978). Children's viewing of television and recognition memory of commercials. *Child Development, 49,* 96–104.

Issues of Outcome Effectiveness: Does it Teach?

12

One story, making the rounds of videodisc conferences, tells of an interactive videodisc to teach American military personnel how to use a voltmeter. A touch-screen input mechanism permitted students to touch the video screen in the two spots where they wanted the video voltmeter contacts placed. Out in the field with a real voltmeter and a real electrical circuit to be tested, students again used their fingers to make contact! Obviously, the videodisc program was not effective in achieving one of its planned outcomes of behavior.

The programs that we are concerned about in this book all have in common their goal to facilitate learning. This chapter briefly reviews the need for defining planned outcomes in educational materials, in light of the problem formative evaluators face of measuring outcomes when materials are incomplete or exposures are limited. The bulk of the chapter discusses methods used to measure outcomes. Although many books describe these same methods, this chapter presents them as they apply to formative evaluation of electronic learning materials.

WHAT OUTCOMES?

To make effective revisions in their programs, developers need to understand in what ways a program is successful or not successful in facilitating outcomes. In a goal-based evaluation, we measure achievement of planned outcomes. One would ask, for example, "in what ways did playing a 3-D tank battle game help or hinder adolescents in improving their spatial-visualization skills?", where these skills are the planned outcomes.

At the same time as assessing the strengths and weaknesses of the program in supporting its intended effects, evaluators keep their eyes open to the possibility of unplanned outcomes. From a goal-free perspective, one looks for all actual effects of the program (Scriven, 1972). In the tank game example, one might observe unplanned positive effects, such as improved hand–eye coordination, and unintended negative effects, such as increased aggression. In their limited timeframe, formative evaluators typically concentrate on those goals that a program plans to achieve. Feedback on planned and unplanned outcomes used as the basis for revisions can increase the potential that the final program will have a successful and positive impact on learners.

Define Outcomes

In order to diagnose strong and weak points effectively, evaluators must know what outcomes are expected by program designers. What are the motor skills, cognitive abilities, or attitudes that developers want to teach or change? Frequently, projects have written objectives, of varying levels of detail, but in cases where objectives are not written or are ill-defined, the formative evaluator works closely with developers in order to understand clearly what it is they want the target audience to be able to do, to know, to feel or believe, after program exposure.

Without recognition of what a student is supposed to learn, evaluators may collect feedback that is easily ignored by developers because it does not address what they felt the program was meant to do. A set of target outcomes agreed upon by producer and evaluator increases the chances that the evaluation data will be useful and used. Note that the ability to evaluate the outcomes easily should not be a determining factor in defining objectives.

Identify Precursor Behaviors

After target objectives are determined, one should identify precursor behaviors, that is, those behaviors that lead to learning of the target objective. Understanding what behaviors might precede acquisition of target objectives is critical for the formative evaluator for three reasons. First, identification of precursor behaviors aids in recognizing the appropriate target audience—those having the entry-level skills to benefit from the program. Second, when an unfinished program or only part of a program is tested, the target objective may be impossible to achieve;

thus, evaluators measure indicators along the way to final achievement of objectives to estimate whether the program is on the right track. Third, formative evaluators want to distinguish what in the program is supporting or interfering with achievement of target objectives, so information on the learning *process*—on attainment of precursor behaviors— helps locate the strong and weak points in the instructional materials. For these reasons, formative evaluators concentrate as much effort on assessing precursor behaviors as assessing target outcome behaviors.

For example, a learning unit for a college-level telecourse on statistics specifies as a target outcome the ability to apply a rule to a new problem. The developer's intention is that students would achieve this outcome after viewing a television program, reading the textbook, and doing homework problems. The rule is presented in the TV program but the application objective is not addressed there, so when testing the rough-cut TV show independently of the other learning unit components, evaluators measure precursor behaviors. These include attention and appeal (as discussed in the previous chapter); recognition and recall of the rule; and understanding of the rule's meaning. If students recall and comprehend the rule from the television program, then they are more likely to be ready to learn how to apply it in problems.

Those who produce programs with long-range goals like attitude formation or attitude change may tend to ignore formative evaluation, offering the argument that the goals are not measurable after short or incomplete program exposure. In these cases, identifying and measuring prerequisite behaviors become particularly important. McGuire (1969) described attitude change as involving:

> at least five behavioral steps, including *attention, comprehension, yielding, retention,* and *action.* The receiver must go through each of these steps if communication is to have an ultimate persuasive impact, and each depends on the occurrence of the preceding step. (p.173)

Taking action or changing one's behavior toward an object conceivably may be achieved through exposure to a series of television programs or a complete computer-based program, but it is unreasonable to expect behavioral responses (i.e., action) as a result of prototype programs and short exposures. Thus, formative evaluators should concentrate on measuring the effectiveness of the communication by examining the steps in McGuire's hierarchy prior to the action step. These include attention (discussed in chapter 11 as message reception); comprehension (i.e., recall and understanding of the message); and yielding (i.e., acceptance of the message). Less often will formative researchers assess Step 4, retention, which requires measuring opinion after a period of time passes.

Summative evaluations of educational programs also examine prerequisite behaviors for attitudinal outcomes. The summative evaluations for a TV series on health, "Feeling Good," and on career awareness, "Freestyle," support this approach as follows:

> The information points conveyed in the "Feeling Good" programs and assessed as part of the evaluation were not stressed as ends in themselves, but as instrumentalities to behavior change; the points were chosen on the assumption that viewers who learned them (or were reminded of them) would be more likely to take the actions recommended. (Mielke & Swinehart, 1976, p.123)

> In the long run, "Freestyle's" creators want children to be free of stereotypes in their choice of activities and roles. But in the short run they are willing to settle for expressions of increased interest in such activities and roles. Of course, interest in an activity or role does not ensure its later selection, but certainly lack of interest greatly hinders its selection. Increased interests are, then, a worthwhile—and measurable—potential effect of "Freestyle." (Johnston & Ettema, 1982, p.115)

In summary, when target outcomes are not measurable due to long-term goals or exposure to incomplete lessons, formative evaluation assesses the achievement of precursor outcomes. Traditional methods of identifying precursors are through task analyses (Desberg & Taylor, 1986; Dick & Carey, 1985; Jonassen & Hannum, 1986); learning hierarchies (Gagné, 1985); or hierarchical taxonomies in motor skills (Harrow, 1972), cognitive outcomes (Bloom, 1956), or affective outcomes (Krathwohl, Bloom, & Masia, 1964).

Which Outcomes to Measure

Once an understanding is reached as to what learning outcomes the program is activating, formative evaluators decide on which outcomes to expend scarce resources:

- Which outcomes are most important?
- Given staff, time, and budget limitations, which outcomes can be reliably and validly measured?
- Which outcomes do program materials actively address?
- Do the developers have ambivalent expectations about certain outcomes?
- Which prerequisite outcomes can be measured to estimate potential effects?

WHEN TO ASSESS OUTCOME EFFECTIVENESS

As described in this book, formative evaluation can occur at various stages in the development of a product. It is logical to argue that outcome effectiveness should be assessed at the end of development, when the program has the best chance of achieving its goals. However, at that time we are usually denied the opportunity to make program changes. To affect decision making, formative evaluators must act early in the development of a product. Thus, during the design phase before production begins, evaluators investigate the broad issues of content and instructional strategies, for instance, by examining effects of existing programs on students or by observing tutorial situations that experiment with alternative teaching approaches.

In the early production phase, scripts, storyboards, and flowcharts serve to obtain feedback on program content and design. Preproduction formative evaluation asks questions like the following: Is the language clear? Is the content presented at the right level of difficulty? Are the major teaching points understandable? Where should overviews occur? How often should practice problems appear?

Testing pilot or prototype programs reveals strengths and weaknesses in the specifics of the media design. Production formative evaluation delves into such questions as: Do the visuals support the verbal presentation? Is the pace of information appropriate? What parts of the program are not understood? Do the instructional pathways in a tutorial actually meet learner needs? Is a simulation's level of fidelity to reality effective?

ASSESSING OUTCOME EFFECTIVENESS

The evaluator develops measures appropriate for the chosen outcomes, for the target audience, and for the kind of test materials available. The goal is to examine what learners achieve and how the program facilitates or hinders progress toward achieving those outcomes. The main categories of measurement are tests, self-report, and observation. The remainder of this chapter discusses each of these categories, providing examples and analyzing their advantages and disadvantages for formative evaluation of educational technologies.

Tests

Formative evaluators measure instructional outcomes with tests. Pretesting before program exposure reveals whether entry-level skills of the target audience are as anticipated. However, the major goal of testing in formative research is to obtain information about effects of program characteristics on outcomes in order to guide revisions. This is in contrast to other evaluation goals such as classifying individuals and groups or assessing the summative impact of a program.

Formative evaluators typically construct tests that are content-referenced (Ebel & Frisbie, 1986). This means that the respondent's performance is referenced to the program content and objectives rather than compared to other respondents, as in norm-referenced interpretations. An analysis of errors renders a profile of the mastery of instructional outcomes, and this diagnostic information locates program areas ripe for revision.

Hofmeister, Engelmann, and Carnine (1987) recount the formative evaluation testing process practiced with Systems Impact's videodisc, "Understanding Chemistry and Energy":

> Most videobased instructional demonstrations used in the science programs are less than a minute long, and the demonstration is usually followed with a written response by the students. During the field tests of prototype versions of each lesson, the written responses of students were collected at the end of each lesson and analyzed to assess the clarity of each instructional demonstration. Such an analysis can pinpoint instructional weaknesses with considerable precision. (p.20)

Much of testing in formative evaluation encompasses paper-and-pencil or oral examinations of simple recall and comprehension of program content, events, and messages. Assessment of low-level information processing, which Palmer (1974) has called *comprehensibility testing*, commonly uses selected-response formats including true–false, multiple-choice, or matching questions. Constructed-response formats, entailing essays, problem exercises, and open-ended questions, yield a richer picture of program comprehensibility and allow for unintended effects to surface, but analysis and summarization are more difficult and time consuming.

For children, the evaluator's creativity is taxed to produce measures that will permit children to demonstrate reliably their comprehension and learning outcomes. For example, researchers of preschool television programming ask children to sequence pictures, revealing their understanding of a televised narrative plot, or to manipulate doll characters or objects in a reenactment of the program story, illuminating their comprehension of character relationships and motives. Children's Television Workshop's researchers measure comprehensibility while the television program is viewed:

One way to do this is to stop the tape at critical junctures and ask the child to explain what is going on at that point in the program. A variation on this is to first view the program in its entirety, then replay the program with the sound turned off, asking the child to provide play-by-play narration. (Mielke, 1983, p.247)

Situational testing assesses performance with simulated or real tasks (Priestly, 1982). For example, for an interactive videodisc program intended to teach recognition and assessment of motor dysfunction in infants, diagnostic skills were tested with video stimuli. Medical students viewed video segments of infants and answered questions about the neuromotor abilities displayed (Huntley, Albanese, Blackman, & Lough, 1985). In another approach, Reeves and Lent (1984) report the use of computer simulation within the instructional program itself to pretest and posttest literacy skills:

Students are . . . put into situations which require them to employ their functional literacy skills to solve military-related problems. For example, a soldier student may travel back in time to the "Battle of the Bulge" where he or she has to follow directions and interpret maps to deliver an urgent message to General Patton. . . . A student enters an instructional lesson if and only if his or her performance in the simulation indicates a need for that instruction. In other words, the problems posed by the simulation serve as the pretests to determine the instructional needs of the students and as the posttests to assess whether they've learned the required skills. (pp. 198–199)

Situational testing is exercised infrequently in formative evaluation because of the difficulty of developing and administering a reliable and valid test, given the quick turnaround time and low budget constraints typical of formative work. Moreover, situational tests evaluate higher level outcomes whose attainment requires exposure to an almost completed program, when changes are less likely to be made. However, if the planned outcomes embrace a set of complex skills, then situational testing may be the most appropriate choice to match the program objectives. A search for existing situational tests that could operate for formative purposes may prove fruitful as computer-based simulations are being developed in different content areas, for instance, to test the clinical judgment and performance of nursing students (Shaw-Nickerson & Kisker, 1984–1985; Sweeney, O'Malley, & Freeman, 1982). Use of existing tests necessitates establishing congruence between the test objectives and the program objectives.

Measures of comprehensibility are common in early phases of formative evaluation when unfinished materials are tested. Comprehension is an important step in the learning hierarchy whether program outcomes are cognitive, attitudinal, or motoric (Bloom, 1956; McGuire, 1969). When almost finished programs are available, one should test higher level outcomes or actual target outcomes because comprehension alone is not sufficient evidence that final goals are achievable with the program.

Despite the time pressures of formative evaluation, every effort, including pretesting measures, should be made to construct good tests. Only evidence seen as credible will convince developers that revision is necessary. For details on how to develop reliable and valid tests, readers should consult the many texts on measurement and evaluation (viz., Ebel & Frisbie, 1986; Roid & Haladyna, 1982). In that development process, however, one should recall that the purpose of the formative evaluation test is to collect timely information that will be useful in determining whether revisions are necessary and in guiding revisions of the program.

Researchers often prefer tests because they are easily administered and analyzed for large samples and give objective, reliable evidence of achievement of prerequisite behaviors or planned outcomes of the program. However, information about why outcomes are not obtained as well as information about the learning process that can facilitate revisions is not readily available from tests. Thus, other methods like self-report and observations supplement test data by pinpointing trouble spots and suggesting remedies.

Self-Report

After viewing a short rough-cut videotape on statistics, college students were tested on their understanding of concepts presented (Flagg & Falk, 1987a). At one point in the program, the host teacher narrates a series of graphic displays about the pattern of residuals or deviations from the least squares line. The pretest results showed that this was a new concept for the students, and posttest results indicated a significant improvement in understanding this concept. However, only 42% of the sample gave the correct posttest answer, a result that was lower than for other concepts and lower than what was desirable outcome performance. Was this result due to an unreliable test question? If not, what factors in the program might have contributed to the difficulty students had in learning the concept?

Self-report data help us find answers to these questions. Students rated the comprehensibility of the material using a continuous-reaction measure. At predetermined points during the running of the videotape, researchers told viewers to check one of two phrases—"I understand" or "I am confused"—with respect to what they just watched. This method gave feedback on viewers' perceptions of their learning process while viewing. The continuous reaction measure showed a low point in comprehensibility after the presentation of the residuals concept, thereby validating the results of the posttest question.

But what should be done about this confusion and lack of learning? Data from a postviewing questionnaire helped define some possible actions. When asked what topics in the program needed further explanation, more than half of the viewers wanted more explanation about the pattern of residuals. Moreover, generally, students rated the pace of statistical concepts as too fast and were only mildly positive about the informal graphic style that was used in the rough-cut videotape. Given these self-report data (and similar analyses related to the other statistical concepts presented), the production staff decided to decrease the number of content objectives per show in order to treat them in more depth at a slower pace; to pay special attention to concepts that were likely to be new to the audience; and to use a sharper and more polished graphic style.

The moral of this tale for formative evaluators is that self-report data are critical to interpretation of test data. Simply finding out what people are learning or not learning is insufficient for effective formative evaluation. Questionnaires, interviews, and continuous reaction measures serve to illuminate the learning process and learner responses to production elements of the program. Inductive analyses of the complementary data sets provide developers with information on which to base revisions of the program.

Continuous-Reaction Measures

Tests give us feedback on whether an outcome was obtained or not, while continuous-reaction measures provide feedback on the process of obtaining that outcome. The purpose of these measures is to understand how specific parts of the program function in facilitating outcomes.

The thinkaloud technique sheds light on problems in the learning process. Details of this continuous reaction measure can be reviewed in the previous two chapters. When the thinkaloud technique is applied to outcome effectiveness, the evaluator asks learners using an interactive program to reflect out loud on the content and structure of the message. What parts of the presentation are exceptionally clear or confusing? Does the feedback provide the information needed? Where is the program persuasive or not? Are the pace and sequencing appropriate? Is the humor distracting or motivating? How relevant or useful is the message? These are a few of the issues that a thinkaloud procedure might address relevant to outcome objectives.

In the escorted trial method, which was introduced and discussed in chapter 10, the evaluator guides respondents through preproduction materials, eliciting reactions about clarity of presentation, learning difficulties, and so forth. For example, at the storyboard stage of one videodisc project, users watched short television segments of two people negotiating a problem. After each video segment, users worked through question and answer branches presented on paper by the researcher. In this preproduction procedure, the researcher acted as the computer, albeit a very slow one. Users' verbal reports, such as the following, revealed which questions and answers needed rewriting:

> Sample comments from students after reading question #10 and alternative answer choices: "It doesn't seem like the question goes with the video segment." "The real answer is not among the options." "Now I'm confused. I'd have to bail out here to repeat the video up till now once or twice more before answering this question." "Up until now I thought I could tell what the questions would be about, but this was a surprise." (Goldie, 1987; Rutstein, 1987)

Through the escorted trial method, developers can obtain users' feedback before production has begun.

Chapter 11 described two methods to evaluate continuously the appeal and reception of television programs: (a) paper-and-pencil viewing response method; and (b) Program Evaluation Analysis Computer (PEAC). Evaluators can adapt these methods to assess program effectiveness, although in practice they have been used infrequently. One use of the paper-and-pencil response viewing method appears in the statistics video example just given. In that case, each time the researcher called out a number while respondents viewed the program, viewers immediately assessed their perception of the comprehensibility of the segment they had just viewed and marked their response sheet next to the phrase "I understand" or "I am confused."

Baggaley (1986) attempted to measure persuasiveness of a televised presentation using the hand-held recording units of the Program Evaluation Analysis Computer (see chapter 11 for details of using the PEAC system). Canadian viewers of the 1980 live televised debate between President Carter and Ronald Reagan answered the question of who was winning the most votes by pressing one of three buttons labeled "Carter," "Reagan," and "Don't Know." Shifts in viewer responses from Carter to Reagan were "found to coincide with verbal points made by Reagan concerning the Carter administration's economic record" (p.32). The PEAC system has been used frequently to measure appeal, but further experimentation is needed to establish its usefulness in assessing processes related to outcome effectiveness.

Summary. Continuous reaction methods obtain respondents' immediate assessment of the comprehensibility and persuasiveness of the program in its early and later production phases. The thinkaloud and escorted trial techniques used to evaluate interactive programs yield verbal, open-ended, and spontaneous comments. The paper-and-pencil and PEAC response methods applied to television programs produce non-verbal, close-ended, regularly elicited comments.

Questionnaires and Interviews

To assess learner outcomes and reactions to program content, questionnaires and interviews query students directly either in written or verbal form. Previous chapters (and other texts in more detail) describe these techniques and discuss the methodological pros and cons of using them, so those issues are not considered again here. Instead we focus on the purposes of questionnaires and interviews in eliciting information related to outcome effectiveness. Formative evaluators use these self-report methods to collect three types of data: (a) demographic data, (b) opinions, and (c) attitudes.

Demographic data. Information about the user's background, such as age, gender, and educational experience, helps validate the sample as representative of the program's target audience. Moreover, with these data, one can discover which aspects of the instructional materials are more or less effective with different subsamples of learners. For example, in response to "Freestyle's" pilot television segments that used counterstereotypical characters to combat sex-role stereotypes, "there was a slight (and expected) bias of boys wanting to imitate male characters more than females and girls modeling females" (Williams, LaRose, & Frost, 1981, p.81).

Opinions. To provide perspective on test results that indicate the outcome effectiveness of the program, evaluators probe with questionnaires and interviews the learners' opinions of and comprehension of the material that supports and surrounds the message. Our concern is with the target students' comprehension of the production techniques that carry the instructional message and their opinion of the effectiveness of those techniques. Can users correctly interpret icons and graphic displays? Are the levels of activity challenging enough? Is the vocabulary too difficult or too slangy? Is the pace in a linear presentation of content too slow or too fast? Do children understand the type of humor used? Are the video techniques and plot easy to follow or do they obscure the educational content? Ease of understanding the production techniques that carry the content is important to comprehension of the content itself.

Further, formative evaluation assists in determining how attributes of the message contribute to the persuasion process. For example, in designing 1-minute TV spots on health, Children's Television Workshop examined "the relative value of plotted drama versus factual narration, or the question of integrating the health messages into the drama versus inserting them in a less organic fashion" (Palmer, 1979, p.9).

In addition to eliciting learners' opinions, evaluators poll the opinions also of those who are involved in the decision to buy or use the product. Is the content right for their curriculum? Is it well paced and are the levels of difficulty appropriate? What would their students learn? Is use of the program feasible and practical in their setting? How would it be used? Faculty or program administrators do not always agree with student assessments, so collecting feedback from both groups is suggested. For example, in evaluating the TV program, text, and exercises associated with a telecourse learning unit on statistics, faculty rated each component as less difficult, clearer, and more appealing than did students (Flagg & Falk, 1987b).

Attitudes. If a program's target outcomes are in the attitudinal domain, evaluators may use existing scales to measure pre- and postprogram attitudes, but more often they develop their own questionnaires and interviews keyed to the program itself. Formative evaluation examines whether students understand the affective and social messages in the program, whether they see them as practical and useful, whether they agree with or accept the messages, and whether they intend to do anything about them.

LaRose (1980) reported using questionnaires for evaluating "Freestyle's" television pilot segments that attempted to reduce stereotypical attitudes toward careers. For example, "children were asked to interpret the "point" of a sequence by selecting the desired objective from statements of other (untreated) project goals" (p.285). Second, "viewers were asked to indicate on a five-point agree-disagree scale whether they would like to perform an activity in the same way as the on-screen model" (p.289). These question formats serve to assess the persuasive impact of the program by investigating two steps in McGuire's (1969) hierarchy of attitude change. LaRose's first question format probes comprehension and the second examines yielding (i.e., verbal agreement with the message).

On occasion, formative evaluation can measure the highest step on McGuire's hierarchy, that of action. For example, Hezel (1982) compared two videotapes designed to encourage viewers to donate kidneys for transplants. The versions presented the same information but differed in the inclusion of emotional scenes. In addition to testing for content recall and opinions, viewers were

> asked to check a donor pledge sheet on which they could indicate their willingness, unwillingness, or uncertainty to donate a kidney while alive or after death. The results showed that individuals who viewed the emotionally-charged version were more likely to express a willingness to donate their kidneys than subjects in the low emotion version. (p.5)

Nevertheless, because attitude change usually takes time, rarely do formative evaluators have the opportunity to assess whether a message is retained over time or whether respondents actually perform recommended behaviors. These tasks are left most often for summative evaluation.

The questionnaire and interview complement each other in collecting data about the learning process and educational outcomes. The questionnaire permits collection of objective information about specific points in the program, while the interview, with its more qualitative open-ended approach, can help us understand why certain results occur. The interview is labor and time intensive yielding small homogeneous samples, while the questionnaire contributes larger diversified samples due to ease of administration and analysis. The questionnaire also provides anonymity for issues where the interview responses might be affected by peer pressure and social conformity.

So which one should be used for a formative evaluation of outcome effectiveness? Preferably a combination of both. However, the more specific one can be in the type of information needed and the faster one needs this information, the more appropriate a questionnaire is. Questionnaires can obtain large amounts of reliable data quickly. On the other hand, interviews are valuable for assessing the variability in feedback and for revealing unintended effects.

Summary.   Questionnaires and interviews allow respondents to report on their own learning process and outcomes, on their opinions about program content and the production attributes that carry the content, and on their attitudes as affected by program exposure. In addition to following the dos and don'ts of good questioning techniques, the formative evaluator checks his or her questions against three more crite-ria: (a) What data will the questions provide that will help locate strong and weak points in the program? (b) Can the expected data be related to program attributes to guide revisions? (c) Are these questions through which unintended effects can emerge?

Observation

Observations of viewers and users can give us insight into the ease with which learners are achieving their objectives. From overt behaviors, we may infer communication successes and failures. It is clear that a TV program is communicating when one sees the young viewer repeating phrases, imitating movements, or shouting responses. It is clear also when the audio punchline comes and is greeted with silence that the program is not communicating. However, the learning process is not always visible in overt behaviors, so observations are best used in con-junction with tests and self-report measures.

The main techniques, advantages, and disadvantages of observation were described in chapters 10 and 11, so our discussion here presents the use of observational data to illuminate the process of outcome achieve-ment. On some occasions observation shows the achievement of planned outcomes, but most often evaluators employ the method to check on the learning process.

Observation is especially useful with children because they frequently produce verbal and nonverbal behaviors from which one infers their comprehension of program segments. Preschoolers spontaneously an-swer questions posed by television characters; pairs of elementary school children commiserate verbally on their inability to understand the task demands of a computer program. As children get older, overt ex-pressions of comprehension or confusion during program exposure dis-appear and evaluators must use other means to observe the learning process.

In the cases of some instructional television shows in the affective domain, classroom discussion after viewing is part of the pedagogical approach. For formative evaluators at the Agency for Instructional Technology (AIT), for example, observation of postviewing discussions reveals the comprehensibility and persuasiveness of the televised mes-sage (e.g., AIT, 1980). Content analysis of these discussions

> allows observers to note the understandings and misunderstandings of both
> students and teachers. . . . It examines the degree to which students and
> teachers focus on the program itself or generalize about their own feelings

or actions in analogous situations. It permits observers to note . . . the degree to which the audience deals with the decision-making process, a desired outcome. (Rockman, 1977, pp. 57–58)

For interactive media, keystroke records furnish an objective way to observe the learning process. One can pinpoint comprehension difficulties by analyzing what segments of the program were accessed in what sequence, by reviewing right and wrong answers in task and test situations, and by examining error messages and help requests. Keystroke records identify what pathways to revise or eliminate and what new branches to add.

Like continuous reaction measures, observation provides a look at the process of learning. Unlike those measures, observation typically does not interfere with normal use of the program in a natural setting and thus is less subject to distortion resulting from respondents wanting to please the researcher. On the other hand, observers must wait for the appearance of behaviors indicating comprehension and persuasion.

Conclusion

The formative evaluator has a diverse set of measurement tools available to investigate learners' acquisition of motor skills, cognitive abilities, and attitudes. Because each measure has different strengths and weaknesses, most evaluators use a combination of tests, self-report techniques, and observations in order to provide as complete and accurate a picture as possible of the outcome effectiveness of the developing program.

UTILIZATION OF RESULTS ON USER FRIENDLINESS, RECEPTION, AND OUTCOMES

This book has presented the philosophy and methods of formative evaluation of educational technologies. The goal of formative evaluation is to inform the decision-making process during the design, production, and implementation stages of an educational program with the purpose of improving the program. Given that one has defined evaluation questions that will yield information usable for decision making and revision, that are answerable within the time demands of the project, and that are relevant to the program objectives and the uncertainties of the developers; and given that one has used a variety of reliable and valid measures with representative target audience members, a further question remains: How can one increase the likelihood that formative evaluation results actually will be used by decision makers? The utilization of evaluation results has become a field of study itself, so this closing section touches only briefly on two major issues relevant to utilization that are important particularly to formative evaluation.

Interpersonal Relations

Creating a working dialogue and trusting relationship between formative researchers and decision makers is critical to the eventual utilization of results. To define research questions, the evaluator must understand the decision needs of the development team. To produce timely results, the evaluator must acknowledge the timeline of production in the research design but also educate developers as to the time and labor requirements of good research. Finally, the formative evaluator should recognize his or her role as that of coach, not judge, providing feedback on strengths and weaknesses in the program so that the strengths can be built upon and the weaknesses eliminated.

Communication

Besides producing results that are timely and relevant to the needs of developers, evaluators must be able to communicate the results in an understandable, nonthreatening, and brief manner. Long printed reports written in the language of evaluation are not easily assimilated by those who work with audiovisuals in a pressured environment. It is crucial that results be summarized and presented in an easily consumable form. Moreover, although formative evaluators do not make the production and design decisions, they can go beyond the data to interpret their findings and direct their communications toward possible alternative solutions to the problems raised in the results. Making recommendations requires that evaluators have knowledge of the constraints on the project—thus, stressing again the necessity of a good relationship with the developers.

In conclusion, effective formative evaluation requires a relationship of trust that is both receptive and responsive. Listen to the needs and uncertainties of the development team. Respond sensitively with timely, relevant, credible, and lucid information. Finally, one might even ask the decision makers to give evaluative feedback on the usefulness of the formative evaluation, so the next research effort can be better.

REFERENCES

Agency for Instructional Television. (1980). *"On the Level" final report on formative evaluation* (Research Rep. No. 77). Bloomington, IN: Author.

Baggaley, J. (1986). Formative evaluation of educational television. *Canadian Journal of Educational Communication, 15*(1), 29–44.

Bloom, B. (Ed.). (1956). *Taxonomy of educational objectives: The classification of educational objectives. Handbook I: Cognitive domain.* New York: David McKay.

Desberg, P., & Taylor, J. H. (1986). *Essentials of task analysis.* Lanham, MD: University Press of America.

Dick, W., & Carey, L. (1985). *The systematic design of instruction* (2nd ed.). Glenview, IL: Scott, Foresman.

Ebel, R. L., & Frisbie, D. A. (1986). *Essentials of educational measurement* (4th ed.). Englewood Cliffs, NJ: Prentice-Hall.

Flagg, B. N., & Falk, J. K. (1987a). *STATMAP linear growth pilot formative evaluation* (Research Rep. No. 87-004). Cambridge, MA: Harvard University, Human Development and Psychology.

Flagg, B. N., & Falk, J. K. (1987b). *Formative evaluation of STATMAP pilot learning unit* (Research Rep. No. 87-006). Cambridge, MA: Harvard University, Human Development and Psychology.

Gagné, R. M. (1985). *The conditions of learning and theory of instruction* (4th ed.). New York: Holt, Rinehart & Winston.

Goldie, J. (1987). [*Hawkins Negotiation* videodisc storyboard evaluation]. Unpublished raw data. Cambridge, MA: Harvard University.

Harrow, A. (1972). *A taxonomy of the psychomotor domain.* New York: David McKay.

Hezel, R. T. (1982, June). *Developing compatibility between functions and techniques in medical television production.* Paper presented at the Fifth International Conference on Experimental Research in Televised Instruction. St. Johns, Newfoundland.

Hofmeister, A. M., Engelmann, S., & Carnine, D. (1987). Developing and validating science education videodiscs. *Teaching with Videodiscs, Special Edition, 2* (3), 1–35.

Huntley, J. S., Albanese, M. A., Blackman, J. A., & Lough, L. K. (1985, April). *Evaluation of a computer-controlled videodisc program to teach pediatric neuromotor assessment.* Paper presented at the American Educational Research Association, Chicago, IL.

Jonassen, D. H., & Hannum, W. H. (1986). Analysis of task analysis procedures. *Journal of Instructional Development, 9*(2), 2–12.

Johnston, J., & Ettema, J. S. (1982). *Positive images: Breaking stereotypes with children's television.* Beverly Hills, CA: Sage.

Krathwohl, D. R., Bloom, B. S., & Masia, B. B. (1964). *Taxonomy of educational objectives: The classification of educational goals. Handbook II: Affective domain* New York: David McKay.

LaRose, R. (1980). Formative evaluation of children's television as mass communication research. In B. Dervin & M. J. Voight (Eds.), *Progress in communication sciences* (Vol. 2, pp.275–297). Norwood, NJ: Ablex.

McGuire, W. J. (1969). The nature of attitudes and attitude change. In G. Lindzey & E. Aronson (Eds.), *The handbook of social psychology: Vol. 3. The individual in a social context* (pp.136–314). Reading, MA: Addison-Wesley.

Mielke, K. (1983). The educational use of production variables and formative research in programming. In M. Meyer (Ed.), *Children and the formal features of television: Approaches and findings of experimental and formative research.* New York: K. G. Saur.

Mielke, K. W., & Swinehart, J. W. (1976). *Evaluation of the "Feeling Good" television series.* New York: Children's Television Workshop.

Palmer, E. L. (1974). Formative research in the production of television for children. In D. R. Olson (Ed.), *Media and symbols: The forms of expression, communication, and education* (pp.303–329). Chicago: University of Chicago Press.

Palmer, E. L. (1979, Fall). Research for the Latin American health minutes. *CTW International Research Notes*, pp. 7–9.

Priestly, M. (1982). *Performance assessment in education and training.* Englewood Cliffs, NJ: Educational Technology Publications.

Reeves, T. C., & Lent, R. M. (1984). Levels of evaluation for computer-based instruction. In D. F. Walker & R. D. Hess (Eds.), *Instructional software: Principles and perspectives for design and use* (pp.188–203). Belmont, CA: Wadsworth Publishing.

Rockman, S. (1977). The functions of evaluation in cooperative projects: The AIT experience. In T. Bates & J. Robinson (Eds.), *Evaluating educational television and radio: Proceedings of the International Conference on Evaluation and Research in Educational Television and Radio* (pp. 56–60). Milton Keynes, England: The Open University.

Roid, G. H., & Haladyna, T. M. (1982). *A technology for test-item writing.* New York: Academic Press.

Rutstein, D. (1987). [*Hawkins Negotiation* videodisc storyboard evaluation]. Unpublished raw data. Cambridge, MA: Harvard University.

Scriven, M. (1972). Prose and cons about goal-free evaluation. *Evaluation Comment, 3*(4), 1–4.

Shaw-Nickerson, E., & Kisker, K. (1984–1985). Computer based simulations in evaluating registered nurse students in a baccalaureate program. *Journal of Educational Technology Systems, 13*(2), 197–213.

Sweeney, M. A., O'Malley, M., & Freeman, E. (1982). Development of a computer simulation to evaluate the clinical performance of nursing students. *Journal of Nursing Education, 21*(9), 28–38.

Williams, R., LaRose, R., & Frost, F. (1981). *Children, television, and sex-role stereotyping.* New York: Praeger.

Author Index

Numbers in *italics* denote complete reference citation

Subject Index